MERLE M. OHLSEN
Indiana State University ——

With a foreword by Harry Joseph

Group Counseling

Holt, Rinehart and Winston, Inc.
New York Chicago San Francisco Atlanta Dallas
Montreal Toronto London Sydney

Foreword

Historically we live in an age of "demand feeding." The desire for immediate gratification of needs begins in infancy and continues into the life of the senior citizen. In many areas of behavior and/or emotional experiences the inability to tolerate frustration results in increasing tension and anxiety; aggression and violence not only have penetrated the university campuses but have also spread throughout our country.

The past quarter century—beginning with the termination of World War II—has brought revolutionary changes to the lives of those to whom Professor Ohlsen's book is addressed. It is simple to analogize from experiments on other members of the animal kingdom and apply them to *Homo sapiens,* but such procedure results in much error. Human behavior and the study of emotions—both normal and abnormal—present specific problems which cannot be studied in an isolated experimental laboratory.

It is difficult to objectify and validate historic facts in the present. It is more difficult to objectify and set criteria for optimum conditions for "mental health." We have learned much: we have much to learn. Emotions are irrational and are not subject to absolute quantification. This indeed is fortunate, negating the possibility of ever relegating emotions to the computer.

We think readily of various periods of "morality," of formulas in bringing up children. We think of the morality of the mid-Victorian era. We think of the rigid and precise schedules and formulas of the first half of the twentieth century by which all children were to be fed and all body functions were to comply; every infant was to be fed on a strict four-hour schedule with predetermined foods.

Demand feeding represented a natural development in infant feeding. It is clear that children vary in their feeding needs. In the absence of verbal communication, the optimum schedule could be determined only by the demands of the child. Parenthetically, although this represented a revolutionary step in infant feeding, and although it represented the most advanced scientifically controlled experiments, it was and is the method used most throughout the world.

But the historic pendulum swings from one extreme to another. Demand feeding is applicable to the first few months of life. It was not and is not meant for the child, the adolescent, the bride and groom, the adult, and the senior citizen. Demand feeding has become the *modus vivendi* in all areas of physical and emotional needs.

The child in elementary school is subjected to a bombardment of audiovisual aids in order for learning to become simpler and easier. Closed circuit television programs allow one teacher to speak to hundreds of children throughout a school. The guidance and stimulus of a teacher is no longer important. Too frequently teachers fear the wrath of the children and the harassment of the P.T.A. Respect for teachers is diminished and in many larger cities completely lacking. Grades are eliminated because they may create competition and frustrate the child.

The adolescent basks in the glory of the assumption that he is at liberty to harass parents and other adults. Rudeness and bad manners are condoned and excused as a natural phenomenon. Parents vie with each other for the affection of the child. Steady dating avoids the possibility of not having a date on Saturday night. Sexual freedom is erroneously proclaimed as a necessity.

Adolescence exists only in *Homo sapiens* and begins with physical maturation at puberty—terminating in the assumption of responsibility for self maintenance. Adolescence cannot be described in terms of age, for a man who is fifty years old may still be an adolescent.

The college student may believe he is an adult. He may insist that he is an adult capable of making his own decisions. Actually he is still an adolescent. The recent violence on campuses often has valid etiological factors, however this does not negate the primary emotional causes—constellations which have revolutionized the lives of many students and many universities—e.g., girls moving into boys' dormitories.

Students feel free to shift from one university to another and are frequently encouraged to do so. They lose a sense of identification, not only with the school but also with their classmates. They are not part of any "family." The primary purpose of a university—education towards a career—is forgotten. In many schools students do not have any "major" curriculum and are dissuaded from pursuing one. They insist on demanding changes in a curriculum without qualifications for determining such changes. Sexual freedom is demanded by the students and encouraged by faculty as a right and necessity. Such freedom simply increases tension and anxiety. The use of drugs and narcotics allows for the temporary withdrawal from reality, to avoid contact with ordinary social needs which are feared. The weekend periods of withdrawal terminate in depression on Mondays when students must awaken. Purposeless aggression in all areas, violence, disrespect, harassment of faculty, and destruction of property are rationalized. The "generation gap" accusations confuse parents and are more confusing to the students—for there is no equating such a "gap." Boys seek to behave as girls and girls behave as boys. It becomes difficult to differentiate them as they walk across the campus. Issues differ on different campuses. The mode of behavior is similar. The fears are the same. The desires are the same—immediate gratification of emotional needs, the fear of becoming an adult and earning a living.

The adult world has changed. The search of the adult is the "security" offered by a position in a paternalistic organization. Ads in newspapers emphasize such "security" with pension plans, profit sharing, sick leave, retirement. Certainly it would be impossible to object to such progress. However, too frequently such paternalistic or more appropriately, "maternalistic" protection leads to monotony, boredom, and loss of incentive. Increased leisure time may be and should be an admirable social gain. However, few know how to use such leisure time for leisure purposes. How painful is a Sunday for many people who do nothing but search for an enjoyable television program. If necessary they watch one they have seen many times because it was a "good one." Passive participation results in boredom.

The "male climacteric" (menopause) is a new syndrome, a new discovery which allegedly occurs in men in the mid-fifties. The female menopause syndrome assumes secondary clinical importance. Actually, the male climacteric is a myth. The depression occurs in men who must shortly retire from their jobs and have nothing to interest them.

The "senior citizen" is politely relegated to a "retired" position. He serves no useful purpose and as a "senior" awaits graduation which is synonymous with death. European senior citizens are respected, and their talents are used in their specific fields. We have not as yet been able to find a resolution for an increasing social problem. There are many cities and developments built specifically for senior citizens. Physical and social needs are carefully planned for. However, the people find themselves emotionally incarcerated, uselessly awaiting death.

A theoretical discussion must also recognize the serious reality problems that must result in "anxiety, pain, discomfort and tension." Housing, racial discrimination, and war all serve to increase such symptoms geometrically. The resolution of these problems is necessary. However, their elimination as problems would still not remove the "anxiety and tension"

which one sees from childhood, through adolescence, adult-
hood, and in retirement.

Any procedure that eliminates anxiety and tension is
therapeutic: And yet there is a large segment of our population with problems not seriously connoting illness but requiring help in various emotional areas. Every university, every
high school seeks well trained counselors and guidance personnel with whom students may consult and find an empathic,
understanding individual who will "listen" sympathetically—
but whose opinion will be helpful by virtue of its objectivity.
But counseling is important at many other times. A counselor
may change a depressed and useless senior citizen into a
constructive, contented individual. This we have learned in
the recent past.

Group counseling is the most recent of psychotherapeutic
procedures. It grew out of necessity. "One to one" counseling
became an impossibility with the increasing recognition of
the need and importance of such help and time requirements.

But the advantages of group counseling in many areas
over individual counseling, the importance of group dynamics,
of group interaction changed previous concepts. Research results and clinical studies are voluminous. Theoretical hypotheses and formulations, techniques, and procedures appear
constantly in the professional literature.

Group counseling arose out of necessity but has grown
into a specific science of its own. One may safely state that
such counseling will effectively change the lives of many from
those of anxiety and insecurity to those of security and continued ego gratification.

Thus the necessity for a book which will review and
describe the many problems that arise in group counseling.
Professor Ohlsen's book serves to fill a gap in our literature
and clinical experience. Not only does it contain thoughts and
conclusions arising from years of experience with such problems, it also includes a most comprehensive review of the
efforts and thoughts of others in the field. I believe that it
should become the definitive text not only in group counseling
but for any group therapeutic situation.

Indeed it may be stated without reservation that group counseling increasingly will serve to dissipate the disharmony, the dissonance, the violence, the anger, the hate, and the unhappiness that exist in many segments of our population.

HARRY JOSEPH, M.D.

Psychiatric Consultant, Board of Education, New York City
Clinical Assistant Professor of Psychiatry, Downstate Medical Center, State University of New York
Professor of Psychiatry, Adelphi University

Preface

In this book I try to help prospective counselors and practicing counselors understand the dynamics of therapeutic groups, to recognize and use the therapeutic forces within a counseling group, to facilitate changes in their clients' behavior, and to help clients learn to assist others while they obtain assistance for themselves. To provide the practical assistance which I believe counselors desire, I have discussed how a counselor can develop treatment goals cooperatively with clients; why specific goals are essential, and how they can be used by clients to assess their own progress; how a counselor can select clients and initiate group counseling; and how beginning counselors can cope with difficult clients (e.g., grievers, hostile clients, and dependent clients). The topics of resistance, transference, and countertransference also are discussed. Frequent illustrations are used to provide counselors with practical assistance in dealing with the problems they meet in group counseling. For these practical suggestions as well as research findings and theory I reviewed the professional literature from counseling and guidance, group dynamics, group psychotherapy, social group work, and social psychology.

This book stresses certain basic conditions for helping individuals in groups. When a person seeks assistance, he must understand what is expected from him, believe that he can be helped, have confidence in the counselor and the treatment method, and conclude the costs and risks involved are worth it. If he is to be helped he must be committed to discuss his problems and to change his behavior, and he must accept responsibility for helping to develop a therapeutic climate within his group. He also must expect others to make similar commitments, help them accept similar responsibilities, and help them change their behaviors. At the same time he does not try to substitute his relationships with the members of his counseling group for his significant others. Instead he applies his new learnings in daily living to improve his relationships with significant others.

Within our profession there are many who have the potential for counseling individuals in groups. Some even have the theoretical background and a knowledge of the techniques but lack either the supervised practice or the support of their supervisors which they feel that they need to initiate group counseling. This book is designed to help qualified counselors, supervisors, and counselor educators to help these counselors expand their repertoire of professional skills to include group counseling.

This book is a product of many years' experience counseling individuals in groups, teaching others to do so, and supervising counselors who are learning to apply in practice what they learned in didactic courses. I have been fortunate to have had excellent students who challenged me, helped me revise and clarify my ideas, and encouraged me to refine my counseling techniques. During the period in which I wrote this manuscript, my colleagues and students at the University of Missouri at Kansas City and the University of Illinois made many suggestions which improved it markedly. For these I am truly grateful.

None of these, however, has influenced me as deeply as a person or as a counselor as the love and companionship of my wife, our daughters, and our son. They have provided me my richest group experiences. Hence, I dedicate this book to Helen, Marilyn, Linda, Barbara, and Ron.

M.M.O.

Terre Haute, Indiana
August 1969

Contents

Chapter Twelve
Appraisal of Group Counseling 240

Chapter One

The Counselor

This chapter is concerned with the counselor as a variable in the counseling process. It defines the counseling relationship, explains how it differs from other group relationships, reviews some of the literature on selection of prospective counselors, and discusses the counselor's professional preparation.

The Counseling Relationship

Counseling is an accepting, trusting, and safe relationship between a counselor and one or more clients. Within this relationship clients learn to face, express, and cope with their most disturbing feelings and thoughts; they also develop the courage and self-confidence to apply what they have learned in changing their behavior. When their new behaviors do not seem to work, they feel sufficiently secure within the counseling relationship to appraise them to determine why they did not work, to modify them, or to identify other approaches to try. Sometimes they must learn new skills to improve their adjustment. Some clients also require assistance to convey their new selves to such significant others as spouses, parents, friends, teachers, and employers and to help these others understand and learn to live with their new selves.

One of the unique characteristics of the relationship is the counselor's ability *to listen*—to focus his attention on his clients' needs, to exhibit genuine caring, and at the same time to maintain a healthy separateness. He also is able to convey his commitment to his clients and to communicate to them what he expects from them in order to help them change their behavior and attitudes.

When he is at his best, a counselor can *feel deeply with* a client without experiencing emotional reactions which are deleterious to the counseling relationship. Such a relationship wins a client's confidence and enables him to discuss problems that he has been unable to discuss, perhaps unable even to accept as his own. Symonds (1956) explained that such a relationship enables a client to be completely honest with himself. When he discovers that he has nothing to fear from his counselor and fellow clients, he can give up the false front he has been portraying to the world, accept himself more completely, and make changes in behavior and attitude that will improve his adjustment.

Rogers (1961) described the counselor's professional psychological stance as genuineness, being open in expressing the feelings and attitudes that flow in him, caring for his clients in a nonpossessive way, and exhibiting empathic understanding.

Carkhuff and Berenson (1967) concluded from their own and others' research that counselors who achieved the best results had these facilitating characteristics:

1. *Empathy.*

> The emphasis, then is upon movement to levels of feelings and experience deeper than those communicated by the client, yet within a range of expression which the client can constructively employ for his own purposes. The therapist's ability to communicate at high levels of empathic understanding appears to involve the therapist's ability to allow himself to experience or merge in the experience of the client, reflect upon this experience while suspending his own judgments, tolerating his own

anxiety, and communicating this understanding to the client. (p. 27)

2. Respect. (Described by Rogers as unconditional positive regard or nonpossessive warmth.)

Respect or positive regard, in turn, has its origin in the respect which the individual has for himself. He cannot respect the feelings and experiences of others if he cannot respect his own feelings and experiences. (p. 27)

3. Genuineness—the degree to which the counselor (or therapist) can reflect his true feelings.

The degree to which the therapist can be honest with himself and, thus, with the client, establishes this base. . . . Again, genuineness must not be confused, as is so often done, with free license for the therapist to do what he will in therapy, especially to express hostility. Therapy is not for the therapist. The therapist does not operate in vacuo. When he crosses the threshold of the conference room, he serves the client and must be guided by what is effective for the client. With a very brittle client leading a very tenuous existence, the therapist may withhold some very genuine responses. Nevertheless, in his therapy he is continually working toward a more equalitarian, fully-sharing relationship. If there can be no authenticity in therapy, then there can be no authenticity in life. (p. 29)

4. Concreteness. A precise, complete response to specific feelings and experiences.

First, the therapist's concreteness ensures that his response does not become too far removed emotionally from the client's feelings and experiences. Second, concreteness encourages the therapist to be more accurate in his understanding of the client, and thus misunderstandings can be clarified and corrections made when feelings and experiences are stated in specific terms. Third, the client is directly influenced to attend specifically to problem areas and emotional conflicts. (p. 30)

The counselor tries to understand each client's perception of himself, of his problem, and of his situation. Although he often tries to help each client to understand the forces at work within himself and his environment in order to help the client to cope with these forces more effectively, the counselor should realize that insight alone is not sufficient for anyone, and for some it is not necessary; clients sometimes improve their behavior without understanding the source of their problems.

Group Counseling Differentiated
from Individual Counseling

To be effective in either individual or group counseling, a counselor must develop the therapeutic conditions and experience the feelings described above. For groups he must select good prospects who have a therapeutic influence on each other, assess their willingness to change, describe and reinforce their helping behaviors, and focus his attention on the speaker while noting and reacting to various clients' reactions to each other. He must detect and therapeutically use nonverbal as well as verbal interactions and teach his clients to do so too.

Frank (1952) reported that clients focused attention on each other rather than on events within their individual pasts or outside their group. Durkin (1964) also found that patients treated in groups tended to focus on the here and now more than those treated individually. Joel and Shapiro (1950) reported that reality testing was an integral part of the treatment for their group patients, and that growth was often unaccompanied by insight. Lindt (1958) stressed treatment *by* the group more than treatment *in* the group. He noted the importance of clients' learning to listen to others, to invest in others, and to react to one another therapeutically. He found that those who profited from his groups made an emotional investment in the group to the extent of making a genuine effort to help at least one or two other members.

Contrary to what those who have never participated in group counseling may think, some clients* find it easier to

* See, for example, Chapter Ten on the counseling of adolescents.

discuss difficult topics in group counseling than in individual counseling. When clients observe and help others discuss their problems openly within a counseling group, and sense others' acceptance and compassion, they discover that they, too, can discuss their problems. Seeing others cope successfully with their problems by discussing them openly, at the same time gaining increased acceptance, decreases resistance and encourages therapeutic action.

What clients discuss is determined by their orientation to their group, their previous experiences in groups, and the way in which group members react to them and their problems. Ohlsen and Oelke's (1962) findings support these observations. Talland and Clark (1954) found that for their therapy groups the topics judged to be most disturbing matched closely those judged to be most helpful. Their patients valued most the topics that could be discussed only within a therapeutic relationship. Although their patients reported that no topic was entirely worthless, some seemed to find a given topic more therapeutic than others. The writer believes that Talland and Clark's findings apply also to counseling groups. When, therefore, clients recognize that a topic is painful for the speaker, the counselor should reflect their feelings for wanting to avoid it as well as speaker's wish to deal with it even though it is painful. Such action enlists the group's assistance and conveys the counselor's confidence in the speaker's ability to cope with the painful material involved.

To harness the full potential of a counseling group, every client must learn to help others as well as to obtain help for himself. He must be sufficiently open to admit when others' problems expose his own, and to encourage others to try solutions that are most appropriate for them. As the therapeutic potency of the group increases, members' personal respect for each other grows so that they can tolerate individual differences and accept quite different solutions for similar problems. From the beginning they must learn to accept responsibility for helping the counselor develop and maintain a therapeutic climate.

How Group Counseling Differs
from Other Group Activities

In this book *counseling* is defined as a therapeutic experience for persons who do not have serious emotional problems. Clients are encouraged to seek a counselor's assistance before they develop serious neurotic, psychotic, or characterological disorders. A counselor works not only with his clients but also with significant others such as parents, teachers, and clergymen in furthering normal social, emotional, and intellectual development. He helps his clients learn normal developmental tasks and also helps significant others teach his clients these tasks, whether they involve adjustment to kindergarten, development of post high school plans, adapting to college, or adjustment to marriage.

Psychotherapy, on the other hand, is defined here as a therapeutic experience for emotionally disturbed persons who seek assistance with pathological problems. In other words, psychotherapy differs from counseling primarily in terms of the persons treated rather than the treatment process. Also, the counselor is less concerned with uncovering the repressed materials that genetically determine the client's problems. Clients may discuss repressed materials which they feel have special relevance for their present problems, but the counselor tends to focus on the present and the solution of the specific immediate problems for which his clients seek help.

For school counselors group counseling also must be differentiated from group guidance. Hinckley and Herman's (1952) definition of social group work can be used as a definition for group guidance: a group activity in which a leader provides information or leads a discussion designed to socialize members or to help them achieve some group objectives. Usually the leader for a school guidance group provides educational, occupational, or social information and encourages members of the group to discuss its relevance for them. Ohlsen (1964) described two types of group guidance activities:

(1) faculty initiated and planned groups such as guidance courses or occupations course, work-experience seminars, college days, career days, and career clubs; and (2) voluntary discussion groups such as student forums. In this sense those who participate in group guidance have a common goal—to obtain specific information or to learn certain skills. Group-counseling clients do not share such common goals. Their objective is to help each client discuss his own, perhaps more private or personal problems and to solve them in his own way.

Inasmuch as the same persons are often expected to provide both group guidance and group counseling in schools and colleges, they must differentiate between the two processes in accepting members for the different groups. In order to provide students with the services they require, these differences must be maintained. When the members of a guidance group seem to want to become a counseling group, and the leader is qualified to do group counseling, he should check with the individual members of the guidance group to insure that they understand the differences and indeed they are ready for and wish to participate in a counseling group.

Another effective type of group experience, often confused with group counseling, is that of T groups, sometimes called sensitivity groups. T groups tend to be brief (from a few days up to two or three weeks), intensive programs designed to improve human-relations skills for consultants or leaders. Bradford, Gibb, and Benne (1964) listed five objectives for the participant: (1) increased sensitivity to emotional reactions in himself and others, (2) improved ability to perceive and learn the consequences of his reactions, (3) clarification and development of personal values and goals consonant with democratic action and decisions, (4) development of insights and concepts that serve as tools in linking personal values, goals, and intentions to actions, and (5) improved behavioral skills to support better integration of intentions and actions. Reinforcement and feedback are crucial teaching tools for T groups. In this sense, T groups have much in common with counseling groups. Both also focus members' attention on the

here and now, changing their behavior, and both use role playing to help members learn to cope with specific situations and
persons.

On the other hand, T groups tend to be less carefully
structured than the counseling groups described in this book;
T-group leaders tend to feel that part of the benefits come
from members' developing a meaningful group relationship.
T groups also tend to give more attention to the analysis of
interactions among members and to the study of group process, to the appraisal of their own group effectiveness, and to
achieving insight (or understanding of what is happening to
them). The way in which members and the leader of a T group
respond to each other also tends to be different from the way
in which they usually respond to each other in a counseling
group. For example, in a T group one would expect A to tell B
how he feels about him and how B is influencing him at the
moment. This also happens in a counseling group, but in a
counseling group member A (or the counselor) would be more
inclined to try to detect and reflect the feelings that B is experiencing, to help him express these feelings, to help him
figure out what he can do about them, and to encourage him
to take action. In other words, T groups tend to stress confrontation and interpretation of behavior, whereas counseling
groups tend to stress empathy with and support for fellow
clients while they are discussing their feelings, planning a
course of action, and implementing it.

Selection of Counselor Education Candidates

Before those who prepare persons to do group counseling
in any setting can develop criteria for selecting candidates
they must agree on the counselor's professional duties and the
program required to prepare him for these duties. With these
criteria they can select those who appear to have promise as
counselors and have a resonably good chance of completing the
program successfully. Actually, those who prepare persons to
do group counseling also prepare them to do individual coun-

seling. Furthermore, most researchers concerned with validating their selection devices have obtained criterion measures on those doing individual counseling, hence these studies are cited here, along with a few theoretical papers on requirements for those who do group counseling.

Good mental ability and demonstrated success in using it are, of course, prerequisites. Those who educate for the professions, however, must be able to identify those *unique* factors which contribute to success in practice, and must develop measuring instruments and standardized observations and/or interviews to predict success prior to admission. Furthermore, they must continue to appraise students' professional development, as well as to reinforce it, as students move through professional education. Increasingly, staff members of approved professional programs are required to screen candidates for certification and/or licensing and to endorse only the competent who complete their institution's program. This procedure makes those who prepare persons for professions accept responsibility for their products, for selective retention as well as for selective admission. This makes sense, for certainly those who have supervised prospective professionals do get to know their students' professional competencies in ways that cannot be assessed by the typical licensing examinations.

The research indicates that counselor educators can predict academic success in professional education better than counseling success. One of the major problems has been lack of adequate criteria for assessing counseling success (this point is developed more fully in Chapter Twelve). Another problem has arisen from the use of data collected during professional preparation rather than performance data concerning employed counselors. It is not sufficient to know how counselors perform within a practicum setting developed for them by their counselor educators; the real test is how well they perform in a setting in which they must establish their own professional role.

Most research done before 1950 tended to select words or characteristics to describe counselors but failed to produce data that could be used effectively to screen candidates, because poor as well as good counselors exhibited these same characteristics, and no adequate measures were developed to appraise them.

A few of the studies that identified general characteristics are reviewed here. Fiedler (1950) concluded that even counselors who hold very different points of view seem to agree on behaviors characteristic of the ideal therapeutic relationship: (1) there is an empathic relationship; (2) the counselor and client relate well; (3) the counselor sticks closely to the client's problems; (4) the client feels free to say what he likes; (5) an atmosphere of mutual trust and confidence exists; (6) rapport is excellent; (7) the client assumes an active role; (8) the counselor leaves the client free to make his own choices; (9) the counselor accepts all feelings that the client expresses as completely normal and understandable; (10) a tolerant atmosphere exists; (11) the counselor is understanding; (12) the client feels most of the time that he is really understood; (13) the counselor is really able to understand the client; and (14) the counselor really tries to understand the client's feelings.

In the same paper Fiedler listed the following as *least characteristic* of an ideal relationship: (1) the counselor is punitive; (2) the counselor makes the client feel rejected; (3) the counselor seems to have no respect for the client; (4) there is an impersonal, cold relationship; (5) the counselor often puts the client "in his place"; (6) the client curries favor with the counselor; and (7) the counselor tries to impress the client with his skill and knowledge.

Fiedler also found that the ability to describe the ideal relationship was more a matter of expertness and experience than of allegiance to any school of counseling. The reason may have been that not all the pertinent items were included in his descriptions of therapeutic relationships.

Sunderlund and Barker's (1962) research certainly suggests that experienced therapists from different schools do behave differently. They divided their subjects into three major groups: Freudian, Sullivanian, and Rogerian. Each group included an equal number of experienced (six years or more) and inexperienced (five years or less) therapists. The persons from the three different philosophical orientations differed at the .01 level of significance on 11 of their 16 dimensions. The Freudians differed from the other two groups on the importance they attributed to early childhood experiences, unconscious motivations, conceptualization, therapist's training, and therapist's goals, planning, and objectivity; they also stressed the importance of the therapist's suppressing his spontaneity. The Rogerians were at the opposite end of the continuum on these dimensions. The Sullivanians usually occupied a position somewhere between the Freudians and Rogerians; however, like Freudians, they were more inclined to stress the necessity for conceptualization, for having therapeutic goals, for planning, and for inhibiting spontaneity and, like Rogerians, they were more inclined to see the therapist personally involved in the treatment and to recognize the importance of the therapist's personality. Sunderland and Barker also found that the inexperienced therapists were a more heterogeneous group than were the experienced therapists.

Four other studies also support the notion that there are observable differences between inexperienced and experienced counselors and therapists: Bohn (1965), Grigg (1961), Mills and Abeles (1965), and Strupp (1955). Grigg found that experienced counselors were less active and less inclined to give advice than inexperienced counselors. Strupp reported that experienced counselors used a greater variety of techniques than inexperienced counselors. Mills and Abeles found that counselors' experience (as practicum students, interns, and senior staff members) influenced their tolerance of their clients' hostility. Both practicum students (the least experienced) and senior staff seemed to cope with hostility better than interns. Interns tended to forego much of their need for nurturance with clients they liked. With more experience they seemed to be able to satisfy this need. Perhaps this explains why for one period in their professional development they tended to exhibit withdrawal behavior rather than to cope with their clients' hostility. Just as the investigators predicted, the need for affiliation and nurturance was found to be positively

related to ability to cope with hostility. For Bohn's study
readers should note that even his experienced counselors were
inexperienced counselors: (1) his experienced counselors were
graduate students who were enrolled in an approved program
in either clinical or counseling psychology and (2) his inexperienced counselors were undergraduates who were meeting their experiment-time requirement for a beginning psychology course. Both were most directive with dependent
clients. His experienced counselors used more restatement of
content and clarification of feelings, whereas his inexperienced counselors used more reassurance, persuasion, direct
questions, and forcing-the-topic responses.

An inference one may make from the studies reviewed
above is that perhaps beginning or inexperienced counselors
are so anxious to do well that they cannot make full use of
their repertoire of newly acquired professional skills. Bandura
(1956) hypothesized that competent psychotherapists are less
anxious and possess a greater degree of insight into the nature
of their anxiety than those judged to be less competent. His
results confirmed only that the competent were less anxious
than the less competent.

Unfortunately, no one has taken findings such as those
reviewed above and developed an instrument that discrimi-
nates clearly between good and poor counselors as beginning
graduate students. Carkhuff and Berenson's (1967) scales,
developed on similar findings, might be used to classify prospective counselors' responses to actors trained to perform as
clients and to bring in critical incidents that counselors meet
in helping clients. Rank's (1966) work may help those who
wish to pursue this notion. Such material could be readily
standardized and presented on video recordings (or on films,
as Rank did), which researchers could then validate as a
screening device. Such materials also would incorporate the
best features of simulated tests used in management training.

A number of investigators have used personality tests to
try to differentiate between best and poorest practicum students. Rarely have personality tests produced adequate differ-
entiation to warrant their use in screening candidates for

counselor education: Bergin and Solomon (1963) MMPI
scores; Brams (1961) MMPI scores and Bill's Index of Adjustment and Values; Demos and Zuwaylif (1966) Allport,
Vernon, and Lindzey Study of Values; Foley and Proff (1965)
MMPI scores; Ohlsen (1967a) MMPI scores; Schroeder and
Dowse (1968) MMPI scores and California Personality Inventory scores; Stefflre, King, and Leafgren (1962) Bill's Index
of Adjustment and Values, and Wasson (1965) MMPI scores.
However, the F scale of MMPI may be useful in screening
counselor education candidates; effective counselors tend to
score lower on it than ineffective ones. Another measure of
authoritarianism or dogmatism is Rokeach's Dogmatism Scale.
Patterson (1967) concluded that Kemp's (1962), Russo, Kelz,
and Hudson's (1964), and Stefflre, Leafgren, and King's
(1962) research all support the notion that effective counselors are less dogmatic than ineffective counselors.

Though little research has been done to validate their use
in screening prospective counselors, the evidence available on
the Wisconsin Relationship Orientation Scale and Cattell's 16
Personality Factor Questionnaire suggests that both show
promise. Wasson (1965) reported that scores on the Wisconsin
Scale correlated higher with his three criterion scores (rated
counseling segments .61, staff ratings .54, and peer ratings
.61) than did any of his other measures (Minnesota Multi-
phasic Inventory, Edwards Personal Preference Scale, Miller
Analogies, Strong Vocational Interest Blank, and NDEA
Comprehensive Examination). Furthermore, the scores obtained on it did not correlate significantly with any of the
other measures. Miller (1965) found a significant relationship
between certain personality characteristics of untrained individuals and their helping behaviors. Helpers were perceived
to exhibit enthusiasm, cheerfulness, openness, expressiveness,
frankness, quickness, ego strength, conscientiousness, and
lower emotional-stability scores than those who were perceived as less helpful. Obviously, one cannot conclude that
these undergraduate males preferred unstable persons; perhaps they saw those who were most helpful as being genuine
and open to their own real feelings.

For the Edwards Personal Preference Scale a number of researchers have identified individual scales that differentiated between most and least effective counselors: Demos and Zuwaylif (1966) found that effective counselors were higher on nurturance and affiliation and lower on autonomy, abasement, and aggression than ineffective counselors; Stefflre, King, and Leafgren (1962) found that effective counselors were higher on deference and order and lower on abasement and aggression; and Truax, Silber, and Warge (1966) found best prospects were higher on change and autonomy and lower on order. Ohlsen's (1967a) findings add further confusion to these ambiguous findings. For his first group of 29 counselors the most effective scored higher on succorance and lower on order, deference, and consistency than the least effective, but these findings were not supported by a similar group of 30 counselors, among whom the most effective scored higher on introspection and lower on dominance and aggression than the least effective. He also pointed out that (1) he had an unusually large pool of good prospects from which to select both groups and (2) Edwards' manifest needs were ranked very similarly for both groups before and after graduate education. Both groups ranked heterosexuality, introspection, change, exhibition, and affiliation high and abasement, endurance, deference, and order low. Furthermore, during graduate education the priority in their hierarchy of needs for heterosexuality and autonomy was raised significantly and for abasement was lowered. Truax, Silber, and Warge also found that students who profited most from their training exhibited a significant decline in abasement and those who profited least raised significantly their abasement scores. Their most-profited students began training with significantly higher autonomy scores and raised them during training, while least-profited students not only began with lower autonomy scores but lowered them. Perhaps these findings relate to Whitely, Sprinthall, Mosher, and Donaghty's (1967) promising findings. Using supervisors' ratings as a criterion for success, they found that their best screening devices were cognitive flexibility-rigidity assessed by projective test responses to critical incidents in case studies.

The Strong Vocational Interest Blank has been widely used in selecting candidates for counselor education. Kriedt (1949), Patterson (1962), and Foley and Proff (1965) found that counselors and students enrolled in counselor education exhibited their highest interest in the social-service block of occupations. Stefflre, King, and Leafgren (1962) and Ohlsen (1967a) reported that effective counselors were more apt to exhibit high scores for these occupations than were ineffective counselors. For Wasson's (1965) study such significant differences were not obtained.

Measures of scholastic aptitude and undergraduate grade point average are useful for predicting academic success in graduate education but rarely predict counseling success: Blocher (1963), Callis and Prediger (1964), Ohlsen (1967a), Patterson (1967), Stefflre, King, and Leafgren (1962), and Wasson (1965). The Miller Analogies is the scholastic aptitude test most often used for screening prospective counselors.

Peer ratings have been widely used as criterion measures for appraising counselors' effectiveness in validating screening devices [for example, Blocher (1963), Dole (1964), McDougall and Reitan (1961), Ohlsen (1967), and Stefflre, King, and Leafgren (1962)]. The last also questioned whether those enrolled in the typical counselor education program know each other well enough to differentiate between best and poorest prospective counselors. Ohlsen and Dennis' (1951) findings with similar subjects would suggest that they do. Ohlsen and Schultz's (1954) research with teachers suggests that sociometric tests also can be used to screen counselor education candidates. Dilley's (1964) findings also offer support for this notion. At least he found that peers' ratings of best and poorest counselors agreed with counselor educators' and supervisors' independent ratings of the same counselors.

In an unpublished study, the writer also found that responses of beginning counselor education students (enrolled in the introduction to guidance course) to the following socio-

metric test items predicted success in practicum: (1) (a) If
you had a problem with which you really needed help and there
was no one else available but the students enrolled in this
class, to which three would you turn first? (b) To which three
would you turn last? and (2) If there are some persons enrolled in this class with whom you are not well enough
acquainted to decide how you feel about them, list their names
here. Currently the writer is involved in a research project in
which he is using these two items along with four others based
on Carkhuff and Berenson's (1967) findings (empathy, respect for others, genuineness, and concreteness) to validate
their effectiveness for screening counselor education candidates. For a class of approximately 25 students he asks them
to name the three whom they would select first and last (the
number they are asked to name varies with the size of the
class). Though students generally agree well on their choices,
the test tends to be threatening. When, however, they realize
that no one else can see whom they have chosen, that no one
will be told who chooses whom, and that the instructor will
interpret the results for them to help them see themselves as
others see them and to help them explore what the results may
mean for their success as counselors, a large majority usually
votes to have the class participate in this sociometric testing.

Another useful source of data in screening counselor education candidates is an intensive intake interview. It may be
used to assess a prospective counselor's ability to experience
his own feelings and accept himself as he is; his attitudes
toward himself and the important others in his life; the degree
to which he has achieved independence; his ego strength; his
goals, and especially his reasons for wanting to become a
counselor. The writer structures this interview as follows: "I
would like to get to know you so that I may help you examine
your plans and make the most of your opportunities to learn
from your graduate education experiences. Try to trust me as
you have never trusted anyone before and tell me about you—
starting with your earliest memories tell me about some of
your happiest and unhappiest moments and the persons who
have had the greatest impact upon your life." If, during their

free response, they fail to mention parents, siblings, early childhood and school experiences, sex, values, or their career development, the interviewer usually asks an ambiguous question such as, "You never mentioned anything about elementary school experiences"—leaving it up to the other to develop the topic in his own way. Of course, some have great difficulty talking about themselves, others tell the interviewer only what they think he wants to hear, and a few cannot or will not reveal themselves. Usually an experienced interviewer can empathize with and convey desire to understand the first type; see through the behavior of the second type; and try to understand but permit escape for the last type. The last type tends to be the poorest bet for counselor education. Obviously, the technique is fallible, but it provides useful data to supplement the other types of data described above.

Careful screening of counselor education candidates should help identify personal values, attitudes, and problems that may interfere with their effectiveness as counselors. Hopefully the type of intake interview described above also will motivate them to become increasingly better acquainted with themselves during counselor education. While enrolled in counseling practicum and internship experiences, in particular, many discover problems which interfere with their effectiveness. For some, merely having a problem called to their attention is sufficient to enable them to cope with it in counseling, but for most the more serious problems require systematic counseling. From his evaluation of a counselor education program Ohlsen (1967b) concluded that group counseling is an effective treatment technique for counselors in training. His subjects reported that group counseling was one of the most profitable experiences in their professional preparation. It increased their self-understanding and self-acceptance and improved their interpersonal relationships, especially with the members of their families and with authority figures.

Group counseling can be one of the most effective ways of helping prospective counselors to better understand themselves, to discover and solve their problems, and to learn how to keep those problems that they cannot solve with reasonable effort from interfering with their effectiveness as counselors. Their experience within a counseling group enables them to express their doubts about the treatment process; to discover that they can be open and trusting and not get hurt (indeed, they feel better and they recognize that they are better accepted by peers); to discover that other prospective counselors have problems, too; to note specific ways in which these other prospective counselors are helped, and thereby increase their confidence in obtaining help; to apply their professional knowledge in understanding others; to observe how a qualified counselor assists various clients; and while functioning as co-counselors to obtain experience in helping others. They experience the therapeutic process and learn to accept it for themselves as well as for others.

Must those who do group counseling have unique personal qualities? Slavson (1962) concluded that those who do group therapy must. He listed the following as essential: poise, judgment, maturity, ego strength, freedom from excessive anxiety, perceptiveness, intuition, empathy, imaginativeness, ability to avoid self-preoccupation, desire to help people, and tolerance of frustration. He contended that unpleasant encounters with groups, especially with the members of their families, makes it very difficult for some persons to accept and to tolerate frank, uninhibited expression of feelings and the confusion that sometimes occurs in groups. Slavson also noted that many are worried about not being able to control the direction and content of interaction among members, and thus not being able to protect some patients from being pushed into uncovering material before they are ready to deal with it or from being hurt by acting-out patients. Some therapists also are concerned about having their own problems and/or professional inadequacies disclosed. On the other hand, Slavson stated that having had a difficult childhood can be an asset for those therapists who have resolved their problems. However, he concluded that these interpersonal conflicts *must be worked through* in psychoanalysis before one attempts to do group psychotherapy. Furthermore, he pointed out how the therapist serves as a model for his clients—that what he is may be as important as what he does. Much of what Slavson said about group therapists applies to those who do group counseling. Though counselors should participate in group counseling for the reasons presented by Slavson and those listed earlier, their clients are not apt to have the pathological impact upon each other noted by Slavson. The counselor's reasonably healthy clients are better able to cope with the problems they discover in groups, and they learn more quickly than Slavson's disturbed patients how to give genuine understanding and support to fellow clients as they struggle with difficult problems.

Professional Preparation

Increasingly, designated members of a profession are assigned the responsibility for doing a taxonomy of their professional duties to determine what knowledge, skills, attitudes, and values are required. Krathwohl, Bloom, and Masia's (1964) model for study of teaching is one effective method. Miller, McGuire, and Larsen (1965) used the critical-incident technique to identify performance requirements for competence in orthopaedic surgery, and concluded that it was valid and reliable for their purpose. Ohlsen (1968) described a technique used by a professional committee to enlist outstanding practitioners in analyzing their professional duties, ranking them in order of their significance, and evaluating their professional preparation. Usually a professional committee develops guidelines for professional preparation and defines criteria that can be used by a faculty for self-study and by accreditation teams to evaluate the calibre of students and faculty, the intellectual climate, laboratories, library, and teaching materials [e.g., Hill (1964)].

Once the essential components have been identified, members of a professional college staff must develop a sequence of didactic and laboratory experiences for each component and

20 GROUP COUNSELING

techniques for evaluating the impact of their program on their students. Mere appraisal of students' mastery of knowledge is not sufficient. Counselor educators must try to assess the development of their students' professional attitudes, interests, values, and clinical skill. Nor is it sufficient to assess the changes that occur in students while they are obtaining professional preparation; an attempt also must be made to assess whether they have developed the professional commitment and skills to implement their professional role and to continue professional development in practice. The latter requires intensive follow-up studies of practitioners.

Merely preparing counselors to do what they are currently doing is not sufficient; they must be qualified to do what can and should be done, and they must be sufficiently sure of themselves to do it. School counselors' recent statement on definition and implementation of role [*Counseling as a Growing Profession* (1964)] supports this stand.

Two other examples of professional statements on the preparation of counselors are: (1) "Standards for the Preparation of Elementary School Counselors" (1968) and (2) "Standards for Counselor Education in the Preparation of Secondary School Counselors" (1964). These programs include the following: developmental and educational psychology, counseling theory and techniques, group dynamics, group counseling, supervised practicum in counseling, career development and vocational guidance, research methods and statistics, tests and measurements, use of tests in counseling, legal status and professional ethics of counseling, development and administration of guidance services, curriculum development, and improvement of conditions for learning within the classroom. More and more programs are also requiring advanced practicum in group counseling and an internship. A master's degree is still accepted by some as a minimum program, but there is a growing support for a minimum two-year graduate program. There also is a strong trend to approve an institution's counselor education program and to make the members of the staff responsible for screening candidates, for practicing selective retention, and for endorsing those whom they prepare who qualify for certification.

Good didactic instruction, clear expectations, and good supervised practice must be supported by meaningful, encouraging relationships with both fellow students and staff. Chenault (1964) stressed the necessity of a nonauthoritarian atmosphere in which a prospective counselor is free to be himself, to experiment with ways of relating to and helping others, and to develop his own professional values. Merton, Reader, and Kendall (1957) found that opportunities for social interaction with fellow students and staff influenced professional development. Ohlsen's (1967b) research subjects cited a number of specific ways in which both their professional and personal development were enhanced by individual assistance and social interactions with fellow students and staff. Schlossberg (1963) argued that these kinds of interactions can be experienced best in full-time graduate education.

Implementation of one's professional role is more difficult for the school counselor, and perhaps for other counselors too, than defining it and developing values consistent with it. Goode and Cornish (1964) concluded that long and carefully planned professional preparation must be reinforced by supportive on-the-job affiliations for most professional persons to establish an image of themselves as professionals. Olsen's (1963) paper supports Goode and Cornish's conclusions. He stated that typical counselor education even with practicum supervision is not sufficient to enable a former teacher to define and implement his counseling role. He made the point that counselors too often merely learn to play the counselor's role within a relatively sheltered environment, and hence they have difficulty in actually living it within a real work setting. When, therefore, counselor educators ask such prospective school counselors to give up attitudes and behaviors that were satisfying to them as teachers, counselor educators must help them recognize and learn to cope with the reinforcers of old attitudes and behaviors. Prospective counselors must define a meaningful professional role, and one they believe they can implement on the job, while they are enrolled in graduate education. Specific assistance and simulated teaching materials also are required during practicum and internship to assist prospective counselors in developing presentations to introduce group counseling, to identify clients, to select clients, and to cope with the problems they meet in counseling their first groups. When prospective counselors have these experiences with fellow students, they develop norms for professional conduct that influence their behavior on the job.

The chance of a counselor's implementing a truly professional role is further enhanced by his accepting a position in a school system with at least one of his fellow students [Hastings, Runkel, Damrin (1961)]. Such fellowship helps a beginner establish and maintain a professional role. Some of these benefits also can be achieved if a student's practicum or internship supervisor helps him get acquainted with other counselors from his school system or from a nearby school system who hold similar professional values and hence can help him establish and maintain his professional role. Follow-up visits on the job by counselor educators from his training institution provide similar aid and also help him face and cope with the problems he meets during early full-time employment [Ohlsen (1967b)]. Besides these aids, good supervision by competent counselors is still needed. Without good supervision and the known support of fellow counselors, beginning counselors find it very difficult to implement a professional role and begin group counseling.

True professionals grow and develop on the job. The degree to which this is achieved is determined in part by selection of candidates for counselor education. Counselor educators should select only those who exhibit intellectual curiosity and seem to have the potential for making a commitment to the profession. Teachers and, later, associates can either hinder or enhance their learning and their intellectual curiosity. Employers should employ counselors who want to grow on the job and are committed to try to improve themselves, and they also should employ supervisors who can help them do so. Finally, counselors have responsibility for their own professional development on the job.

Because so few counselors have had systematic didactic preparation and supervised practice in group counseling, many will have to take the initiative to obtain this work after they are employed as counselors. Even those who have good professional preparation in social psychology, group dynamics, leadership training, and group counseling and/or group psychotherapy methods rarely have had supervised practice in group counseling. After they feel reasonably secure doing individual counseling, the writer recommends that they conduct some voluntary discussion groups (described in Chapter Ten) to develop their skills as discussion leaders and to increase their understanding of groups. Participating in group counseling as clients also increases their readiness to cope with groups.

For school counselors who have had these group experiences and formal instruction in group counseling methods, the writer has developed a two-semester, on-the-job seminar, "Supervision in Field-Trial Experiences." It is an internship kind of experience for groups of eight to ten employed counselors. During the first semester they meet biweekly to discuss their goals for group counseling, the problems they expect to meet in group counseling, methods for presenting the idea of group counseling to prospective clients, and criteria for selecting clients. They also select with the help of seminar members the clients that *each will counsel* in his first group. The second semester of the seminar is devoted to discussion of the problems they meet counseling this first group, including critiquing recordings between seminar sessions. For the second year of on-the-job training the seminar group breaks up into two groups, each consisting of half of the old group and an equal number of new members who are interested in beginning group counseling. While the new members are obtaining help carrying their first group, the old members obtain help with their second group. Substantially less consultant help is required the second year. Most members also do considerable professional reading. This is merely an example of how supervision can encourage growth on the job. Often it is best to begin this field-trial work with supervisory personnel.

Best results are obtained by the supervisor when the counselors respect him and believe that he is concerned about them as people as well as about the service he obtains from them. To fulfill this leadership role the supervisor must help his counselors define their professional role, implement it, and develop criteria that they can use by themselves, or with his assistance, to appraise their own effectiveness. He encourages them to make audio recordings, and where possible even video recordings, for self-study. A counselor is most apt to seek this kind of help when he is secure enough to recognize his mistakes, when he wants to correct them, and when he feels that his supervisor respects him, wants to help him, and will try to understand why he behaved as he did. The supervisor must accept responsibility for regular supervision of his counselors and for developing the kinds of working relationships that enable counselors to accept supervision. Whether or not these conditions are met, every counselor must accept professional responsibility for his own growth on the job.

Summary

Counseling is defined as a therapeutic experience for reasonably healthy persons, psychotherapy as one for emotionally disturbed persons who seek, or are referred for, assistance with pathological problems. Thus, the primary difference is in the persons treated rather than the treatment process. A counselor's clients are encouraged to seek assistance before they develop serious neurotic, psychotic, or characterological disorders. Besides counseling his clients, a counselor assists significant others in furthering his clients' normal social, emotional, and intellectual development; hence, his services are preventive and developmental as well as therapeutic.

Counseling is an accepting, trusting, encouraging relationship between a counselor and one or more clients. A counselor knows how to listen, to feel and convey empathy and respect, and to respond to the feelings a client is experiencing. Furthermore, in group counseling, he is able to help his clients accept responsibility for developing a therapeutic relationship, for maintaining it, and for helping fellow clients while they are obtaining assistance for themselves. Clients not only *try to change* their own behavior and attitudes, they *expect* to change them, and they expect fellow clients to change theirs, too. Within this relationship clients learn to face and to cope with their problems, and they develop the courage and self-confidence to apply what they learn in daily living.

Many clients, especially adolescents, find it easier to discuss their most private thoughts and feelings in groups than in individual counseling. What, however, a client discusses in his counseling group seems to be determined by his orientation to his group, his own previous experiences in groups, and the way in which the members of his group react to him and his problems.

The counselor is an important variable in the treatment process. Hence, those who prepare counselors must accept the responsibility for selecting the very best available prospects, for preparing them well, and for encouraging their growth in practice. This chapter reviews the research on screening candidates for counselor education. Some of the most promising screening devices described include sociometric tests, simulated tests, and an intensive screening interview. Though most personality tests have not differentiated between effective and ineffective counselors, the following show more promise: Cattell's 16 Personality Factor Questionnaire, the Edwards Personal Preference Scale, Rokeach's Dogmatism Scale, and the Wisconsin Relationship Orientation Scale. Certain scores on the Strong Vocational Interest Blank also tend to differentiate between effective and ineffective counselors. Miller Analogies and undergraduate grades also are usually used to screen candidates for counselor education. These last two are of little or no value in predicting counseling success, but they do seem to help in predicting academic success during professional preparation.

Careful screening of counselor education candidates also

should help prospective counselors come to understand themselves and to identify personal values, attitudes, and unsolved problems that may interfere with their effectiveness as counselors. This process should continue in professional education and in practice. Group counseling is one of the most effective ways of stimulating this process as well as personal development during counselor education.

Increasingly, designated members of every profession are assigned the responsibility for analyzing the duties of a practitioner to determine what knowledge, skills, attitudes, and values are required. Once the essential components have been identified, members of a professional college staff must develop a sequence of didactic and laboratory experiences for each component and techniques for evaluating the impact of their program on their students. They also must try to assess whether their students have developed the professional commitment and skills to implement their role and to continue professional development in practice. Counselor educators must do intensive follow-up studies and encourage continued growth on the job.

Good didactic instruction, clear expectations for professional development, and even good supervised practice are not enough in themselves. They must be supported by encouraging meaningful relationships with students and staff during professional preparation and by professional assistance and encouragement on the job. Even when these are missing, a professional must accept responsibility for his own development. He must accept responsibility for providing the best services within his power.

References

Bandura, A. "Psychotherapists' Anxiety Level, Self-Insight, and Psychotherapeutic Competence," *Journal of Abnormal and Social Psychology*, 1956, 52:333–337.
Bergin, A. E., and Sandra Solomon. "Personality and Performance Cor-

relates of Empathic Understanding in Psychotherapy," *American Psychologist*, Convention Abstract, 1963, 18:393.

Blocher, D. H. "A Multiple Regression Approach to Predicting Success in a Counselor Education Program," *Counselor Education and Supervision*, 1963, 3:19–22.

Bohn, M. J. "Counselor Behavior as a Function of Counselor Dominance, Counselor Experience and Client Type," *Journal of Counseling Psychology*, 1965, 4:346–352.

Bradford, L. P., J. R. Gibb, K. D. Benne (eds.) *T-Group Theory and Laboratory Method*, New York: John Wiley & Sons, Inc., 1964.

Brams, J. M. "Counselor Characteristics and Effective Communication in Counseling," *Journal of Counseling Psychology*, 1961, 8:25–30.

Callis, R., and D. J. Prediger "Predictors of Achievement in Counseling and Guidance," *Counselor Education and Supervision*, 1964, 3:63–69.

Carkhuff, R. R., and B. G. Berenson *Beyond Counseling and Therapy*, New York: Holt, Rinehart and Winston, Inc., 1967.

Chenault, Joann "The Education of the School Counselor," *Phi Delta Kappan*, 1964, 45:450–452.

Counseling as a Growing Profession, a joint ACES-ASCA publication, Washington, D.C.: American Personnel and Guidance Association, 1964.

Demos, G. D., and F. H. Zuwaylif "Characteristics of Effective Counselors," *Counselor Education and Supervision*, 1966, 5:163–165.

Dilley, J. S. "Supervisory Ratings of Counselor Trainees in a Simulated Work Setting as Compared with Peer and Instructor's Ratings of Some Trainees in an Academic Setting," *Counselor Education and Supervision*, 1964, 3:70–73.

Dole, A. A. "The Prediction of Effectiveness in School Counseling," *Journal of Counseling Psychology*, 1964, 11:112–121.

Durkin, Helen E. *The Group in Depth*, New York: International Universities Press, Inc., 1964.

Fiedler, F. E. "The Concept of an Ideal Therapeutic Relationship," *Journal of Consulting Psychology*, 1950, 14:239–245.

Foley, W. J., and F. C. Proff "NDEA Institute Trainees and Vocational Rehabilitation Counselor: A Comparison of Characteristics," *Counselor Education and Supervision*, 1965, 4:154–159.

Frank, J. D. "Group Methods in Psychotherapy," *Journal of Social Issues*, 1952, 8:35–44.

Goode, W. G., and Mary J. Cornish *Professions in American Society*, New York: Columbia University Press, 1964.

Grigg, A. E. "Client Responses to Counselors at Different Levels of Experience," *Journal of Counseling Psychology*, 1961, 8:217–223.

Hastings, J. T., P. J. Runkel, and Dora E. Damrin *Effects of Tests by Teachers Trained in NDEA Institute*, Cooperative Research Project #702, College of Education, University of Illinois, 1961.

Hill, G. E. "How to Define the Functions of the School Counselor," *Counselor Education and Supervision*, 1964, 3:56–62.

Hinckley, R. G., and Lydia Hermann *Group Treatment in Psychotherapy*, Minneapolis: University of Minnesota Press, 1952.

Joel, W., and D. Shapiro "Some Principles and Procedures for Group Psychotherapy," *Journal of Psychology*, 1950, 29:77–88.

Kemp, C. G. "Influence of Dogmatism on the Training of Counselors," *Journal of Counseling Psychology*, 1962, 9:155–157.

Krathwohl, D. R., B. S. Bloom, and B. B. Masia *Taxonomy of Educational Objectives*: The Classification of Educational Goals, Handbook II, Affective Domain, New York: David McKay Company, Inc., 1964.

Kriedt, P. H. "Vocational Interests of Psychologists," *Journal of Applied Psychology*, 1949, 33:482–488.

Lindt, H. "The Nature of Therapeutic Interaction of Patients in Groups," *International Journal of Group Psychotherapy*, 1958, 8: 55–69.

McDougall, W. P., and H. M. Reitan "The Use of Peer Rating Technique in Appraising Selected Attributes of Counselor Trainees," *Counselor Education and Supervision*, 1961, 1:72–76.

Merton, R. K., G. G. Reader, and Patricia L. Kendall *The Student Physician*, A Report from the Bureau of Applied Research (Columbia University), Cambridge, Mass.: Harvard University Press, 1957.

Miller, G. E., C. H. McGuire, and C. B. Larsen "The Orthopaedic Training Study—A Progress Report," *Bulletin of American Academy of Orthopaedic Surgery*, 1965, 13:8–11.

Miller, T. K. "Characteristics of Perceived Helpers," *Personnel and Guidance Journal*, 1965, 43:687–691.

Mills, D. H., and N. Abeles "Counselor Needs for Affiliation and Nurturance as Related to Liking for Clients and Counseling Process," *Journal of Counseling Psychology*, 1965, 12:353–358.

Ohlsen, M. M. *Final Technical Report on Institute for Elementary School Counselors*, College of Education, University of Illinois, 1967a.

Ohlsen, M. M. *An Evaluation of a Counselor Education Program Designed for Prospective Elementary School Counselors Enrolled in 1965–1966 NDEA Institute*, U. S. Office of Education Project #6-8087, College of Education, University of Illinois, 1967b.

Ohlsen, M. M. *Guidance Services in the Modern School*, New York: Harcourt Brace & World, Inc., 1964.

Ohlsen, M. M. "Standards for the Preparation of Elementary School Counselors," *Counselor Education and Supervision*, 1968, 7:172–178.

Ohlsen, M. M., and C. Dennis. "Factors Associated with Education Students' Choices of Classmates," *Educational Administration and Supervision*, 1951, 277–290.

Ohlsen, M. M., and M. C. Oelke "An Evaluation of Discussion Topics in

Group Counseling," *Journal of Clinical Psychology*, 1962, 18:317–372.

Ohlsen, M. M., and R. Schultz "A Study of Variables for Use in Selection," *Journal of Teacher Education*, 1954, 5:279–283.

Olsen, L. C. "Success for New Counselors," *Journal of Counseling Psychology*, 1963, 10:350–355.

Patterson, C. H. "Test Characteristics of Rehabilitation Counselor Trainees," *Journal of Rehabilitation*, 1962, 28:15–16.

Patterson, C. H. "The Selection of Counselors," a paper read at Washington University Conference on Research in Counseling, St. Louis, Missouri, January 10–13, 1967.

Proposed Statement of Policy for Secondary School Counselors and Proposed Guidelines for Implementation of the ASCA Statement of Policy for Secondary School Counselors, Washington, D.C.: American School Counselor Association, A Division of American Personnel and Guidance, 1966.

Rank, R. C. "Counseling Competence and Perception," *Personnel and Guidance Journal*, 1966, 45:359–365.

Rogers, C. R. *On Becoming a Person*: A Therapist's View of Psychotherapy, Boston: Houghton Mifflin Company, 1961.

Russo, J. R., J. W. Kelz, G. R. Hudson "Are Good Counselors Open Minded?" *Counselor Education and Supervision*, 1964, 3:74–77.

Schlossberg, Nancy K. "A Sociological Framework for Evaluating Guidance Education," *Personnel and Guidance Journal*, 1963, 42:285–289.

Schroeder, Pearl, and Eunice Dowse "Selection, Function, and Assessment of Residence Hall Counselors," *Personnel and Guidance Journal*, 1968, 47:151–156.

Slavson, S. R. "Personality Qualifications of a Group Psychotherapist," *International Journal of Group Psychotherapy*, 1962, 12:411–420.

"Standards for Counselor Education in the Preparation of Secondary School Counselors," *Personnel and Guidance Journal*, 1964, 42:1061–1073.

"Standards for the Preparation of Elementary School Counselors," ACES Publication, Washington, D.C.: American Personnel and Guidance Association, 1968.

Stefflre, B., P. King, and F. Leafgren "Characteristics of Counselors Judged Effective by Their Peers," *Journal of Counseling Psychology*, 1962, 9:335–340.

Strupp, H. H. "Psychotherapeutic Technique, Professional Affiliation, and Experience Level," *Journal of Consulting Psychology*, 1955, 19:97–102.

Sunderland, D. M., and E. N. Barker "The Orientation of Psychotherapists," *Journal of Consulting Psychology*, 1962, 26:403–409.

Symonds, P. M. *Dynamics of Psychotherapy*, New York: Grune and Stratton, Inc., 1956.

Talland, G. A., and D. H. Clark "Evaluation of Topics in a Therapy Group Discussion," *Journal of Clinical Psychology*, 1954, 10:131–137.

Truax, C. B., L. D. Silber, and D. G. Warge *Personality Change and Achievement in Therapeutic Training*, Arkansas Rehabilitation Research and Training Center, University of Arkansas, 1966.

Wasson, R. M. "The Wisconsin Orientation Scale in the Assessment of Applicants for Counselor Education," *Counselor Education and Supervision*, 1965, 4:89–92.

Whiteley, J. M., N. A. Sprinthall, R. L. Mosher, and R. T. Donaghty "Selections and Evaluation of Counselor Effectiveness," *Journal of Counseling Psychology*, 1967, 14:226–234.

Wrenn, C. G. *The Counselor in a Changing World*, Washington, D.C.: American Personnel and Guidance Association, 1962.

Chapter Two

Goals for Group Counseling

Group counseling, as indicated in Chapter One, is concerned with helping normal people recognize their problems and solve them before they become serious. It is also concerned with helping clients learn to generalize from their counseling experiences and to apply these learnings in daily living. School counselors are concerned about furthering the social, emotional, and intellectual development of children and youth by helping teachers and parents to understand them better and to provide appropriate developmental experiences for them. In this latter sense the counselor's services are preventive, focusing on helping children and youth discover their problems early, counseling them, and teaching the important others in their lives to contribute to their normal development and to obtain assistance for them before their problems become debilitating.

Before a counselor initiates group counseling, he must decide whom he can help best under what circumstances. Next, he and each client must define specific goals for the client. These decisions are influenced by the degree to which he understands and accepts prospective clients and their perceptions, respects their judgments, and understands their impact upon him. Since these matters are discussed in Chapters One and Seven, they will not be discussed here.

A counselor's goals for his clients also are influenced by his definition of mental health. In this book adjustment is perceived as a dynamic process. As an individual gradually improves his adjustment, he discovers who he is, what he would like to do, what he can do, what gives him the greatest satisfaction, and how to recognize conflict and cope with it. He discovers that he is able to face and cope with life's crises. Good adjustment also includes improved ability to accept oneself and others, to give and accept love, to work with others and to feel and show concern for their welfare, to accept responsibility for one's behavior, to enjoy work and play, and to accept reality. A well-adjusted person realizes that he is gradually becoming his wished-for self. He achieves increasing congruence between his real self and his ideal self as he redefines his perception of ideal self and learns to behave increasingly like his ideal self. [These statements show the influence of Jahoda (1958) and Maslow (1954), who recognize that mere absence of mental illness is not mental health.]

Does such a definition of mental health agree with counselors' and therapists' general goals for treatment in groups? To what extent do counselors and therapists who are committed to different theoretical orientations seem to agree on general treatment goals? The next section reviews the general goals for group treatment given by six authors holding different theoretical points of view. Readers should note the extent to which they agree reasonably well on all goals except the importance of insight.

The remaining two sections of this chapter are concerned with (1) an evaluation of goals for counseling and (2) suggestions for defining idiosyncratic goals.

General Goals

In defining criteria for terminating analytically oriented groups Bross (1958) revealed the following goals for her groups: development of ego resources, ego integration, improved functioning as a group member, resolution of transference and resistance, ability to gain pleasure from purposeful activities, development of self-confidence, achievement of self-assertion and self-realization with one's contemporaries, and ability to formulate and act on one's plans. Increased insight, a commonly stated goal for classic analysis, was not stated, but is clearly inferred from her goals for resolution of resistance and transference.

Adlerians perceive group treatment primarily as an educative process. Dreikurs (1957) stated that Adlerians try to help clients give up the faulty premises that have produced their feelings of inferiority and isolation, their guilt feelings, and their desire to gain prestige and change their life style. Though their clients experience genuine and meaningful emotional interchange, Adlerians stress intellectual understanding. Through encouragement and support they teach clients to cooperate, to relate more wholesomely, to seek healthier sources of personal satisfaction, to achieve genuine security, and to take life in stride. Perhaps the most important feature of their treatment is the increase of self-respect, or stated differently, the removal of feelings of inferiority.

Frank (1957) stressed five goals for his treatment groups: (1) to facilitate constructive release of feelings, (2) to strengthen patients' self-esteem, (3) to encourage patients to face and resolve their problems, (4) to improve their skills for recognizing and resolving both interpersonal and intrapersonal conflicts, and (5) to fortify them to consolidate and to maintain their therapeutic gains.

Glasser (1965) contended that those who do group treatment must be concerned about helping each client satisfy two basic needs: (1) the need to love and to be loved and (2) the need to feel that he is worthwhile to himself and to others. However, one may infer two other goals from his discussion of teaching clients to be responsible for themselves: (1) helping each client learn to fulfill his needs without depriving others of the ability to fulfill their needs; and (2) helping each

client to behave in a responsible manner and to accept responsibility for his behavior.

> To illustrate, a responsible person can give and receive love.
> If a girl, for example, falls in love with a responsible man, we
> would expect him either to return her love or to let her know in
> a considerate way that he appreciates her affection but that he
> does not share her feelings. If he takes advantage of her love to
> gain some material or sexual end, we would not consider him
> responsible.
> A responsible person also does that which gives him a feeling
> of self-worth and a feeling that he is worthwhile to others. He
> is motivated to strive and perhaps endure privation to attain
> self-worth. (p. 13)

From Kelman's (1963) discussion of outcomes the following goals were identified: (1) to overcome feelings of isolation,
(2) to enhance self-esteem and increase acceptance of self,
(3) to develop hope for improved adjustment, (4) to help each
client learn to be himself and to express his real feelings, (5)
to accept responsibility for himself and for solving his problems, (6) to develop, practice, and to maintain new relationship
skills, (7) to enhance his commitment to change his attitudes and behaviors, and (8) to generalize his insights and
skills by applying them in his daily life. A quotation from Kelman highlights his emphasis on using insights to generalize
psychotherapeutic learnings:

> The ultimate goal of psychotherapy is achieved when the
> patient generalizes therapeutic insights to specific situations in
> his daily life. He addresses himself to interpersonal situations
> in which he has problem situations in which he is ineffective,
> self-defeating, and uncomfortable. He examines these situations
> from the point of view of his own contributions to them, the
> attitudes and expectations that he brings to them, the elements
> of distortion and unrealism with which he approaches them,
> and the kind of interaction patterns in which he typically be-
> comes involved. In this examination, the patient applies the in-
> sights he derived from corrective emotional experiences in the

therapy situation to the real-life situation with which he is now
confronted.

The significance of this part of the process lies in the fact
that insights are applied to specific situations. That is, the
patient does not merely adopt some general formulation about
himself and interpersonal relationships which he then carries
with him into his real-life situations. . . . Rather, he goes a step
beyond that and involves himself in a more active and idosyn-
cratic process, not just taking over and expounding an explana-
tory system and a language but deliberately applying them in
a concrete and unique situation. (p. 428)

Hobbs (1962) seemed to accept most of the others' goals,
but he challenged the notion that insight contributes to improved adjustment:

The problem of the contemporary neurotic is not lack of insight
but lack of a sense of identity, of purpose, of meaning in life. . . .

I suggest that insight is not a cause of change but a possible
result of change. It is not a source of therapeutic gain but one
among a number of possible consequences of gain. It may or
may not occur in therapy: whether it does or not is inconse-
quential, since it reflects only the preferred modes of expression of the therapist or the client. It is not a change agent, it
is a by-product of change. . . . (p. 742)

Joel and Shapiro (1950) observed from their experience
as group therapists that their patients' growth was often unaccompanied by insight.

For his subjects who were treated by client-centered methods Vargas (1954) reported that self-awareness (or insight)
is not related to therapeutic success. One also may intimate
from his findings that his clients' increased understanding of
their needs may not be as important as changes in their feelings
about themselves.

Lewis' (1959) findings support Vargas' findings. He compared hospitalized maladjusted veterans with a similar group
of hospitalized veterans with medical-surgical diagnoses. His

findings indicated that the adjusted group experienced significantly more need satisfaction than maladjusted, but chance could account for any observed differences in understanding of their needs.

Perhaps counselors and therapists have accepted too literally the charge: "Know thyself." Vargas' and Lewis' findings certainly make sense. These findings also support a therapeutic focus on clients' current feelings in preference to discussion of either early childhood experiences or why they behave and feel as they do today. Chapter Seven explains how it may be easier for clients to understand themselves and their behavior than it is to accept themselves, change their behavior, and experience greater need satisfaction. On the other hand, Hobbs', Lewis', and Vargas' clients were neurotics. Though insight may not be essential for improved emotional adjustment of neurotics, it may be essential for educational and vocational planning.

An Evaluation of Goals for Counseling

Walker and Peiffer (1957) wrote a very critical review of counselors' and therapists' treatment goals. Their four principal criticisms were: (1) a client's happiness is not sufficient as a treatment goal; (2) goals are guided too much by the counselor's own personal values and middle-class values; (3) goals focus almost entirely on self-actualization of the client without expressing enough concern for society's best interests; and (4) goals tend to be too vague and general. Though at first one may find Walker and Peiffer harsh, on a second reading of their paper few will miss their deep concern for counselors' plight in defining goals for clients. They argue for replacing pious hopes with more realistic goals, and the writer argues further for specific, idiosyncratic goals stated in terms of measurable outcomes.

What is wrong with happiness as a goal for a client? Was not counseling developed to enable clients to find greater happiness and satisfaction in their daily lives, to learn to live more richly? Should not a counselor obtain self-reports from clients in appraising the effectiveness of counseling? Yes—but these are not sufficient. A client could report increased happiness and yet lose contact with reality and evade normal responsibilities. Furthermore, a client can better assess the effect of counseling when he has helped to formulate very specific goals and can look for specific changes in attitudes and behaviors. Even then he may have difficulty detecting and reporting changes within himself because insight is not always associated with gains achieved in counseling. Zax and Klein (1960) made another point that is relevant here: a client may distort negatively when he tries to gain admission to a counseling group and distort positively either when he wants to terminate but doubts that his counselor and fellow clients will let him or when he is afraid to face a threatening problem. A classic analyst would probably call the latter mere flight to health or transference cure. Walker and Peiffer also pointed out the dangers of symptom removal and substitution. The present writer, however, agrees with behavioral therapists who question that symptom substitution occurs when symptoms are removed by effective treatment [for example, Paul (1966); Ullman and Krasner (1965)]. In spite of all the difficulties involved in using clients' self-reports, most counselors and researchers agree that they will be used (Chapter Twelve elaborates on this point). If they are used effectively, clients need goals stated in more precise terms than increased happiness.

Are goals for treatment unwholesomely influenced by counselors' and therapists' own middle-class values? Do they fail to convey genuine respect for clients' values that differ from their own? Walker and Peiffer stated that these are real dangers—and their warning should be considered. However, these factors also can be used therapeutically. Unfortunately, counselors do not always realize the extent to which their personal values influence the definition of goals for their clients. Wolberg (1954) pointed out that no matter how objective a therapist tries to be in order to permit a patient to develop his own values, the patient's new superego will be patterned after the therapist as he is perceived by the patient. He is somebody special in a client's (or patient's) life, hence he tends to be used as a model. Even counselors who deny that they have goals for their clients must have some goals in mind; they must use some criteria to determine to which feelings and behaviors they respond. If, therefore, such counselors could accept the need for specific goals, and could be flexible enough to alter goals during the course of treatment, they might detect and cope with therapeutic material more effectively, recognize and use their clients' tendency to use them and other clients in the group as models, and detect when a client's use of others' values is not in his best interest.

Some who seek counseling, and perhaps even more of those who seek psychotherapy, need to learn to recognize and use models. Kvaraceus (1959) concluded that juvenile delinquents surely need positive models to offset the reinforcement of their antisocial behavior by neighborhood gangs, their family, and even some of their community's most law-abiding citizens:

> In understanding the delinquent's behavior and in assisting him in buying and living by the legal-societal rule book, professional and lay workers will need to be aware of the delinquent's primary reference groups, the interplay of the forces within this milieu, and finally how the child can be weaned from his rule book and helped to adopt the code of conduct of another reference group. . . . (p. 192)
>
> The adults in the community are explicitly and implicitly involved in the delinquency story. Norm violations by youngsters tend to fulfill a number of psychological functions for older and more law-abiding members of the community. In the sanctimonious cluckings of many parents can be heard a half-concealed vicarious thrill and delight in escapades of youth. One can almost sense the adult smack his lips as he bemoans the "awful" norm-violating conduct of the less inhibited young. If delinquency is to be prevented and controlled, it will be necessary for many adults to inspect their own emotional needs, their own problems, and their own pleasures in the delinquency phenomenon. (p. 198)

Such youngsters need a new reference group: one that will provide positive models, expect them to change their behavior, and reinforce the new behavior. Beck (1958) concluded that the norms set by a group of peers in a counseling group fulfill these functions—that the group becomes a place where new norms for behavior are set and reinforced. These new norms are gradually integrated as old norms are rejected and set aside. Discovery of living models (or even models from literature, especially biographies) can be utilized by both fellow clients and the counselor to further this process in individual clients.

Cartwright (1951) describes the impact of the group upon the individual as follows:

> Now if we try to discover how the level of aspiration gets set, we are immediately involved in the person's relationship to groups. The groups to which he belongs set standards for his behavior which he must accept if he is to remain in the group. If his capacities do not allow him to reach these standards he experiences failure, he withdraws or is rejected by the group and his self-esteem suffers shock. (p. 384)

When a delinquent elects to join a counseling group after he has had an opportunity to learn what will be expected from him and what he can expect from the group, he discovers that the other clients are trying to understand and accept him, and that he can expect unconditional acceptance from the counselor. He feels a strong pressure to change, but it is not so threatening or devastating that it drives him from the group. Much as his fellow clients want him to change, they provide genuine support and encouragement through their efforts to understand him and empathize with him. They also exhibit patience with his efforts. As the counseling group becomes attractive to him, a client often finds among his fellow clients at least one prestige figure whom he can use as a model. In fact, the counselor should consider this possibility in selecting clients for a group. Therefore, the counselor must be conscious of the extent to which goals for his clients are determined not only by his own values but also by the values of the other clients whom he assigns to a counseling group.

Since both the counselor and clients serve as models, the counselor must be conscious of his ethical responsibilities in selecting clients. He must not only try to convey acceptance of values that are different from his own, but he must try to help clients do the same as they try to understand and help each other. The writer's experience with clients treated in groups suggests that they do become increasingly tolerant of others' values. These impressions are verified by studies made of even less intensive discussion groups. Miller and Biggs (1958) reported that, by comparison with control subjects, undirected discussions of secondary school students increased significantly their tolerance toward specific nationalities. Weider (1954) conducted similar studies with college classes. Two groups were used: (1) student-centered instruction accompanied by sociodrama and (2) the traditional lecture-discussion. He found that student-centered instruction modified students' attitudes associated with racial, religious, and ethnic prejudices and also increased their own self-acceptance scores.

The fact that the counselor exhibits tolerance for values different from his own does not mean that either he or clients condone unlawful or irresponsible behavior. When someone may be hurt by a client's planned antisocial behavior, a counselor may ask permission of the group to break confidence to protect the person who may be hurt. Very, very rarely are those who do individual counseling required to break confidence for this reason. It is even less likely that they will be required to do so in group counseling, because even delinquents in a counseling group point out the consequences of hurtful acts and try to help fellow clients accept and adjust to society's expectations. Sometimes, in fact, they put pressure on fellow clients to conform when perhaps they should discuss what they can do to improve laws and school regulations that they feel are unfair or ineffective. Mere conformance is not good enough: group counseling also should help youth learn to behave in a responsible way in solving social problems that affect them adversely.

Walker and Peiffer's third major criticism of counselors' goals was their failure to exhibit adequate concern for what is good for society. They argued for a balance between what is required for self-actualization of clients and what is good for society. Obviously, counselors must be conscious of what is good for society as well as what is good for the individual. However, the author's experiences with school counselors suggest that as former teachers they are too concerned about what is good for society; many of them find it easier to present what society expects than to empathize with the individual student and help him actualize himself. Furthermore, all counselors should note Papanek's (1958) point that self-interest and society's interest need not be perceived as opposing values. In fact, the nation's current interest in early identification and development of the gifted is based upon the notion that their self-actualization is to the nation's as well as to these individuals' own best interest.

Perhaps Walker and Peiffer also exhibited too little faith in clients' (at least in the normal adolescent's) concern for what is good for society. Rarely are clients satisfied with their antisocial behavior. For example, the writer found that when a group of juvenile delinquents established a safe relationship in which they could discuss what really bothered them, even they exhibited deep concern about their actions. It is true that they began by boasting about their antisocial behavior, but when they discovered that the counselor and the other members of the group really wanted to help them change, and expected them to change, they talked about how they wished they could behave differently and they began to accept responsibility for their behavior. In the same vein Glasser (1965) described his clients' acceptance of responsibility and its impact upon their growth. Corsini (1954) had a similar experience in treating prison outcasts; once he demonstrated that he could understand them and accept them in spite of what they had done, they began trying to accept responsibility for their behavior and for trying to change it.

Finally, the writer agrees enthusiastically with Walker and Peiffer's criticism of vague, general goals. Specific goals are necessary for effective counseling as well as for appraisal of outcomes of counseling. Heretofore researchers have been seriously handicapped by counselors' failure to define goals in specific, measurable terms. Such goals are necessary in order to define adequate criteria, and subsequently for selecting and/or developing appraisal instruments to evaluate clients' growth (this point is discussed more fully in Chapter Twelve). When a counselor accepts a client's reasons for seeking counseling, helps him translate these reasons into clearly and simply stated changes in behavior and attitudes, and helps him recognize and state new goals, it helps the counselor identify therapeutic material and helps his client obtain feedback on his own growth.

Definition of Goals for Counseling

When a client asks to participate in group counseling, the writer encourages him to discuss whatever is bothering him, to describe what he expects from group counseling, and to ask whatever questions he wishes to ask to clarify what will be expected of him and what he may expect from others (Chapter Five describes more fully how clients are selected and how the writer tries to assess readiness for group counseling). He accepts his client's goals for group counseling, tries to help him state his goals in terms of specific attitudes, behaviors, and skills, and tries to help him define precisely how he may determine whether, and to what extent, he is being helped by group counseling. They also discuss what data may be collected to help the client assess his own progress during and following termination of his group. When specific goals are developed cooperatively in this manner, the writer has found that his clients seek feedback on their own progress and use their own successes and failures therapeutically within their group.

Every counselor also must try to appraise the effectiveness of his services. Even if he is not a researcher, he must try to determine at least informally whom he can treat most effectively, with whom, and under what circumstances. When a counselor encourages his clients to participate in defining treatment goals, he is honor-bound to help them try to assess the success of treatment on the basis of their idiosyncratic goals. Obviously this complicates a counselor's statistical analysis of his data, but it can be done. For example, a measure of anxiety is used to appraise outcomes for two opposite types of clients: (1) a client who does poorly on examinations because he becomes too anxious while preparing for and taking them to function efficiently and (2) another who does poorly because he does not become anxious enough to prepare for examinations and to attend fully to the task while taking them. Both are helped; but to grow, they move in opposite directions. In this instance signed numbers may be used to retain gains achieved by each.

To make his data easier to handle statistically, a counselor may be tempted to use vague general goals, to select for groups only clients with some common goals, and to ignore individuals' unique goals when appraising clients' growth (research techniques for handling these problems are discussed in Chapter Twelve). Such errors often account for a counselor's failure to obtain significant results when he tries to assess the outcomes of group counseling. Carefully defined, precise goals stated in terms of measurable or observable outcomes are necessary if the counselor is adequately to assess changes in clients.

The two most common questions asked by practitioners are: (1) How do you define clients' goals or how do you involve clients in defining their goals? and (2) Are specific idiosyncratic goals necessary? Krumboltz (1965) made a case for a yes to the second question. He also provided a good answer to two other common questions: (1) What should a counselor do when a client states a goal that may involve the counselor in unethical behavior? (2) What should a counselor do when he is asked to assist with a problem that does not lie within his professional competencies or interests?

Some people may be offended by the notion that we should permit the wishes of our clients to determine the criteria of our success and would prefer to establish universal criteria applicable to all clients. It should be remembered that all professional groups and all professional persons are ultimately evaluated by the extent to which they bring about the conditions desired by their clientele. When a client requests his lawyer to write out a last will and testament, the client expects the lawyer to write the document in such a manner that the client's requests will eventually be executed in precisely the manner that he wishes. In a like manner a physician is successful if, let us say, a patient with a broken leg can walk normally again as he desires.

In the case of both the lawyer and the physician there come times when the professional man cannot carry out the wishes of his client either because the request is not within the scope of his interests, or because it is beyond his power, or because it violates his ethical standards. In such cases the professional man explains the reasons why he cannot carry out the specific requests of the client, perhaps indicating alternate courses of action including referrals when appropriate. When a professional man does accept a client, however, he is implicitly agreeing to exert whatever efforts he can to accomplish what his client requests. The use of clients' requests as a basis for generating the criteria of success is as appropriate for counselors as it is for lawyers and physicians. In the case of counselors it means that the same criterion measures cannot be applied to evaluate all counseling contacts. (pp. 383–384)

Additional goals also are defined during counseling. Sometimes the needs for new goals are disclosed and defined within the group. At other times a client will request an individual session to examine whether or not he wishes to define new goals.

Is it appropriate for a counselor to define goals for clients over and beyond those which they set for themselves? By responding to therapeutic material most counselors do in fact disclose the need for new goals. When, for example, a student asks to join a group to learn how to relate to peers and to make friends, and the counselor recognizes and responds to that client's feelings of inadequacy with reference to his academic aptitudes as well as ability to relate to his peers, he should realize that he is opening up a new topic, and thereby disclosing the need for new goals for that client. Fellow clients also detect and respond to therapeutically significant material. As long as the client realizes that he can decide what he will deal with, and without coercion, the counselor has protected the client's personal rights. This may not be as simple as it first appears, because members need to be taught to recognize and deal with resistance (a topic dealt with more fully in Chapter Six).

The discussion of clients' rights leads directly to the final topic for this chapter. From the very beginning of treatment clients should realize what they can expect from each other and the counselor and what the counselor can expect from them. Among other things they should be encouraged to help develop and maintain a therapeutic relationship. Whenever this calls for guidelines for behavior to enable them to function efficiently, they should be encouraged to help formulate such guidelines. For example, they should define criteria governing a client's decisions on what topics he will discuss and when he may terminate counseling. Reasonably healthy youth usually will elect to terminate when a majority believe they have achieved their goals or whenever an individual concludes that his goals cannot be achieved within the group. When a group terminates before some clients have achieved their goals, they may be counseled on an individual basis or combined with others to form a new group. Among those who achieve their goals sooner than others, most, especially adolescents treated within a school setting, accept responsibility for remaining in their group to help the others. Besides gaining experience helping others, they often uncover new therapeutic material and obtain additional assistance.

Sometimes, especially within a group of lonely adolescents, a group will resist termination. On such occasions the counselor detects the search for new meaningful topics. Though they seem to have covered all the topics they can or wish to discuss, they try to find a reason to continue this meaningful relationship. Whenever the counselor discovers such efforts to justify continuation, he responds to these feelings as he would to other feelings, helping the clients to express their need for each other and their disappointment with terminating the relationship.

Summary

Group counseling is concerned with helping reasonably healthy persons recognize their problems, solve them, and apply these learnings in daily living. Before a counselor initiates group counseling he must have some idea whom he can treat best in group counseling, under what circumstances, and with whom. In order to be most effective in counseling and in appraising its outcomes, specific goals must be developed for each client in precise measurable or observable terms.

When a counselor can accept his clients' reasons for seeking counseling, can involve each in stating clearly and simply the changes he desires in his behavior and attitudes, and can help each recognize and state new goals during counseling, the counselor can use such goals to detect and respond to therapeutic material and to help each client obtain feedback on his own progress. When clients define specific goals in such a cooperative manner, they do seek feedback on their own progress and use their successes and failures therapeutically within their counseling group. Such specific goals also are needed for appraisal of outcomes of group counseling.

References

Beck, Dorothy F. "The Dynamics of Group Psychotherapy as Seen by a Sociologist, Part I: The Basic Process," *Sociometry*, 1958, 21:98–128.
Bross, Rachel B. "Termination of Analytically Oriented Psychotherapy in Groups," *International Journal of Group Psychotherapy*, 9:326–337.

Cartwright, D. P. "Achieving Change in People: Some Applications of Group Dynamics Theory," *Human Relations*, 1951, 4:381–392.

Corsini, R. "Group Therapy with a Hostile Group," *Group Psychotherapy*, 1954, 6:168–173.

Dreikurs, R. "Group Psychotherapy from the Point of View of Adlerian Psychology," *International Journal of Group Psychotherapy*, 1957, 7:363–375.

Frank, J. D. "Some Determinants, Manifestations, and Efforts of Cohesiveness in Therapy Groups," *International Journal of Group Psychotherapy*, 1957, 7:53–63.

Glasser, W. *Reality Therapy*, New York: Harper & Row, Publishers, 1965.

Hobbs, N. "Sources of Gain in Psychotherapy," *American Psychologist*, 1962, 17:741–747.

Jahoda, Marie *Current Concepts of Positive Mental Health*, New York: Basic Books, Inc., 1958.

Joel, W., and D. Shapiro "Some Principles and Procedures for Group Psychotherapy," *Journal of Psychotherapy*, 1950, 29:77–88.

Kelman, H. C. "The Role of the Group in the Induction of Therapeutic Change," *International Journal of Group Psychotherapy*, 1963, 13: 399–432.

Krumboltz, J. D. "Behavioral Counseling: Rationale and Research," *Personnel and Guidance Journal*, 1965, 44:376–382.

Kvaraceus, W. C. "Nature of the Problem of Juvenile Delinquency in the United States," *Journal of Negro Education*, 1959, 28:190–198.

Lewis, W. A. "Emotional Adjustment and Need Satisfaction of Hospital Patients," *Journal of Counseling Psychology*, 1959, 6:127–131.

Maslow, A. H. *Motivation and Personality*, New York: Harper & Row, Publishers, 1954.

Miller, K. M., and J. B. Biggs "Attitude Change through Undirected Group Discussion," *Journal of Educational Psychology*, 1958, 49: 224–228.

Papanek, Helene "Change in Ethical Values in Group Psychotherapy," *International Journal of Group Psychotherapy*, 1958, 8:435–444.

Paul, G. L. *Insight vs. Desensitization in Psychotherapy:* An Experiment in Anxiety Reduction, Stanford, Calif.: Stanford University Press, 1966.

Ullman, L. P., and L. Krasner (eds.) *Case Studies in Behavior Modification*, New York: Holt, Rinehart and Winston, Inc., 1965.

Vargas, M. J. "Changes in Self-Awareness during Client-Centered Therapy," in C. R. Rogers and R. F. Dymond (eds.) *Psychotherapy and Personality Change*, Chicago: University of Chicago Press, 1954.

Walker, D. E., and H. C. Peiffer "The Goals of Counseling," *Journal of*

Counseling Psychology, 1957, 3:204–209.

Weider, G. S. "Group Procedures Modifying Attitudes of Prejudice in College Classroom," *Journal of Educational Psychology,* 1954, 45: 332–344.

Wolberg, L. R. *The Technique of Psychotherapy,* New York: Grune & Stratton, Inc., 1954.

Zax, M., and A. Klein "Measurement of Personality and Behavior Changes Following Psychotherapy," *Psychological Bulletin,* 1960, 57:435–448.

Chapter Three

Group Dynamics

Every effective leader tries to understand forces within his group that contribute to and interfere with the group's goals. The extent to which he trusts members and shares his leadership responsibilities with them determines the extent to which he can enlist their assistance in identifying the resources of the group, in discovering problems that interfere with the group's success, in diagnosing these problems, and in taking action to solve them. Group dynamics is concerned with the study of these forces to improve the effectiveness of groups.

Even such excellent books as Bradford, Gibb, and Benne's (1964) *T-Group Theory and Laboratory Method*, Cartwright and Zanders' (1968) *Group Dynamics: Theory and Practice*, and Kemp's (1964) *Perspectives on the Group Process* do not include all the findings from this exciting, relatively new field of study. In this text, the material for two chapters is drawn primarily from the literature on group dynamics: Chapter Four discusses the implications of this literature for understanding the therapeutic forces within counseling groups and the present chapter discusses the development of groups. The subject at hand is divided into seven discussion topics:

characteristics of effective groups, leadership, influence of group size, developmental phases of groups, participation, congruence, open communication, and a group's self-study.

Characteristics of Effective Groups

To meet the minimum requirements for a group those persons assembled must cooperate to fulfill some meaningful purpose. For Bradford and Mial (1963) a group exists when: (1) it knows why it exists; (2) it has created an atmosphere in which its work can be done; (3) it has developed guidelines for making decisions; (4) it has established conditions under which each member can make his unique contributions; (5) it has achieved communication among its members; (6) its members have learned to give and receive help; (7) its members have learned to cope with conflict; and (8) its members have learned to diagnose its processes and improve its functioning.

A mature and effective group has good reasons for meeting [Thelen and Stock (1949)]. These may include diagnosing community difficulties, dissemination of information, teaching new skills, motivating members to act on problems, and planning action to alleviate specific problems. Thus, a meeting of a group is expected to accomplish the goals its members seek. To accomplish their purposes group members must hammer out agreements on such things as:

> . . . what is expected from each member (definition of member role and responsibility); how freely emotion is to be expressed (climate); the degree and quality of performance expected from individuals, and what behaviors are to be rewarded or punished (standards); whose words or experiences will be used to settle disputes (authority); how wide a range of individual behaviors will be tolerated (individuality); how tentatively actions will be taken and how easily agreements and policies can be modified (experimentalism, flexibility); on what basis prestige will be given (status system); and many other problems.
> A mature and effective group is one in which people know

what to expect with regard to these questions. This knowledge, whether explicitly or implicitly known, is required for self-discipline. Until these things are known, much energy goes into the effort to find out. Spontaneity is limited, self-consciousness enhanced, and any effort of a member to help the group or influence its direction is felt to be loaded with risk. . . .

Each individual member will be willing to subordinate his own needs to the group only if he knows that there will be some opportunity at some point for some more direct expression and satisfaction of his own wants. Conditions of flexibility and the expectation of ultimate satisfaction make group members willing to commit themselves to difficult tasks and to maintain their commitment to group work during periods of minimal reward. (pp. 105–106)

Lifton (1966) made the additional point that the group must be a safe place in which a member can express his ideas and expect honest reactions from others. Members must be able to convey acceptance of a person even when they cannot accept a given idea or behavior, to exhibit tolerance for individual differences and values, and to recognize nonverbal as well as verbal communication. Lifton also recognized that the leader plays an important role in the development of a mature group:

The basic responsibility for the initial group leader is to be responsive to the real goals of the group, including those not yet articulated. Since the security of group members depends upon clearly defined limits, he defines the initial purpose of the group. Because under stress people tend to be unable to communicate, it is the leader's role to help the group develop and use their resources to provide support to group members.

One of the major differences in the role of the leader in a democratic society from other types is that he derives his authority from the group. At any point where his perceptions of group goals deviates beyond the limits of group acceptance, he is no longer able to function. It is, therefore, the group's responsibility to give the leader the help he needs to shoulder the roles needed by the group. It is also their responsibility constantly to share their ideas and feelings so that the hidden agenda can come to light. (p. 27)

Leadership

A leader is a facilitator of action or change. If he is an autocratic leader, he defines his goals and facilitates group movement toward them. If he is a democratic leader, he helps the members of his group define their own goals and facilitates action toward those goals. In some instances he is elected or appointed to provide general leadership for a specific term. In other instances he may be selected informally by members to help them solve a specific problem for which he possesses special knowledge or skills.

Most of the research on leadership has been done with task groups and T groups. Lewin was a central figure in early research on such groups. His own and his colleagues' findings [Lewin (1944)] support democratic leadership. Some of his most important findings were: (1) democratic behavior cannot be taught by autocratic methods; (2) democratic leadership can improve group efficiency; (3) a discussion can be used to clarify issues better than a lecture, but it does not necessarily produce either a decision or action; and (4) improved production (or changed behavior) follows member participation in defining specific production goals. He also reported specific ways in which members were influenced positively by a democratic working relationship. For example, hostile and competitive behaviors were replaced by friendliness and cooperative behaviors. A we-feeling was evident in his democratically led group. He concluded that even the same group members learned to relate differently when they were assigned a leader who behaved differently. Cartwright and Zanders (1960) concluded that subsequent research has supported these findings.

As free men most current writers in this field support Lewin's endorsement of democratic leadership. They agree that it is essential for our way of life. If our nation is to use its resources wisely in solving its problems, both leaders and members must be taught by meaningful experiences to function within a democratic group. Bradford (1960) explained how democratic methods can be used in the classroom to help students establish meaningful goals for learning, to teach them to help one another achieve their goals, to increase learning, and to improve classroom morale. Bradford, Gibb, and Benne (1964) reviewed the research on group dynamics and described various ways in which democratic leadership can be used in T groups. Dreikurs (1959) presented a case for using the family council to provide meaningful experiences in a democratic group and to enlist everyone's assistance in solving a family's problems. Gordon (1955) used his experiences with religious workers to develop group-centered leadership. Grater (1959) described and evaluated his adaptation of Gordon's method in training college leaders. Ohlsen (1964) developed a similar program for training secondary school and college leaders.

In all the examples cited above the leader is committed to help members define and accept responsibility for achieving their goals. Gordon's perception of the leader's role and his basic attitude toward members are most congruent with the counselor's role. He respects members, trusts them, exhibits confidence in their ability to achieve their goals, recognizes and encourages each member's problem-solving skills, and *finds relevance in each member's contributions*. He listens empathically, tests his understandings, tries to discover relevance in their contributions for solving the problem being discussed, detects and conveys linkage to others' contributions, and helps members become increasingly independent. He recognizes members' leadership skills and encourages them to use them. Although members at first perceive the leader as someone special who possesses more status and power, Gordon begins at once to share the leadership and to develop members' independence and leadership skills. Though Gordon seems to be willing to give up his special leadership status, the writer doubts that a leader can ever become just another member. By his example, however, and perhaps by teaching, he can develop members' leadership skills as he helps them achieve their goals.

Gordon stated beautifully why such leadership is crucial for our nation:

> The challenge that democracy faces is to discover a conception of leadership more consistent with the fundamental democratic principles we have learned to cherish. When discovered, it will need to be so injected into the blood stream of the social organism that it will reach every group and institution in our society.
>
> It is our thesis that society is searching for a kind of leadership that puts human values first. Traditional leadership, based as it is upon authority and power, has often restrained the individual through submission to that authority, and consequently has failed to release all the creative and constructive forces within the individual. . . . (p. 7)

Nevertheless, some of the research evidence seems to suggest that for certain groups autocratic leadership is more effective than democratic leadership. For example, Hare (1962) concluded that autocratic leadership seems to produce greater quantitative results, whereas democratic leadership seems to produce better morale and qualitative results. Fiedler (1964) reasoned that directive leadership is more effective for a group in which the situation is either highly favorable or highly unfavorable for the leader, whereas the nondirective leader is more effective in the intermediate stages of favorability, and he offered good supporting evidence for his conclusions. Two brief quotes help to clarify his position: "The leader is defined as the individual in the group who directs and coordinates task-relevant activities, or who, in the absence of a designated leader, automatically performs these functions in a group." (p. 153) "Factors other than strong, centralized control or the quantitative vs. qualitative nature of task performance are likely to play an important role in determining the type of leader attitude or behavior which is most appropriate in a particular situation." (p. 151)

Shaw and Blum (1966) tested Fiedler's basic thesis on relative effectiveness of directive vs. nondirective leaders:

When the group task situation is either highly favorable or highly unfavorable for the leader, controlling, managing directive leadership is most effective, whereas permissive, considerate, nondirective leadership is needed for moderately unfavorable group-task situations.

According to this theory, the favorableness of the group-task situation is determined by three dimensions: the affective relation between the leader and his members, the power inherent in the leadership position, and the degree to which the task is structured. Although it is recognized that the interaction of these dimensions is complicated, Fiedler suggests that the leader's relations with his members is the most important, the structure of the task is next most important, and inherent power of the leadership is least important for the favorableness continuum. Once measures of the three dimensions are available, it is possible to order group-task situations along the favorableness continuum, by first ordering the group-task situation on the basis of the leader's relationship with his group, then on the basis of the task structure, and lastly on the basis of position power. This ordering may be considered to be an operational definition of the favorability continuum. The most favorable group-task situation is one in which leader-member relations are good, the task is highly structured and the position power is strong; the most unfavorable group-task situation is one in which leader-member relations are very poor, the task is unstructured and the position power is weak. (pp. 238–239)

Regardless of their implications for the contingency model, the results of this experiment show clearly that direct leadership is more effective than nondirective when the task is highly structured; that is, when there is only one solution and one way (or only a few ways) of obtaining this solution. The requirements for leadership are quite limited, and nondirective leader behaviors may only interfere with the problem-solving process. However, on tasks that require varied information and approaches, nondirective leadership is clearly more effective. On such tasks the requirements for leadership are great. Contributions from all members must be encouraged, and this requires motivating, advising, rewarding, giving support—in short, nondirective leadership. (p. 241)

What Fiedler has called nondirective leadership should more appropriately be called democratic leadership. The democratic leader need not be passive; he can be active, but he must respect the members, convey this respect, realize that the group needs everyone's ideas to obtain the best possible solutions, and know how to solicit members' assistance in achieving the group's goals. Unlike the laissez-faire leader, both democratic and autocratic leaders recognize the need for structure and limits. However, the latter two do not agree on how expectations should be defined and maintained. Whereas a democratic leader encourages members to determine what they should expect from each other, including the leader, the autocratic leader decides these things for himself or tries to manipulate the members into approving his ideas on how the group should function. This author believes that a democratic leader not only can contribute his ideas and help evaluate alternative solutions but should be expected to do so. If the group is to make the best possible use of all its resources, it needs everyone's ideas. However, such a leader should expect his ideas to receive the same critical evaluation as everyone else's; he should accept others' criticism and demonstrate that members may safely criticize him as they would anyone else.

Influence of Group Size

Psathas' (1960) review of the literature suggests that with increase in group size, members experience less direct involvement and participation. Instead of interacting with each other, they tend to direct communication to the highest-ranking initiator, who in turn responds to them as a group rather than as individuals. Most communications flow through the top man.

Loeser (1957) reported that as groups increase in size, transference reactions become weaker and weaker until members experience no meaningful relationships with each other. Any real relationship that they experience occurs with the leader, speaker, or performer. This situation gives the central figure great potential power. To the degree that he can establish a meaningful relationship he can use his influence to arouse emotion or to quiet unrest.

Loeser also noted the problems involved in establishing effective working relationships for a group of three: two members pair up against the third. Even a child learns quickly to use these relationships to his advantage. He learns to play one off against the other to obtain what he wants. However, the triad can be used therapeutically. If, for example, a couple seeking marriage counseling are really committed to make their marriage succeed, a counselor can so structure the relationship that when one (say, the husband) discusses on a feeling level the problems that really bother him, the wife can function as the counselor's helper. Instead of criticizing his wife as he often does in marriage counseling, he discusses his own feelings of inadequacy, tells what he wishes he could do to improve their marriage, and describes the kinds of help he needs from his wife to achieve his goals. While the husband talks, the counselor listens and responds therapeutically and teaches the wife to respond therapeutically. When she talks about herself, the husband learns to do the same thing for his wife. As each listens, each gradually experiences empathy and compassion for the other. The desire to help the other *become what he wants to become* is substituted for self-pity. As each becomes increasingly aware of the other's needs, learns how to help him satisfy his needs, and tries to communicate, they develop a more meaningful relationship, learn to encourage each other and to reinforce desired behaviors. Obviously, it is difficult to help each to trust the other and to talk openly about himself rather than to merely complain about the other, but it can be done—and must be done to enable them to develop a meaningful relationship. This same technique can be used in other situations—for example, to help an adolescent develop an improved relationship with one or both parents.

If a counseling group is to function effectively, a member must be able to capture the floor to speak, to feel safe in discussing his feelings, to interact meaningfully with others, and to obtain feedback. When making a decision on group size, a counselor must consider each client's maturity, attention span, and ability to invest in others. Each client must recognize that adequate time has been allowed for him, that he will not have to wait too long in order to speak, and that the group is small enough for him to become deeply involved with other members. Hence, those who counsel children in groups tend to work with smaller groups and for shorter work sessions than those who counsel adults (see Chapter Eleven). Even adults must have sufficiently small groups to accept considerable responsibility for their own behavior and for developing and maintaining a therapeutic climate.

Loeser concluded that a group of four to eight is ideal for group counseling and group therapy, and most writers have agreed with him. He pointed out that it is a natural grouping —the largest group that can function without a leader and some strong rules—and that larger groups will break up into subgroups without strong leadership. As a group moves up from eight to thirty, Loeser noted that they tend to function like a class with greater dependence on the designated leader. In order to reap the full benefits of group counseling, clients must be able to accept considerable responsibility for themselves and function as a total group.

Developmental Phases in Groups

Chapter One pointed out how a counseling group differs from other groups. Unlike an academic department, in which members are expected to learn to work together to improve their programs and to encourage each other's professional development, a counseling group is a temporary group designed to improve its members' personal adjustment. Though they deal with their feelings for each other, they do so to learn to cope with others and to generalize to daily lives outside the group rather than to solve their common problems as a group and to develop permanent working relationships. Since it is a temporary, safe relationship, one would expect clients to take more risks and to deal more openly with their feelings than they would in their permanent groups. Research does not support this point. Perhaps it would if counselors selected their clients for group counseling with greater care.

On the basis of their research on eight groups, each of three weeks' duration, at the Second National Training Laboratory in Group Development, Thelen and Dickerman (1949) identified four phases through which a group passes:

1. *Individually centered, competitive phase.* Members tried to establish themselves in the leadership hierarchy or peck order. They wanted a strong leader to take over and to accept responsibility for them.

2. *Frustration and conflict phase.* When the T-group leader failed to take over for them, they felt hostile toward him, perceived him as inadequate and inefficient, and blamed him for their frustrations and failures. They tended to blame others rather than to accept personal responsibility for developing relationships in which they could achieve their group goals.

3. *Group-harmony phase.* During this phase cohesiveness developed, but it was accompanied by complacency, smugness, and sweetness. Members were supportive, but tended to avoid or gloss over conflict, and were not very productive. They curbed impulse, especially negative reactions, and tried to repress individual needs to satisfy group needs.

4. *Group-centered, productive phase.* Members still exhibited concern for others but not to the degree that they would ignore or gloss over conflict in order to achieve harmony. Members faced conflict and learned to deal with it. They accepted responsibility for their behavior, participated in solving their group's problems, and developed productive working relationships. They also developed increasingly greater tolerance for others' values and behaviors. They became the kind of group-centered groups described later by Gordon (1955).

Thelen and Dickerman also reported that these four phases do not always appear in sequential order. Interpersonal relationships in the fourth phase are very similar to those in a counseling group. With careful selection of clients and the kind of structuring described in Chapter Five, the writer has found that a counseling group can move quickly into phase four.

Psathas (1960) used Bales' categories to compare members' interactions in two therapy groups of four patients each, conducted by a psychoanalytically oriented therapist, with interaction of members in problem-solving groups. His therapy groups met twice a week for approximately ninety minutes each session for a year. His primary findings were: (1) therapy groups are confronted with more than a single problem to resolve in the course of a ninety-minute discussion, and therefore single meetings rarely showed up the phase sequence exhibited in a task-oriented or problem-solving group, but when a number of meetings were added together a similar sequential pattern was noted; (2) therapy groups did not exhibit the pressure for group decision; (3) members of a therapy group tended to bring up a substantive problem, discuss it and analyze it, but seldom pursue it to open evaluation; (4) more positive acts were exhibited through all phases of therapy groups; (5) the therapist, and also patients, expressed, both verbally and nonverbally, many simple acts of agreement that seemed to be perceived by the speaker as support and encouragement for him to go on to deal with his problems [Noble, Ohlsen, and Proff (1961) found that a school counselor used a similar category, which they called simple acceptance, for the same purpose]; (6) unlike the problem-solving group, the therapy groups showed an increase in negative acts over phases, probably because of the greater freedom within the group to disagree; and (7) disturbance remained higher in therapy groups, but the balancing of actions and reactions did seem to occur even though solutions were not obtained within the ninety-minute period. However, techniques for attacking the problems were discovered and solutions were developed and applied over a series of sessions.

Finally, here are Psathas' succinct observations on channels of communication:

> Communication channels in these groups show the same pattern as that observed in laboratory groups. The rate of interactions is an important determinant of differentiation within the group. Participators are responded to in proportion to the

frequency of their initiation of actions. These tendencies appear despite the fact that individual contributions to discussion are not focused on a single problem confronting the group and the tendency therefore to react to a contributor may not be as great as it is in a laboratory group engaged in problem-solving discussion. One implication of these findings for the therapeutic process is that the sheer amount of participation by patient or therapist will produce some structuring of the interaction process which could conceivably affect the therapeutic process as well. Therapists are often very concerned with the participation rates of patients and make efforts to stimulate low participators and restrict, to some extent, excessively high participators, in order to be certain that some opportunity exists for all patients to present some material. Beyond this is the question of whether the structuring of interaction will affect the progress of therapy. As some patients achieve high rates and are responded to proportionately, interaction rates of others are depressed. Reactions of patients to their own inability to break into the discussion or reactions to others because of their high (or low) participation rates introduce additional variables into the therapeutic process. Whether, and in what way, imbalance in the distribuion of participation among patients obstructs or contributes to the therapeutic process is an important question for research to explore. The therapist's own participation rate must also be considered, since his rank as an originator will affect the amount of action addressed to him. (p. 193)

Psathas' observations raise a number of important questions for further research on the treatment process, and possibly for the selection of clients: (1) How may a counselor help clients recognize and cope with the monopolist? (2) How may he help clients become sensitive to and involve the low participator? (3) How may he recognize these types and take account of these characteristics in selecting clients for a group? (4) To what extent must clients participate verbally in order to profit from the therapeutic experience? (5) How does group size affect participation? Methods for coping with the low participator and the monopolist are discussed in Chapter Nine. Nevertheless, perhaps some clients do not need to talk as much as others to experience a feeling of belonging and genuine involvement.

The differences Psathas noted between task-oriented and therapy groups are what one would expect. A group of clients have not been assigned the task of solving a specific problem within a specified period; their task is to create a climate that will enable every client to deal with the problems that concern him. Very quickly they recognize the need for understanding and acceptance of others and by others. Within such a climate one would expect to find supportive acts, greater spontaneity, and clients' willingness to express their real feelings, including open discussion of disagreements and negative feelings as well as positive feelings for each other.

Bion (1948) also found that his therapy groups passed through stages similar to those noted in task-oriented groups. Inasmuch as he provides very little structure, one would expect his groups to follow a pattern more like the one described by Thelen and Dickerman (1949) than that of the more structured therapy groups described by Psathas. Bion defended his lack of structure on the grounds that members of a therapy group must discover and learn to use their own therapeutic resources. Though Bion presents some sound arguments for his approach, the writer believes that with more structure time could be saved, and perhaps clients could be spared some unnecessary tension and some of the confusion Bion's patients experienced. Powdermaker and Frank's (1953) work supports the writer's view. They found that in the initial stages too little direction resulted in intense competition, which in turn upset their patients, and that too much direction encouraged patients to do what the therapist wanted them to do and inhibited the therapeutic process.

Participation

Man wants to become meaningfully involved in solving his own problems, in improving his social order, and in making the decisions in every group that affects him, whether it be his family or his nation. When he is not allowed or does not know how to participate fully, or he does not believe that he can make his influence felt, Allport (1945) said that he becomes reactive. He attacks, complains, looks for a scapegoat. He also becomes an easy prey for a demagogue. On the other hand, when he can help shape the events which influence his life, he finds life more meaningful and more readily accepts responsibility for himself and for improving conditions within his environment. Allport described this phenomenon as follows:

> Friendly, unaffected social relations are the most indispensable condition. Patronizing hand-outs and wage-incentive systems alone do not succeed. Opportunities for consultation on personal problems are, somewhat surprisingly, found to be important. And as members of this society have shown, group decision, open discussion, and restraining of leaders in accordance with democratic standards yield remarkable results. . . . In other words, a person ceases to be reactive and contrary in respect to a desirable course of conduct only when he himself has had a hand in declaring that course of conduct to be desirable. (pp. 122–123)
>
> In insisting that participation depends upon ego-involvement, it would be a mistake if we were to assume that we are dealing with a wholly self-centered and parasitic ego that demands unlimited status, and power for the individual himself. Often, indeed, the ego is clamorous, jealous, possessive, and cantankerous. But this is true chiefly when it is forced to be reactive against constant threats and deprivations. We all know "power people" who cannot, as we say, "submerge their egos." The trouble comes, I suspect, not because the egos are unsubmerged, but because they are still reactive toward some outer or inner features of the situation which are causing conflicts and insecurity. Reactive egos tend to perceive their neighbors and associates as threats rather than as collaborators. (p. 123)

Open Communication

A democratic leader provides the kind of involvement described above. He enlists members' assistance in developing open relationships in which members can discuss the issues as they perceive them and give each other honest feedback. They have no hidden agenda, and pluralistic ignorance cannot persist.

When the members of a committee or a task force accept a decision that only a few members believe is the best one because each feels that he alone is displeased with the decision, the group is experiencing pluralistic ignorance. Shaw and Blum (1965) found that pluralistic ignorance occurred when there was a discrepancy between publicly stated positions and privately held positions. They also reported that this reaction was most apt to occur when members were confronted with difficult tasks—or, in other words, when everyone's contributions and genuine reactions were needed most. Their findings agreed with Shaw and Caron's (1965) findings that frank feedback on dissatisfaction is associated with group effectiveness. However, they disagree on the nature of feedback. Though Shaw and Blum agreed on the desirability of open feedback, they found that their research subjects were more likely to signal their true feelings when they could report them anonymously. Shaw and Caron found that dissatisfaction feedback was more valid when reported overtly than when reported covertly. When members are secured, they can afford to discuss issues as they perceive them. When they do not feel safe, they tend to report their satisfactions and to withhold reporting their dissatisfactions. When covert reports do not agree with overt reports, the leader must try to involve members in determining what must be done to make the group a place where open communication is possible.

Congruence

In order to function well a group needs a real purpose, clear expectations, effective leadership, meaningful participation, the necessary security to enable members to contribute openly their ideas and reactions, and the ability to communicate with each other. Rogers (1961) concluded that congruence is essential for effective communication. He used the term *congruence* to indicate an accurate matching of those feelings of which an individual is aware with those which he is experiencing. To illustrate lack of congruence Rogers used the example of a man whose flushed face, angry tone of voice, and pointing finger clearly suggested anger, although his words denied his anger:

> What is happening here? It seems clear that at a physiological level he is experiencing anger. This is not matched by his awareness. Consciously he is not experiencing anger, nor is he communicating this (so far as he is consciously aware). There is a real incongruence between experience and awareness, and between experience and communication.
>
> Another point to be noted here is that his communication is actually ambiguous and unclear. In its words it is a setting forth of logic and fact. In its tones, and in the accompanying gestures, it is carrying a different message—"I am angry at you." I believe this ambiguity or contradictoriness of communication is always present when a person who is at the moment incongruent endeavors to communicate.
>
> Still another facet of the concept of incongruence is illustrated by this example. The individual himself is not a sound judge of his own degree of incongruence. Thus the laughter of the group indicates a clear consensual judgment that the man is experiencing anger, whether or not he thinks so. Yet in his own awareness this is not true. In other words it appears that the degree of congruence cannot be evaluated by the person himself at that moment. We may make progress in learning to measure it from an external frame of reference. We have also learned much about incongruence from the person's own ability to recognize incongruence in himself in the past. (pp. 339–340)

On the basis of his knowledge of the research evidence and his experience as a therapist Rogers presented a tentative statement of a general law:

> Assuming (a) a minimal willingness on the part of two people to be in contact; (b) an ability and minimal willingness on the part of each to receive communication from the other;

and (c) assuming the contact to continue over a period of time; the following relationship is hypothesized to hold true.

The greater the congruence of experience, awareness and communication on the part of one individual, the more the ensuing relationship will involve: a tendency toward reciprocal communication with a quality of increasing congruence; a tendency toward more mutually accurate understanding of the communications; improved psychological adjustment and functioning in both parties; mutual satisfaction in the relationship. Conversely the greater the communicated incongruence of experience and awareness, the more the ensuing relationship will involve: further communication with the same quality; disintegration of accurate understanding, less adequate psychological adjustment and functioning in both parties; and mutual dissatisfaction in the relationship. (pp. 344–345)

If, therefore, the sender is to send a clear message, he must experience congruence while he is sending his message, and if the receiver is to receive the message clearly and accurately, he must be congruent while he is receiving.

Roger's general law on congruence seems to apply to both task-oriented groups and counseling groups. In fact, members' failure to experience the kind of congruence described by Rogers, the openness described by Shaw and Blum, and the quality of participation described by Allport may explain, at least partially, why informal groups develop within a formal group such as a school faculty. Even when members are invited to participate in solving problems, they may appear to accept the leader's proposals, and then meet later in an informal, safer group in which they can gripe and state somewhat more honestly what they really think. Within such a group there are usually a few who previously have accepted the challenge to participate in solving the group's problems and have been penalized for disagreement with the leader. These persons tend to be cautious; they do not want to be hurt again. To involve them the leader must convince them that he needs their assistance and that members can afford to disagree with him.

To illustrate how this problem can develop in industry, Bass (1960) described a problem within one department of a large plant:

> If a department head fails to meet regularly with his group to
> discuss mutual actions and problems, he may be surprised by
> the development of active cliques sharing their guesses about
> various motives and future actions. The informal organization
> may serve to disrupt the formal relations established by author-
> ity. Communication by the informal interaction is less likely
> to be accurate. Material unfavorable to the formal system is
> likely to be disseminated informally. . . . A group of tech-
> nicians from different departments may band together to share
> grievances concerning their dissatisfaction with an immediate
> supervisor and his boss, leading eventually to some deleterious
> action. (p. 85)

Though members of an informal group can help solve
problems of the formal group, they tend to become primarily
concerned with the best interests only of themselves. Frequently they focus their attention on a scapegoat, such as a
foreman or his boss, within the formal group. When they
devote a lot of time to expressing negative feelings without
contributing to the solution of the problems for the formal
group, they tend to pity themselves and become bitter—thus
interfering with the solution of the group's problems and
perhaps with their own self-actualization.

Whenever an individual accepts employment in an organization, or joins a church, or even joins a social club, he gives
up some aspects of personal freedom for the rewards the formal organization provides. An informal organization often
develops to help members restore some of the personal freedom
the individuals surrendered. It also may develop because
members' needs are not being met in the way they expected
to have them met within the formal structure. Such a group
also may develop to rally around a splinter group when there
are basic differences in opinion concerning what is best for the
entire group. When these events occur, the leader must be
able to enlist members' assistance in diagnosing the group's
problems, in developing strategies to cope with them, and in
conveying why all must cooperate to achieve the entire group's
objectives.

A Group's Self-Study

If the members of a task-oriented group accept their full responsibility for developing and maintaining an effective working relationship, they will learn to study their own behavior in order to understand why they function well when they do and to diagnose and remedy their difficulties when they function badly.

Identification and classification of the roles played by members is one effective method for self-study. In fact, Newcomb (1950) concluded that the study of roles may be used to understand an individual's personality as well as members' behavior in a group. By observing how an individual functions in varied roles such as father, husband, host, employer, employee, and guest, an observer can discover much about that person's interests, values, relationship skills, problems, and self-consistency. Newcomb also concluded that a study of roles played by members may be used to identify groups that are similar or different. He also noted that when the nature of a group changes (or persists), the roles played by members tend to change (or persist). When, for example, a quarterback repeatedly calls a play in which he carries the ball and gains on a winning football team, players assume supporting roles, but when his team begins losing and he does the same thing, they tend to take critical roles.

From their studies of the First National Training Laboratory in Group Development, Benne and Sheats (1948) identified and classified member roles that can be used to study task-oriented groups:

1. *Group-task roles.* Initiator contributor, information seeker, opinion seeker, information giver, opinion giver, elaborator, coordinator, orienter, evaluator-critic, energizer, procedural technician, and recorder.

2. *Group-building and maintenance roles.* Encourager, harmonizer, compromiser, gate-keeper, standard setter, group observer, and follower.

3. *Individual roles* (members trying to satisfy their individual needs). Aggressor, blocker, recognition-seeker, self-confessor, playboy, dominator, help-seeker, and special-interest pleader.

Ohlsen and Pearson (1965) selected from Benne and Sheats' roles, adapted them, and redefined some of them for a study of members' (including the counselor's) behavior in counseling groups: aggressor, ameliorator, blocker, clarifier (subdivided into four roles pertaining to clarification of relationships within the counseling group, clarification of relationships between clients and persons outside the counseling group, and demands for clarification in the two other categories), catharter, dominator, evaluator, expositor, expediter, giver of information, giver of advice, help seeker, initiator, intellectualizer, interpreter of behavior for clients' important others, interpreter of members' behavior, information seeker, opinion seeker, prober, reflector, role player, recognition seeker, supporter, support seeker, structurer, and sympathy seeker.

Ohlsen and Pearson also were interested in appraising the impact of the person playing these various roles upon other members. To do this they identified the principal actor and tried to assess independently the impact of the role and the person who played it. For this study they defined the principal actor as the person who had the attention of at least the majority of the group. Usually he was the speaker, but occasionally another individual attracted and maintained the attention of the majority of the group for at least ten seconds. Horney's (1945) work was used to develop and define the four responses of members to the principal actor: approach behavior, attack behavior, withdrawal behavior, and passive attendance behavior.

Except for the most disorganized moments of group interaction with children's groups, Ohlsen and Pearson found that trained observers could identify the principal actor, classify the role he played, and record the other group members' reactions to the role. They used two observers: one to identify the principal actor and classify his role and the other

to classify members' reactions to the role. For two judges
working independently for each task, percentages of agreement between judges for principal actor roles varied from
72 to 93 percent and for reactions to the roles the agreements
varied from 76 percent for attack to 87 percent for passive
attendance. Chief disagreements occurred initially with regard
to interpreter and clarifier roles. Though the evidence presented by Ohlsen and Pearson indicated that live interactions
can be reliably classified, these researchers preferred to work
from video recordings, which enable observers to control the
flow of stimuli and, where necessary, to replay parts of the
interaction in order to be more certain of classification
decisions. They concluded that their method can be used for
better understanding of the treatment process and the management of counseling groups; that clients responded differently
to different individuals who played various principal-actor
roles; and that in future studies investigators should take
account of the general therapeutic climate in which the specific
interaction occurs. The fact that these clients did play a
number of helping roles suggests that even young clients
(underachieving, bright fifth graders) can learn to help
others as well as obtain help for themselves. Perhaps clients
also can learn to use a simplified version of this system to
study the group dynamics within their own counseling group.

   As a less complicated system for the study of group
dynamics within both a task-oriented group and a counseling
group, the writer recommends the use of Benne and Sheats'
recorder and observer roles. The recorder keeps a running
account of disagreements, agreements, decisions, topics discussed, and issues mentioned but left unresolved. The observer,
on the other hand, tries to help members determine why they
behaved as they did, why they succeeded or failed. As he
observes, he tries to answer such questions as: Do members
seem to know and accept the group's goals? What was done
that aided or interfered with their achieving their goals? Who
participated in the discussion? What was the nature of each
one's contributions? Who actually made the decisions? How

did the group deal with controversial issues? How did members deal with personal conflict between members? Who helped resolve conflict? How was it resolved? What did the group expect from its designated leader? What other leader roles emerged? What purpose did each serve? Who was assigned special responsibility for the study of group process? How did members seem to react to these specialists' contributions? How did members seem to feel about what was being accomplished? How did they seem to feel toward each other? What needs to be done to improve the efficiency of this group?

An observer often finds that he can use an end-of-meeting reaction sheet to encourage members to look at themselves. He also can involve them in contributing entries for such an evaluation sheet. Most sheets of this nature seek responses to the kinds of questions listed above; usually the first item requests a general reaction to the session:

> 1. How do you feel about this session?
>   a. It was as successful as most such meetings.
>   b. It was better than most such meetings.
>   c. It was less successful than most such meetings.
>   d. It was one of the best I ever attended.
>   e. It was one of the poorest I ever attended.

Such reaction sheets usually attempt to assess how members feel about each other:

> 2. How do you feel toward the other members of the group?
>   a. I am not sure how I feel about the others.
>   b. They did not seem to be interested in what I had to say, but most of them seemed to accept me as a person.
>   c. They did not seem to be interested in what I had to say, and most of them did not seem to accept me as a person.
>   d. They were interested in what I had to say, and most of them accepted me as a person.
>   e. They were interested in what I had to say, but most of them did not seem to accept me as a person.
>   f. If none of the above applies, write your reaction to the others here.

Such an end-of-meeting reaction sheet can be used success-fully with task-oriented groups such as student councils and leadership training groups in which the members either elected, or asked the leader to choose from volunteers, a recorder and observer. Tape-recorded sessions also can be used to provide a group with live case materials from their own experience for analysis. Video recordings are even better for this purpose: with a record of the nonverbal behavior asso-ciated with verbal responses they learn to detect even the subtle nonverbal cues that influence group effectiveness. Benne and Sheats' roles also can be used effectively for such self-study with task-oriented groups.

Use of such specialists as observer and recorder must be introduced with care in counseling groups, especially with adolescents, who are very sensitive to external evaluation. To be effective, counseling must be perceived as an understanding, accepting relationship. If clients are to discuss the topics that really bother them and express their genuine feelings, they must feel that they are reasonably well protected from hurtful evaluations. Now this does not mean that such special roles cannot be used in group counseling, but it does mean that the clients must see the need for self-study, want it, and realize that the roles are used to help them study themselves. When these conditions are met, they also may use recordings effec-tively for self-study. Recordings also can be used for research purposes when the clients know why recordings are being made and they *are convinced that confidences will be kept.*

Summary

Every effective leader helps members understand those forces within the group which contribute to and interfere with their achieving their goals. It is not sufficient if he alone understands these forces. He must be able to help members identify and use the group's resources, to recognize behavior that suggests difficulty, to diagnose the difficulty, and to enlist everyone's assistance in solving the group's problems. For this he needs a knowledge of group dynamics and the ability to help members apply its findings in self-study.

Task-oriented groups and counseling groups seem to pass through similar phases as they develop. Members of both groups must know what to expect and must learn to function in these roles to perform effectively. As some members participate more, and are responded to proportionately, others' participation rates are depressed, setting up participation expectations. This applies also to the leader. The extent to which he structures and permits the group to depend upon him seems to determine the amount of discussion directed to him and the amount of responsibility members will assume. On the other hand, too little direction can waste time and create unnecessary tension among members.

Although most readers can cite examples of autocratic leaders who have been effective, democratic leadership is preferred. Even when the autocratic leader seeks and uses members' advice on difficult problems, as most effective ones do, such efforts are not sufficient; participation in the decision-making process seems to be essential to enlist members' full cooperation in the solution of the group's problems. Discussion in itself will not change behavior: Members must become deeply involved to make the necessary commitment to help the group achieve its goals.

Mere talking is not sufficient. Members must be able to talk openly about how they feel, make a commitment to change their behavior, and obtain honest feedback. Another necessity for good communication is congruence of experience, awareness, and expression. The greater this congruence on the part of the speaker, and the more transparent the listener is to himself, the better the former will communicate and the latter will receive.

When members either elect, or ask the leader to choose from among volunteers, an observer and recorder, these roles can be used effectively by members to study their own behavior and increase group efficiency. Their effectiveness is enhanced, and the threat of evaluation is decreased, when the observer uses end-of-meeting evaluation sheets and encourages members to study behavior within the group as it is exhibited on recordings. Video recordings are even better than tape recordings, because they enable members to recognize and use subtle nonverbal responses. With counseling groups, however, these special roles must be used with care, lest such self-study deteriorate into harsh evaluations and interpretations that can destroy the therapeutic climate. Such threats should be kept to a minimum. Members must feel that the counseling group is one place where they can be themselves—where they can express what they feel without fear of evaluation.

References

Allport, G. W. "The Psychology of Participation," *Psychological Review*, 1945, 52:117–132.

Bass, B. M. *Leadership, Psychology, and Organizational Behavior*, New York: Harper & Row, Publishers, 1960.

Benne, K. D., and P. Sheats "Functional Roles of Group Members," *Journal of Social Issues*, 1948, 4:41–49.

Bion, W. R. "Experiences in Groups: I," *Human Relations*, 1948, 1:487–496.

Bradford, L. P. "Developing Potentialities through Class Groups," *Teachers College Record*, 1960, 51:443–450.

Bradford, L. P., J. R. Gibb, and K. D. Benne *T-Group Theory and Laboratory Method*, New York: John Wiley & Sons, Inc., 1964.

Bradford, L. P., and Dorothy Mial "When Is a Group?" *Educational Leadership*, 1963, 21:147–151.

Cartwright, D., and A. Zanders *Group Dynamics: Research and Theory*, New York: Harper & Row, Publishers, 1968.

Dreikurs, R. "Basic Principles in Dealing with Children," Chapter 4 in Dreikurs, Corsini, Lowe, and Sonstegard, *Adlerian Family Counseling*, Eugene, Ore.: University of Oregon Press, 1959.

Fiedler, F. E. "A Contingency Model of Leadership Effectiveness," in L. Berkowitz (ed.), *Experimental Social Psychology*, New York: Academic Press, Inc., 1964.

Gordon, T. *Group-Centered Leadership*, Boston: Houghton Mifflin Company, 1955.

Grater, H. A. "Change in Self and Other Attitudes in a Leadership Training Group," *Personnel and Guidance Journal*, 1959, 37:493–496.

Hare, A. P. *Handbook for Small Group Research*, New York: Free Press of Glencoe, 1962.

Horney, Karen *Our Inner Conflicts*, New York: W. W. Norton & Company, Inc., 1945.

Kemp, C. G. *Group Process: A Foundation for Counseling with Groups*, Boston: Houghton Mifflin Company, 1964.

Lewin, K. "The Dynamics of Group Action," *Educational Leadership*, 1944, 1:195–200.

Lifton, W. M. *Working with Groups: Group Process and Individual Growth*, New York: John Wiley & Sons, Inc., 1966.

Loeser, L. H. "Some Aspects of Group Dynamics," *International Journal of Group Psychotherapy*, 1957, 7:5–19.

Newcomb, T. M. "Role Behaviors in the Study of Individual Personality and of Groups," *Journal of Personality*, 1950, 18:273–289.

Noble, F., M. Ohlsen, and F. Proff "A Method for the Quantification of Psychotherapeutic Interaction in Group Counseling," *Journal of Counseling Psychology*, 1961, 8:54–61.

Ohlsen, M. M. "A Leadership Training Program," in *Guidance Services in the Modern School*, New York: Harcourt, Brace & World, Inc., 1964, pp. 380–388.

Ohlsen, M. M., and R. E. Pearson "A Method for the Classification of Group Interaction and Its Use to Explore the Influence of Individual and Role Factors in Group Counseling," *Journal of Clinical Psychology*, 1965, 21:436–441.

Powdermaker, Florence B., and J. D. Frank *Group Psychotherapy*, Cambridge, Mass.: Harvard University Press, 1953.

Psathas, G. "Phase Movement and Equilibrium Tendencies in Interaction Process in Psychotherapy Groups," *Sociometry*, 1960, 23:177–194.

Rogers, C. R. "A Tentative Formulation of a General Law of Interpersonal Relationships," in *On Becoming a Person*, Boston: Houghton Mifflin Company, 1961.

Shaw, M. E., and J. M. Blum "Group Performance as a Function of Task Difficulty and Group Awareness of Member Satisfaction," *Journal of Applied Psychology*, 1965, 49:151–154.

Shaw, M. E., and J. M. Blum "Effects of Leadership Style Upon Group Performance as a Function of Task Structure," *Journal of Personality and Social Psychology*, 1966, 3:238–241.

Shaw, M. E., and P. Caron "Group Effectiveness as a Function of the Group's Knowledge of Member Dissatisfaction," *Psychonomic Science*, 1965, 2:299–300.

Thelen, H. A., and W. Dickerman "Stereotypes and Growth of Groups," *Educational Leadership*, 1949, 6:309–316.

Thelen, H. A., and Dorothy Stock "Basic Problems in Developing the Mature and Effective Groups," *National Education Association Journal*, 1955, 44:105–106.

Chapter Four

Therapeutic Forces
within a Counseling Group

A successful counselor must understand, recognize, and know how to use the therapeutic forces within a counseling group, and he must be able to teach his clients to recognize and use these forces. Likewise he must recognize and feel competent to deal with the antitherapeutic forces, and he must teach his clients to recognize, cope with, and accept responsibility for dealing with these forces. Intelligent use of the therapeutic forces tends to prevent much antitherapeutic behavior, or at least enables clients to cope with it. This chapter discusses the nine major therapeutic forces within a counseling group: commitment; clear expectations; clients' acceptance of responsibility to change, to help others change, and to help develop a therapeutic climate; genuine acceptance within the group; an attractive group; a feeling of belonging; security; productive tension; and meaningful norms.

Some counselors are deeply bothered by the notion of the counselor's using the therapeutic forces to achieve change in clients. They are bothered by the authoritarian connotations of the implied manipulation; and they are rightly concerned with the inappropriate use of these powers. They must be cautious lest they manipulate clients to behave in ways that serve the counselors' values rather than the clients' self-actualization in terms of their own values and goals. Perhaps some counselors will be relieved to know that when clients are given responsibility to function as the counselor's helpers as well as to obtain help for themselves, clients come to accept a client's goals for himself and become more tolerant of values that differ from their own.

Whenever an individual joins a group, accepts its norms and its goals, makes a commitment to help its members achieve their goals, and invests of himself in helping them, he can expect, even in a short-term, task-oriented group, that he will have some impact upon the other members, and they upon him. This holds especially for members of a counseling group. Selection criteria stress each client's commitment to discuss his own problems openly, to help fellow clients discuss their problems, to change his own behavior and attitudes, and to become deeply involved in helping others change their behaviors and attitudes, too.

But is not this expectation to change threatening? Cartwright (1951) claims that the expectation to change is more threatening than either education or therapy; the mere goal of change does not either suggest respect for values or insure positive change. On the other hand, to most persons, education and therapy imply the authority to insure good change. The counselor may allay fears by selecting clients carefully, encouraging them to state clear and precise goals, helping them develop criteria to appraise changes that occur in them, and giving straightforward answers to their questions about what to expect.

As Frank (1961) said, clients' faith in a healer is an important variable in developing a therapeutic climate. Nevertheless, sometimes clients wonder whether facing up to their problems and learning to behave differently is worth the risks and the pain involved. Most seem to realize that it is much easier to talk about how they got to be the way they are or even what they would like and, perhaps, could be, than it is *to change their own behavior*. The enabling conditions for change require wise use of the therapeutic forces within the group. Beck (1958a) observed that a client's very introduction into an artificially structured, temporary subculture in which change is expected, supported, and reinforced not only encourages changes but also breaks down the barriers to change associated with former group loyalties.

Kelman (1963) introduced some other related ideas on permanence of change. He identified three sources of social influence within groups: compliance, identification, and internalization. A counselor must understand and be able to recognize how these forces influence clients' behavior—both within and outside the counseling group. Although changes in behavior and attitudes may at first be motivated by compliance, the counselor must try to establish internalized motivation. The following quotations from Kelman (1963) develops the rationale for this point of view:

> Compliance can be said to occur when an individual accepts influence from another person or from a group in order to attain a favorable reaction from the other, that is, to gain a specific reward or avoid a specific punishment controlled by the other, or to gain approval or avoid disapproval from him. Identification can be said to occur when an individual accepts influence from another person or a group in order to establish or maintain a satisfying self-defining relationship to the other. In contrast to compliance identification is not primarily concerned with producing a particular effect in the other. Rather, accepting influence through identification is a way of establishing or maintaining a desired relationship to the other, as well as the self-definition that is anchored in this relationship. By accepting influence, the person is able to see himself as similar to the other (as in classical identification) or to see himself as enacting a role reciprocal to that of the other. Finally, internalization can be said to occur when an individual accepts influence in order to maintain the congruence of his actions and beliefs with his value system. Here it is the content of the induced behavior and its relation to the person's value system that are intrinsically satisfying. . . . (p. 400)

> On the consequent side, the framework proposes that the changes produced by each of the three processes tend to be of a different nature. The crucial difference in nature of change between the three processes is in the conditions under which the newly acquired behavior is likely to manifest itself. Behavior accepted through compliance will tend to manifest itself only

under conditions of surveillance by the influencing agent, i.e., only when the person's behavior is observable (directly or indirectly) by the agent. The manifestation of identification-based behavior does not depend on observability by the influencing agent, but it does depend on the salience of the person's relationship to the agent. That is, the behavior is likely to manifest itself only in situations that are in some way or other associated with the individual or group from whom the behavior was originally adopted. Thus, whether or not the behavior is manifested will depend on the role that the individual takes at any given moment in time. While surveillance is irrelevant, identification-based behavior is designed to meet the other's expectations for the person's own role performance. The behavior, therefore, remains tied to the external source and dependent upon social support. It is not integrated with the individual's value system, but rather tends to be isolated from the rest of his values, to remain encapsulated. In contrast, behavior accepted through internalization depends neither on surveillance nor on salience but tends to manifest itself whenever the values on which it is based are relevant to the issue at hand. Behavior adopted through internalization is in some way, rational or otherwise, integrated with the individual's existing values. It becomes part of a personal system, as distinguished from a system of social-role expectations. It becomes independent of the original source and, because of the resulting interplay with other parts of the person's value system, it tends to be more idiosyncratic, more flexible, and more complex. (p. 402)

Commitment

Those who profit most from group counseling recognize and accept the need for assistance and are committed to talk about their problems, to solve them, and to change their behavior when they are accepted for group counseling. They also seem to understand what will be expected from them, have some notion how they can be helped by group counseling, and expect to be helped. In the intake interview (see Chapter Five) a prospective client is not pressured to accept group counseling. In fact, the very opposite is true; he must convince the counselor that he is ready for group counseling and that he can make the necessary commitments.

In addition to selecting the most highly motivated volunteers, Beck (1958b) identified three other criteria for group membership that support the necessity for commitment: (1) a prospective client's awareness of his own emotional difficulties, (2) open admission of his need for help, and (3) surrender of his defenses. According to her review of the literature on group dynamics, a client must want assistance, be able to accept it, and want to get well.

Kelman (1963) agreed on the importance of each client's commitment to treatment and to his group's norms:

> If the patient, then, is to continue in therapy long enough so that he can get to the point of having corrective emotional experiences, he must develop a commitment to the therapeutic situation as one that is potentially beneficial to him and to which it is worth making certain sacrifices. . . . When he is asked to conform to the therapeutic norms by exposing himself and expressing his feelings without censorship he is placed in a very difficult situation. He runs the risk of criticism, rejection, and condemnation after he has divested himself of his defenses and laid himself bare before others. If the patient is to feel free to engage in the therapeutic process and talk about himself, then he must regard the situation as one in which he is safe from attack and condemnation and in which he can afford to relax his customary protective mechanisms. In short, then, if the patient is to engage himself in the therapeutic process and open himself to the possibility of therapeutic experiences, he must develop a commitment to the situation: an attitude of trust and a willingness to accept its terms, based on his conviction that he will be protected in this situation and that he will benefit from it. (p. 410)

Since the school counselor's prospective clients for group counseling have many opportunities to get to know him, to hear him and their teachers describe his services, and to learn from their peers how they have been helped by group counseling, the school counselor should be able to obtain committed clients somewhat more easily than those who practice privately or work in community agencies. He also has the advantage of working with persons who can be helped more easily and more quickly. When, however, he selects poor prospects, and consequently does not help them, this fact also becomes known quickly.

Expectations

Clients profit most from a counseling group when they understand what is expected before they decide whether to join. They need an opportunity to learn what kinds of decisions they may make for themselves, what will be expected from them, what they can expect from the other clients and the counselor, and what benefits they may expect from the group counseling experience. When prospective clients realize what is expected of them in order to increase the chances for the success of the group, and what decisions they can make, they tend to take more responsibility for helping to create a therapeutic climate, for functioning as the counselor's aides in the treatment process, and for enforcing the limits they defined. (Relevance of expectations for a T group was discussed in Chapter Three.)

Chapter One pointed out that the counselor must understand himself, feel qualified for his counseling responsibilities, and know how he functions best in order to define the therapeutic relationship for prospective clients. He also must have some clear notions on who can be helped by group counseling, have confidence in those whom he selects and in the treatment process, and feel secure in encouraging them to help define relevant limits for the group.

School counselors who have well-established counseling services and who have conveyed to the faculty what they are trying to do have a decided advantage in introducing group counseling. In such a setting the principal will usually allocate some time at a regular faculty meeting for a counselor to describe group counseling and the kinds of students who are most apt to profit from it, and to give the staff members a chance to react to the idea (including expressing their doubts about it and challenging its value), to ask questions about the treatment process, and to find out how they may help introduce the service. Besides increasing the staff members' understanding of the treatment process so that they can make more intelligent referrals and interpret the service to others, such meetings give the counselor a chance to explain why he would like to be invited into the teachers' classes to describe group counseling for students, to answer their questions, and to explain how they may arrange to join a counseling group. Even where the counselor is not given the opportunity to present the idea to the entire faculty, he is usually permitted to describe group counseling to interested faculty at a voluntary meeting. Usually he is also permitted to speak to students in the library or study halls.

When this process is followed, prospective clients tend to come to intake interviews with a better understanding of what is expected, with specific questions to clarify what is expected, and with more commitment than they would have otherwise. Thus, insofar as it can be done in advance, prospective clients have an opportunity to learn what is unique about interpersonal relationships within a counseling group, what they will be expected to do to develop and maintain such relationships, and what they will be expected to talk about if the meaningful participation, congruence, and openness described in Chapter Three are to be experienced. Frank (1961) concluded that for an effective counseling group the clients' two most important expectations are: (1) free, honest expression of feelings and (2) opportunity to discuss their own and others' problems constructively. Clients learn to value cooperation more than competition—to value another for what he is rather than for what he has achieved.

Responsibility

Increased responsibility for themselves and the therapeutic process increases clients' chances for growth within a counseling group.

Meaningful involvement and participation in making decisions that affect them encourage most persons to accept responsibility and discourage them from becoming reactive and hostile (see Chapter Three). When, therefore, only those who wish to participate are accepted for counseling, each helps to formulate his own treatment goals, and each makes a commitment to change, then each tries to accept responsibility for helping members achieve their goals.

Cartwright reported that strong pressure for change can be developed in a group by creating a shared perception of the need for change—so that pressure for change comes from within the group. Marrow and French (1945) illustrated how data alone cannot create such pressure for change: decision-makers must participate in solving their own problems. In this case, on the grounds of absenteeism and poor training risk, management defended a policy of not hiring women over thirty. Even though the staff psychologist presented convincing contrary evidence, they refused to budge until they themselves helped to design a study and to collect the data that supported the need for a change.

Hobbs (1962) presented a similar case for making clients feel responsible for themselves. Though he was discussing the sources of gain in individual psychotherapy, his conclusions obviously apply to group counseling: (1) the locus of control must be placed in clients rather than in the counselor, and (2) clients must accept responsibility for developing and modifying their cognitive structure in order to make personal sense out of the world. Nevertheless, Hobbs denied that insight was an important source of gain in psychotherapy. Instead, he said that emphasis must be placed upon clients' immediate experiences and their learning of specific behaviors. Clients must practice making decisions, learn to accept responsibility for themselves, learn new ways of relating to others, and discover that they are capable of managing their own lives.

Current practices in courts and hospitals that excuse irresponsible behavior encourage it and reinforce it. Glasser (1965) said that patients must accept responsibility for their irresponsible past behaviors and for helping themselves get well. He claimed that the more irresponsible a patient is, the more he must learn to satisfy his needs in an acceptable, responsible way.

For most clients, and especially adolescents who have been pressured to accept counseling because of some conflict with important others such as parents or teachers, voluntary participation makes them feel more responsible. When they are given the right to decide whether or not to participate and the responsibility for convincing the counselor that they are ready for group counseling, they feel respected, and they are encouraged to help develop and maintain a therapeutic climate. As they become increasingly involved in the therapeutic process, they learn to help others as well as to obtain help for themselves. Moreover, Lindt (1958) found that only those who accepted this responsibility for helping others within their group profited from the group treatment experience.

However, acceptance of responsibility for enforcing the group norms that clients have helped to develop does not mean that the norms will never be ignored or challenged. Sometimes most members will have difficulty disciplining themselves, accepting group discipline, suppressing their own needs, and listening to others. When this happens and clients do not recognize the problem, the counselor has responsibility for helping clients recognize and cope with these antitherapeutic behaviors. Usually a reflection of underlying feelings is sufficient: "Joe seems to be unhappy with the idea that he is expected to ———." Occasionally the counselor may find it necessary to ask the group to review what is expected and to decide whether or not they wish to change the group norms. Usually, however, most members are so committed to the group that they will try to adjust to its norms when they realize that they are deviating. Though it may be difficult for a client to accept an agreement that he does not like or to listen to another when he wants to talk, he eventually learns to do this because he participated in defining the agreements and he realizes that reasonably soon he will be given a chance to talk. Bach (1954) reported that the patients' participation in building group norms is one of the most effective factors in producing the optimal degree of cohesiveness in the group.

Acceptance

Genuine acceptance by his fellow clients enhances self-esteem and encourages a client to change his behavior. When a client discovers that he has been accepted for treatment in a group with other persons who expect to profit from group counseling, who really try to understand and to accept him and who reach beyond mere talk to uncover the problems that bother him, they convey to him that they have confidence in his ability to solve his problems.

> Needless to say, such acceptance enhances the patient's self-esteem as well as his feeling that he can somehow be reclaimed. While acceptance from the group is not as predictable nor as unconditional as that from the therapist, when it does occur it is likely to have a powerful impact. For here is acceptance not by a professional, who has been trained to take this role and is being paid for it, but by the person's own peers who, despite their deviancy, are more representative of society at large. [Kelman (1963), p. 413]

Attractiveness

"The more attractive the group is to its members, the greater is the influence that the group can exert on its members." [Cartwright (1951), p. 388]

Cartwright reported that a group's attractiveness is determined by the importance of its perceived goals, the extent to which it meets its members' needs, whether its members are liked, and whether it includes prestige members.

Later Cartwright (1968) reported that a group is attractive when: (1) its members are valued and accepted [Dittes (1959), Jackson (1959)]; (2) its members are similar [Newcomb (1953), Festinger (1954)]; (3) it is small enough to enable members to communicate and relate effectively [Porter and Lawler (1965)]; (4) it provides opportunities for social life and close personal associations [Hagstrom and Selvin

(1965)]; and (5) it provides at least two of these three sources of satisfaction: personal attraction, task attraction, and prestige from membership [Back (1951)]. With reference to Back's research, Cartwright noted that these three different sources of attraction did have some common effects, but led to different styles of communication:

> When cohesiveness was based on personal attractions among members, they made their discussion a long, pleasant conversation in which they expected to be able to persuade one another easily. When cohesiveness was based on effective performance of the task they were given to do, the members wanted to complete the activity quickly and efficiently and discussed only those matters which they thought were relevant to achieving their purposes. And when cohesiveness was based on the prestige obtainable from membership, the members acted cautiously, concentrated on their own actions, and in general were careful not to risk their status. (p. 106)

Festinger and Aronson (1960) reported that even a dull group is more likely to be attractive when one must undergo considerable stress to become a member than when he can be admitted with little or no effort.

The findings above certainly apply to counseling groups as well as task-oriented groups. When a counselor has an opportunity to describe group counseling for prospective clients, as is suggested in Chapter Five, he can increase the attractiveness of a counseling group by (1) using examples of problems that previous clients have discussed in groups to convey that the clients treated in these groups are reasonably healthy persons struggling with problems like those of prospective clients; (2) including within his description the problems of prestige figures such as athletes or student leaders; (3) telling how he tries to identify persons with some common problems; (4) giving examples of how clients have been helped; and (5) explaining why clients are required to convince the counselor that they are ready for group counseling. Obviously, a counselor must be careful not to break confidence with any previous clients or to cast himself in the

role of selling a service or putting pressure on prospective
clients to join a counseling group. Instead, his task is to convey
what is expected and for whom the services seem to be most
relevant. Usually, when this is done well, more clients volunteer for the first group than the counselor can accept. By
selecting the very best prospects and arranging for appropriate assistance for the others until a new group can begin, he
also increases the attractiveness of counseling groups. Those
who have been helped reinforce the attractiveness of subsequent counseling groups.

Cartwright (1951) reported that the greater the prestige
of a group member *in the eyes of other members,* the greater
is his influence within the group. If, therefore, a counselor is
to select a prestige figure for one of his first groups, he must
select someone who is perceived as prestigious *by clients.* For
example, a school counselor must select a prestige figure
admired by fellow students rather than one who may be
admired only by teachers. In any case, a prestige figure must
not be merely used. Only those who genuinely want help and
are committed to change their behavior must be selected.

Whenever a counselor selects clients for a group, he must
always ask himself whether he believes that they can be
helped *best within his counseling group.* For his first counseling groups this is even more critical—especially when he is
the first to use the treatment method within his work setting.
However, his relationships with his clients and his ability to
help them in groups will always affect the attractiveness of his
counseling groups, within which he is one of the prestige
figures.

Belonging

*"Both those who are to be changed and those who
influence change must sense a strong feeling of belonging in
the same group."* [Cartwright (1951)] As the feeling of
belonging increases, clients become more ego-involved in the

interaction, participate more meaningfully, and increase their commitment for change.

Frank (1961) observed that the rootlessness of many Americans has deprived them of the emotional support formerly provided by the large and close family. With their obvious competition for status and prestige, the social club and associations at work (or at school) have not proven to be adequate substitutes for these family relationships. In fact, however, conflicts within the very primary groups from which persons expect to experience genuine belonging and support, such as the family, often motivate prospective clients to seek group counseling. From it they hope to learn how to escape from their devastating loneliness and to develop satisfying relationships within their primary groups. Frank said that the way in which treatment groups enable clients to be themselves and express themselves honestly facilitates improved adjustment: such a group diminishes feelings of isolation, heightens hope, and increases self-esteem.

Dreikurs (1957) said that in order for a client to be open, to look at himself as he really is, to lower his defenses, and to search for more appropriate goals, he must feel that he truly belongs; he must experience within his treatment group genuine human fellowship in which persons give of themselves without ulterior motives: "Unlike any other group, here, individual differences and particular deficiencies do not lower the patient's status." (p. 374)

Beck (1958a) said that membership with others struggling with similar problems helps develop a feeling of belonging.

Kelman (1963) reported that the presence of persons with shared problems increases clients' identification with the group and their commitment to the therapeutic situation. The feeling of belonging also is bolstered by the intimacy of discussion topics and the support provided by fellow clients.

The importance of intimacy in individual therapy, described by Hobbs (1962), makes it an even more powerful therapeutic force within a counseling group:

. . . psychotherapy is a situation carefully designed to make it possible for a client to learn to be close to another person without getting hurt. . . .

He has an experience of contact, of engagement, of commitment. He learns directly and immediately, by concrete experience, that it is possible to risk being close to another, to be open and honest, to let things happen to his feelings in the presence of another, and indeed, even to go so far as to dare to include the therapist himself as an object of these feelings. The neurotic, on the basis of earlier attempts at intimate relationships with important life persons, primarily his mother and father, has come to the deep-seated conviction that other people cannot be trusted, that it is terribly dangerous to open oneself up to them. . . . Or he may get engaged with others in intense relationships that should lead to intimacy but always with reservations, always on terms that guarantee that he is really not exposed. These are the counterfeit friendships and marriages of the neurotic. And in all of this, of course, he will not even be intimate with himself; he cannot let himself feel how he actually feels about himself and others. Now I argue that human intimacy is necessary for survival. . . . (p. 743)

What Hobbs and Kelman have said about the importance of belonging for neurotics certainly applies to adolescents. When a school counselor tries to let adolescents know what they can expect before they elect to join a group, allows them to help define guidelines for their behavior within the group, conveys that the group will be made up of persons like themselves, and expects them to help develop the therapeutic climate, they sense genuine membership in the group—they feel that they belong. Within the counseling sessions the feeling of belonging can be further enhanced by affiliation responses by the counselor. For this purpose Powdermaker and Frank (1953) recommended emphasizing the similarity among individual clients' problems, experiences, and emotions and generalizing from one client's remarks in order to help others see the implications for them.

Belonging to a group in which he experiences intimacy desensitizes a client to the fear of intimacy, teaches him relationship skills, and provides experiences that reinforce his efforts to achieve such meaningful relationships. But, as Hobbs indicated, it is not sufficient to experience these relationships only in counseling. A client also must learn to relate to significant others in this meaningful way outside of counseling. His investment in the other clients, their investment in him, his commitment to change, their expectations for him to change, and his experiences in relating meaningfully to varied personalities in his group convey to him that he can belong and help him develop the will and self-confidence to change his behavior outside his counseling group. Knowing that he has such membership also makes it safer to apply outside the group what he has learned in it; he knows that the other members will help him analyze his failures as well as enjoy his successes.

Security

When clients come to feel reasonably secure within their counseling group, they can be themselves, discuss the problems that bother them, accept others' frank reactions to them, and express their own genuine feelings toward others. The safer a client feels in the group, the easier it is for him to be open and transparent. Although he realizes that at times the experience will be painful, he is willing to tolerate the pain within this safe environment to reap the potential benefits.

The setting for group counseling meets the optimal conditions for learning described by Seeman (1963): "It is a safe environment; it is an understanding environment; it is a caring environment; it is a participating environment; and it is an approving environment." (p. 8) It is a safe place where clients can be open, honest, and frank and can discover new ways of behaving, practice these new behaviors, and solicit frank evaluations of their efforts to change.

Beck (1958a) presented a number of reasons why the treatment group is a safe place for self-revelation: (a) it is more easily learned with a group of peers; (b) untrained peers provide an uncensored, more realistic response to it; (c) they accept it with a minimum of threat and provide feedback that enables the speaker to see through his defenses (or to merely lower them); and (d) they listen, accept his problems as real, and offer assistance. From others' discussions of problems each client also discovers that others have problems as bad or worse than his own, and that they expect to be helped in the group.

Beck's rationale for self-revelation in treatment groups can be extended to include one of Hobbs' (1962) sources of gain in psychotherapy: to divest clients of the symbols that produce anxiety and guilt. The counseling group is a safe place in which a client can identify the specific symbols, discuss them with accepting peers, become desensitized to them, and learn to cope with them. Where coping with these symbols involves practice in dealing with specific persons or situations, role playing can be used to provide desired practice.

Tension

Clients' growth in counseling usually involves some tension. There must be enough tension and dissatisfaction to motivate change but not so much that it interferes with a person's use of his resources in achieving change.

Hulse (1950) claimed that some tension is necessary to initiate counseling and to maintain a therapeutic relationship:

> In a well-planned therapeutic group, tension will be present from the very beginning, because the patients have been so selected as to stimulate each other and to maintain interpersonal exchanges of material loaded with affect. Tension is the motor which keeps the therapeutic group going; anxiety is the fuel that makes the motor run. The group therapist becomes the responsible conductor of this vehicle. (p. 834)

With the counselor's help clients can learn to detect and

reflect therapeutic material, and thereby help each other recognize their problems so that they may be faced and solved. Such acts do create tensions, but such tension is not nearly so debilitating as that caused by confrontation and interpretation.

Group Norms

When a client understands and accepts the necessary conditions for a therapeutic group, he is reluctant to ignore his group's norms, because he wants to be helped and he does not want to be perceived as a deviant within his counseling group.

Most counselors agree that group norms are powerful. Bach (1954) reported that patients enforce group norms and do not reinforce antitherapeutic behavior. His emotionally or psychosomatically disturbed patients tried to maintain a relationship in which improved mental health could be achieved. He also described the therapist as the initiator and gate-keeper of norms.

Kelman (1963) noted that therapeutic groups have powerful resources for enforcing group norms:

> The group has powerful techniques at its disposal for controlling the behavior of individual members and maximizing their conformity. Desirable behavior can be rewarded by praise, encouragement, support, or by giving the individual visible signs that he is a valued member of the group and that his status is secure and may, in fact, be enhanced. Undesirable (nonconforming) behavior can be discouraged by direct criticism, ridicule, ostracism, loss in status, and other signs of rejection. (p. 408)

When clients are selected in the manner described earlier in this chapter, they see the group as attractive and expect to be influenced by fellow clients. They also know what decisions they will be encouraged to make before they elect group counseling. Hence, they accept responsibility for helping to develop and maintain group norms. They also become increasingly tolerant of personal values and treatment goals that differ from their own.

Nevertheless, the counselor is a powerful person in establishing group norms. He is a professionally qualified person who knows the conditions under which he has helped others in groups; he has a reputation for helping people; he initiates group counseling; he answers prospective clients' questions about what they can expect and how similar clients have been helped; and he selects clients for the groups. By his behavior as well as his words he reinforces expectations and teaches clients to help others.

Consideration also must be given to the antitherapeutic effect of group norms. A client is confronted with their powerful influence in his out-of-counseling groups when he tries to apply what he has learned. Cartwright (1951) stated his relevant principle as follows: "Efforts to change individuals or subparts of a group which, if successful, would have the result of making them deviate from the group will encounter strong resistance." (p. 389)

Cartwright also explained why some individuals who profited from T-group experiences had such difficulties applying their new knowledges and skills on the job and in their community leadership roles:

> During the past few years a great deal of evidence has been accumulated showing the tremendous pressures which groups can exert upon members to conform to the group's norms. The price of deviation in most groups is rejection or even expulsion. If the member wants to belong and be accepted, he cannot withstand this type of pressure. It is for this reason that efforts to change people by taking them from the group and giving them special training so often have disappointing results. This principle also accounts for finding that people thus trained sometimes display increased tension, aggressiveness toward the group, or a tendency to form cults or cliques with others who have shared their training. (p. 389)

Cartwright's principle explains why some counselors have had the difficulties described in Chapter One in implementing their professional role on the job. After learning new professional skills and developing a new professional role definition, they met with resistance in changing their function to use their new professional knowledge and skills. Learning these skills and developing a commitment to use them is not sufficient. Counselors also need to be taught to cope with blocking forces on the job.

Several examples illustrate why this phenomenon must be considered during counseling. When, for example, juvenile delinquents have been removed from negative neighborhood influences to be counseled, they have often responded well to treatment but have been unable to return to their old neighborhoods and apply the gains achieved during treatment. Hence, treatment must be continued while they are learning either to change group norms within their primary neighborhood groups or to develop new associations that will reinforce the desired behaviors. Of course, still another alternative is to develop the courage to leave the old neighborhood and develop reinforcing associations within another setting.

A similar phenomenon can be observed when a person responds well to treatment within a hospital setting and returns home to lose his gains within the old setting that created his psychosis. This is why some mental hospitals are involving members of a patient's family in family group treatment to improve the mental health of the family unit, to change their expectations in regard to the hospitalized family member, and to develop positive reinforcers for the newly learned behaviors within the family.

In Chapter Ten consideration is given to adolescents who achieved significant improvement but required assistance to convey their new selves to significant others and to enlist their assistance in reinforcing their new behaviors. For even better results adolescents can be helped to convey treatment goals to significant others, so that these others can help them learn and practice new behaviors during counseling. Involving significant others early also tends to help clients change the norms within their out-of-counseling groups.

Summary

An effective counselor recognizes and uses the therapeutic forces within a counseling group and is able to teach his clients to recognize and use them. He also recognizes antitherapeutic forces, knows how to cope with them, and knows how to enlist his clients' assistance in dealing with them.

A group's therapeutic potential is realized best when: (1) clients begin with a commitment to discuss their problems openly, to change their behavior, and to help others change their behavior; (2) they know, before they begin counseling, what is expected of them, insofar as this is possible in advance; (3) they accept responsibility for helping to develop and maintain a therapeutic climate, for their own behavior within their counseling group and outside of it, and for changing their behavior; (4) they sense genuine acceptance within their counseling group; (5) they perceive their group as attractive; (6) they feel that they truly belong; (7) they feel safe enough within their group to discuss whatever bothers them; (8) they experience enough tension to want to change, believe that they can cope with their tension, and are convinced that the results will be worth the pain and effort; and (9) they accept their group's norms.

References

Bach, G. R. *Intensive Group Psychotherapy*, New York: The Ronald Press Company, 1954.
Back, K. "Influence through Social Communication," *Journal of Abnormal and Social Psychology*, 1951, 46:9–23.
Beck, Dorothy F. "The Dynamics of Group Psychotherapy as Seen by a

Sociologist, Part I: The Basic Process," *Sociometry*, 1958a, 21:98–128.

Beck, Dorothy F. "The Dynamics of Group Psychotherapy as Seen by a Sociologist, Part II: Some Puzzling Questions on Leadership, Contextual Relations, and Outcomes," *Sociometry*, 1958b, 21:180–197.

Cartwright, D. "Achieving Change in People: Some Applications of Group Dynamic Theory," *Human Relations*, 1951, 4:381–392.

Cartwright, D. "The Nature of Group Cohesiveness," Chapter 7 in D. Cartwright and A. Zanders, *Group Dynamics: Theory and Research*, New York: Harper & Row, Publishers, 1968.

Cartwright, D., and A. Zanders. *Group Dynamics: Theory and Research*, New York: Harper & Row, Publishers, 1968.

Dittes, J. "Attractiveness of Group as Function of Self-esteem and Acceptance by Group," *Journal of Abnormal and Social Psychology*, 1959, 59:77–82.

Dreikurs, R. "Group Psychotherapy from the Point of View of Adlerian Psychology," *International Journal of Group Psychotherapy*, 1957, 7:363–375.

Festinger, L. "A Theory of Social Comparison Process," *Human Relations*, 1954, 7:117–140.

Festinger, L. and E. Aronson "The Arousal and Reduction of Dissonance in Social Contexts," Chapter 12 in D. Cartwright and A. Zanders, *Group Dynamics: Theory and Practice*, New York: Harper & Row, Publishers, 1960.

Frank, J. D. *Persuasion and Healing*, Baltimore: The Johns Hopkins Press, 1961.

Glasser, W. *Reality Therapy*, New York: Harper & Row, Publishers, 1965.

Hagstrom, W. O., and H. C. Selvin "The Dimensions of Cohesiveness in Small Groups," *Sociometry*, 1965, 28:30–43.

Hobbs, N. "Sources of Gain in Psychotherapy," *American Psychologist*, 1962, 17:741–747.

Hulse, W. C. "The Therapeutic Management of Group Tension," *American Journal of Orthopsychiatry*, 1950, 20:834–838.

Jackson, J. M. "Reference Group Processes in Formal Organization," *Sociometry*, 1959, 22:302–327.

Kelman, H. C. "The Role of the Group in the Induction of Therapeutic Change," *International Journal of Group Psychotherapy*, 1963, 13:399–432.

Lindt, H. "The Nature of Therapeutic Interaction of Patients in Groups," *International Journal of Group Psychotherapy*, 1958, 8:55–69.

Marrow, A. J., and J. P. R. French "Changing a Stereotype in Industry," *Journal of Social Issues*, 1945, 1:33–37.

Newcomb, T. M. "An Approach to the Study of Communication Acts," *Psychological Review*, 1953, 60:393–404.

Porter, L. W., and E. E. Lawler "Properties of Organization Structure in Relation to Job Attitudes and Job Behavior," *Psychological Bulletin*, 1965, 64:23–51.

Powdermaker, Florence B., and J. D. Frank *Group Psychotherapy*, Cambridge, Mass.: Harvard University Press, 1953.

Seeman, J. "Motivation to High Achievement," Summer Lecture in Guidance at University of Colorado, 1963.

Chapter Five

Establishing a Group

This chapter is designed to help a counselor describe group counseling for prospective clients, help them decide whether they want to participate, select the best prospects for group counseling, assign the best prospects to groups, structure the counseling relationships, and help clients learn to help the counselor as well as themselves. Though school and college counselors have the advantage of being able to reach organized groups of prospective clients in order to introduce group counseling, the principles herein presented also apply to the introduction of group counseling in other settings.

Introducing Group Counseling

One of the best ways to introduce group counseling is to describe it for clients and answer their questions about what to expect and what will be expected of them (see Chapter Four). In institutions such as schools and colleges counselors should accept the responsibility for describing their professional services, especially when they introduce a new treatment method like group counseling. Wattenburg (1953) claimed that this increases the counselor's chances for identifying those who are most likely to profit from counseling. He encouraged school counselors to try to describe for teachers and administrators those whom they can help best, and when they accept a referral who is a poor bet, to accept him on a trial basis after explaining their reservations to the one who made the referral. In such cases a counselor is obligated to explore with the referrer other sources of help for the student, including what the two of them can do to achieve the desired behavior without counseling—for example, by using behavior-modification techniques in the classroom.

When counselors fail to communicate about the kinds of people they can and cannot help, and try instead to accept whoever is referred, Wattenburg said that they tend to be judged by their failures:

> Two particular harmful side-effects grow out of this state of affairs. As he finds himself working on refractory cases with little progress, the counselor's own morale can be shaken. Even more serious for the growth of a guidance program within a school system or a business concern, the principal or super-intendent who has given the counselor "a tough nut to crack" may later point to the consequent "failures" as evidence that "guidance is over-rated." (p. 202)

Should one conclude that only volunteers may be accepted for group counseling? Should not the counselor sometimes include in a counseling group those who are referred by significant others? Certainly, although a counselor may describe group counseling for prospective clients who have been referred by colleagues or parents, he should put no pressure on them to join a counseling group. The counselor should merely state why he was asked to contact them, what would be expected from them in group counseling, and how it may help them, and then go on to answer their questions. He should not seriously consider such clients for membership in a counseling group until they ask to join. Prospective clients should realize that only those who can convince the counselor that they are ready for counseling will be admitted. From both their review of others' findings and their own data, Ewing and Gilbert (1967) concluded that those who volunteer for counseling are more apt to profit from it (at least in terms of significantly improved grades) than those who do not volunteer. Furthermore, some who do not recognize the need for counseling, when it is presented as described above, will think about it and later volunteer for it. With such recognition seems to come the acceptance of greater responsibility for improving themselves.

If, however, students are to volunteer for counseling, they must know about the services. By speaking to students in a required course such as English, the counselor can reach all students systematically. Since, however, he usually will prefer to begin with only one or two groups, he should not approach more than one or two class sections until he is ready to make the service available to most of his prospective clients. After he has worked with several groups, he may wish to prepare a written description to be distributed to students to stimulate discussion when he visits their classes.

Typical questions asked by high school students on the occasion of such visits are:

1. Why do students join a counseling group?
2. What do they talk about in such groups?
3. Who usually joins such groups?
4. How does one get into such groups?
5. Who decides which pupils are assigned to each group?
6. What can members expect of each other? of the counselor?
7. How does one know whether the others can be trusted with confidential information?
8. Where does the group meet? How often does it meet? Is attendance required?

Since some of these questions have been answered in Chapters One and Four, only a few illustrative answers will be given here:

"Students join a counseling group to talk with others like themselves about the problems that really bother them. They also learn to behave and feel differently and help others do so, too."

"A counseling group is a safe place in which you can talk about anything or anybody. However, the purpose is not to blame others or even to determine who is at fault. Instead, your purpose should be to express how you really feel; to discover how things need to be changed, including how you need to change; and to make the necessary changes. Besides feeling better from having talked out your problems, you learn to change your behavior and at least some of the situations that upset you."

"Before participating in group counseling, many are concerned about whether they can trust others. Usually they discuss what they can expect from each other on this matter and agree on some rule. They often agree not to discuss anything outside the group that is discussed in the group except when it involves what they themselves have said or agreed to do. Usually they also allow individuals to arrange for private conferences with the counselor.

"Another thing that helps group members trust each other is the fact that the counselor tries to select only those who can be trusted, who will talk openly about themselves, and who want to help others. If, however, there is anyone whom you would not like included in your group, give his or her name to your counselor when you have your intake interview [the intake interview would have been defined earlier]. Most prefer not to be in a group with close friends, relatives, or enemies. They wonder whether or not their friends will continue to like them when they find out what they are really like and whether or not their enemies will use what they learn to hurt them. Though having them in your group may help you face up to your real problems with them, you may find it more difficult to *tell it as it is* with such persons present. Whatever you decide, your fellow members will try to help you learn to trust them and to deal with whoever is included in your group."

Since those who attend regularly tend to profit most from group counseling [Spielberger, Weitz, and Denny (1962)], regular attendance should be expected. Usually, failure to arrive regularly or on time results from a client's indifference or his inability to face his problems. Hence, sessions should begin on time (and end on time) ; let the group deal with a dilatory client as they perceive him. Naturally, they will tend to react differently to what they perceive as norm violations than to what they perceive as resistance.

The length and frequency of counseling sessions should be adapted to clients' maturity (see Chapter Eleven).

Whether prospective clients ask about it or not, the counselor should describe the room in which the group will meet and the precautions taken to insure that no one can overhear what is said during group sessions. All that is really required is a soundproof room large enough to allow the group to sit in a circle (preferably without a table) with enough extra space so that they can move in closer or slide somewhat away from the action. Such an arrangement enables everyone to see everyone else, to pick up subtle nonverbal cues, and to react to everyone. A tape recorder is essential, and occasional use of a video recorder is highly desirable (see Chapters Three and Eight). Obviously, a well-furnished room conveys that the counselor has a successful practice or that his services are highly regarded.

The Intake Interview

The counselor's purpose in the intake interview is to get to know the prospective client in order to determine the likelihood of helping him; to decide with which of the other prospective clients he would fit best; to give him a chance to reveal the problems with which he would like assistance; to assess his willingness to discuss these problems within a counseling group and his commitment to change his behavior and to help others change their behavior; and to answer any questions he may have about expectations. He also is encouraged to discuss any doubts that he may have concerning participation. Thus, a prospective client must convince not only the counselor but also himself that he is ready for group counseling.

Such an intake interview may be structured as follows:

"Though we do our best to insure that everyone obtains the assistance he needs, we admit to a counseling group only the person who can convince the counselor that he has some problems that he will talk about in his group, that he will change his behavior, and that he will help his fellow clients change their behavior. I also must try to know each one who is accepted so that I can place him with the best possible combination of persons to maximize his chances for obtaining the help he wants and for effectively helping others. Hence, I would like you to trust me as you have never trusted anyone before and tell me about you. Begin with something that is bothering you right now and tell me about it. If you are bothered about something that is very difficult for you to discuss, and perhaps even for you to admit to yourself, it may help to tell me why it is difficult to talk about it. I will listen very carefully, really try to understand how you feel, and help you express your feelings."

Such screening takes time, but it is worth it. To those who are accepted it conveys the extent to which they must accept responsibility for improving themselves and helping others improve themselves. It also enables them to develop cooperatively specific goals and criteria for appraising growth.

The interview also gives the counselor a chance to explore with those who are not accepted what they can do to increase their readiness for group counseling, to decide whether it is the best way for them to be helped, and to explore other sources of assistance. When a client agrees that group counseling offers promise for him, the counselor should report when other groups will be begun and how the client may apply for the next one. Thus, he can exhibit caring even when he does not accept a client for the group. He also can teach prospective clients to accept increasing responsibility for getting themselves ready for counseling and the further responsibility that counseling will bring.

Selection of Clients

By careful selection of clients a counselor can increase his chances of helping them. He must be free to accept only those clients whom he feels reasonably certain can be helped in his group, and preferably only those who request membership after they realize what will be expected of them and what they can expect from others in the group. Fiedler (1949) and Broedel, Ohlsen, Proff, and Southard (1960) found that even one strong, antitherapeutic client can block the development of a therapeutic climate within a counseling group. This very rarely happens when prospective clients are carefully screened in the intake interview.

Who are the best prospects for treatment in groups? Beck (1958), Ewing and Gilbert (1967), Johnson (1963), and Rickard (1965) concluded that those who volunteer and exhibit high motivation for membership are the best bets. Johnson said that it is easier to help those who are experiencing pain and seek treatment on their own, than those who have been coerced by family and friends to seek treatment. Stranahan, Schwartzman, and Atkin (1957) concluded that youngsters who can profit from group treatment must have some capacity for insight, a degree of flexibility, desire for growth, and some experiences early in life with an authority figure who possessed some measure of steadiness, helpfulness, direction, and maturity. Lindt (1958) found that unless his patients made an emotional investment in helping other members of the group, it was difficult for them to make progress. Allport (1960) claimed that ability to become ego-involved is an essential characteristic of any good member. Such a member can invest in others and reap satisfaction from seeing another solve his problems. Ryan (1958) discovered that ability to become meaningfully involved in a treatment group was related to a member's ability to empathize with others, to form relationships with others, to delay gratification of one's own needs, and to derive satisfaction from gratifying others' needs.

Powdermaker and Frank (1953) found that feelings of affiliation enhanced the quality of the therapeutic relationship for their patients. Hence, selecting clients with common problems, or at least problems to which they have assigned a common name, should increase their feelings of affiliation.

Spielberger, Weitz, and Denny (1962) reported that those anxious college freshmen who attended regularly improved their academic performance significantly, but only a third of those who volunteered attended a sufficient number of sessions to benefit from the program: "Group counseling may be of value for those students who possess personality characteristics which make it possible for them to participate fully and thereby benefit from such counseling." (p. 203)

These findings lend further support to the principles stated in Chapter Four concerning expectations, commitment, belonging, acceptance, attractiveness, responsibility, and security.

Nash, Frank, Gliedman, Imber, and Stone (1957) found that most patients who rejected group therapy after a brief exposure to it were more ineffective socially, irresponsible, withdrawn, and impulsive than those who accepted it. Parloff (1961) concluded that premature termination seemed to be related to the patient's perception of his relationship with the therapist. Bach's (1954) criteria for exclusion of prospective patients (insufficient reality contact, culturally deviant symptomatology, chronic monopolist, and impulsiveness) include two characteristics that may be relevant for school counselors: being impulsive and monopolizing. On the other hand, perhaps the monopolist can best be counseled in a group; a case is made for doing so in Chapter Nine.

Peck and Stewart (1964) found that nearly all of the institutions utilizing group play-therapy considered homogeneity with reference to sex and age essential in selecting children for treatment; 76 percent considered intellectual level important, while less than 50 percent regarded socioeconomic status or religion as relevant variables. Except for extremely withdrawn children, for whom there was a tendency to use homogeneous grouping, there was a general tendency to use heterogeneity with reference to personality dynamics.

To what extent should those who work with reasonably healthy clients try to select homogeneous clients? If they try to select homogeneous clients, which characteristics should they consider?

1. *Age.* Most school counselors who work with children in groups tend to select clients from the same grade, although the critical factor is social maturity, not chronological age. Even many counselors who work with adults seem to feel that a wide age range may at first impede open discussion of problems and reduce chances for affiliative responses.

2. *Intellectual ability.* Bach (1954) found that failure to consider intelligence can create problems in selecting clients: "If such patients [less educated and less intelligent] are placed in groups predominated by the more verbally fluent, better educated individuals, they have been observed to feel out of place. Careful attention to the factor of verbal fluency in the case of relatively uneducated or relatively less intelligent persons helps to offset mistakes in placement in this respect." (p. 27)

Those who work with children from a wide intellectual range should take cognizance of Bach's point. However, this need not mean that only those at the same intellectual level be included in a group. To the extent that an individual's intellectual ability hampers his communication with his fellow clients, it becomes an important factor to consider in selecting group members. When most members have greater verbal facility than a given member, they may tend to talk over his head. When, on the other hand, a client talks down to the rest of the group, he often rejects, and is rejected by, his fellow clients. For some bright clients it may be desirable to learn to communicate with those less intelligent than themselves. If they are interested in using their superior ability to solve social and political problems, they must learn to communicate with all the people.

3. *Sex.* Ginott (1961) reported that prevailing practice

in clinics is to separate boys and girls for treatment during the latency period. Ohlsen and Gazda (1965) noted that in their groups girls were more mature, showed more interest in boys than boys did in girls, tended to handle topics related to sex better than boys, were more verbal, and tended to dominate the discussion. Though it may be easier to treat boys and girls separately at this age, the counseling group may be one of the most effective places in which to help boys and girls deal with their problems, and thereby further normal social-emotional development. For adolescents mixed groups are essential. They want and need reactions from the opposite sex in discussing the problems they face in defining their sex roles and in learning to relate to the opposite sex. Moreover, they seem to be able to discuss issues more frankly in a mixed group and exhibit less need to test limits with obscene language.

When adolescents cannot be treated in mixed groups, Joel and Shapiro (1950) recommended that a counselor of the opposite sex be assigned to the group. Daniels' (1958) and Staples' (1959) findings support this idea. Daniels treated 24 upper-middle-class eighth-grade boys under three conditions and compared his results with a control group: (1) received group therapy by a male therapist; (2) received group therapy by a female therapist; and (3) received group therapy with both a male and a female therapist. The members of the control group failed to improve on any measure, continued to lose interest in school work, and deteriorated in arithmetic. The boys treated by the male exhibited no deterioration and improved social, emotional, and intellectual behavior. The boys treated by the female exhibited no deterioration and improved their social behavior, attitude toward male peers, self-confidence, faith in the future, and acceptance of male sex role. Those treated by both a male and a female simultaneously became less defiant and improved their social behavior, but became more hostile toward school, less confident of themselves and the future, and more reluctant to adopt a male sex role. Staples replicated Daniels' study with eighth-grade girls and obtained very similar results. Best results were obtained by the male therapist. Results obtained by the two therapists were more unfavorable than Daniels' results with boys. Both questioned the value of using two therapists simultaneously with a group of adolescents; only superior results could justify this practice.

4. *Common problems.* Discovering that other members of the group have similar problems helps clients of all ages feel that they belong and that they are more readily understood. When clients share common problems, the counselor also can more readily identify affiliation responses. For the adolescent period, when they cherish being like their peers, it is very supportive to discover that fellow clients have similar problems. To identify students with similar problems a counselor may have prospective clients complete a problem check list. Although this may aid the counselor in identifying students with problems to which they have assigned the same name, absolute sameness does not exist. Clients may sense genuine affiliation because they have assigned the problem the same name, but even they soon realize that their problems tend to be unique and often have very different underlying causes. Nevertheless, when a client discovers that others can discuss a problem similar to his own, and that his fellow clients try to understand and help each take some positive actions to solve his problems, he is motivated to discuss his problems, too.

Homogeneity with reference to personality dynamics can account for resistance. Freedman and Sweet (1954) stated their guidelines thus:

> Within broad limits attempts are made to arrive at relatively homogeneous group composition with respect to age, educational level, and socioeconomic background. On the other hand, it is considered desirable to avoid homogeneity with respect to diagnosis. It has been our experience that members of groups uniform with respect to personality structure tend to reinforce each others' defenses. (p. 357)

For this reason it is rarely advisable to treat within a single school group a single type of client, such as gifted under-achievers. Such clients can be treated more effectively with peers whom they admire who are concerned about and are searching for ways to improve their academic performance.

Bach (1954) argued for heterogeneity on another ground: to give his patients experience in learning to relate to different kinds of persons and in helping them solve their problems. From the earlier quotation it is evident, however, that he sought some homogeneity with reference to intelligence. He also recognized the need for some homogeneity with reference to social maturity and a matching member with similar problems:

> For example, with respect to the age range, we find it necessary to exclude very young adults with little sexual and social experience from more experienced adult groups. While we definitely like to mix married and unmarried members in the same group, we see to it that we have at least two of each category in the same group. In general, we limit excessive heterogeneity by trying to place a patient in a group where he can find at least one other patient in circumstances which are similar with respect to some other central phase of his own life. (p. 26)

Obviously, counselors need information about their prospective clients in order to make essential decisions in selecting them. Though the psychological tests used by Bach (1954) to screen prospective patients may be appropriate for his groups, they are not generally recommended for screening reasonably healthy clients treated by counselors within a school or college setting. In the intake interview, however, the counselor should try to assess his prospective client's adjustment and to determine whether each can be best treated within the group setting. When he feels he needs additional diagnostic information, he should obtain it.

From what other sources may a school counselor obtain data on prospective clients? He may begin with the cumulative folder. These data may be supplemented by conferences with parents and by a case conference with colleagues who know the student best [Ohlsen (1964), chap. 6]. Besides giving colleagues a chance to share what they know about a student and deciding cooperatively what all of them may do to improve his school adjustment, a counselor can obtain essential data on roles that a prospective client plays in the classroom and in extracurricular activities. Colleagues may also be able to describe problems with which a prospective client seems to require assistance and the types of students from whom he can most readily accept such assistance. However, the usual diagnostic labels are of little value in the selection of clients.

Once the counselor has the essential data, he must try to select from the pool of clients the best prospects for successful group counseling and assign to each group the best combination of individuals. Where a number of counselors know the prospective clients, this decision can be best made in a staffing session. As indicated in Chapter One, at this point most beginning counselors need the help of a supervisor or consultant.

Structuring and Setting Limits

Structuring begins when a counselor describes group counseling for prospective clients and answers their questions about what will be expected from them. During the intake interview he answers questions to further clarify expectations. In both of these instances prospective clients are interested in learning what decisions they will be permitted to make. For example: To what extent will they be given any choices on group membership? With whom may members discuss outside the group what is discussed within the group? Who will decide when the group will terminate? Can anyone drop out whenever he wishes?

At the beginning of the first meeting of the group, clients are encouraged to ask any other questions they may have and to define any operational guidelines that they feel they need. Most clients want to develop a clear statement on keeping confidences. Some will still have questions: How do relationships in the counseling group differ from those in the home or the classroom? Why must they help develop and maintain a therapeutic climate? How can they help each other? Important as they are, the counselor should not encourage a long, involved discussion of these topics. At the group's first meeting the counselor merely helps them clarify what is expected and encourages them to begin discussing what is bothering them and what help they would like. When, for example, the need for limits arises, he reflects this need. When it seems appropriate, he also may reflect their wanting him to define and enforce limits rather than doing so themselves. Thus, he conveys to them that it is their group and that they must accept responsibility for making it work if they are to be helped.

School counselors often fail to see the difference between the teacher's role and the counselor's role. The school counselor may have to spell out these differences, and more importantly exhibit the differences in his attitudes and behaviors. The real structuring is done by the way the counselor lives the role and responds to clients' behavior—knowingly, or unknowingly, encouraging certain behaviors and discouraging others. Readers may recall Psathas' (1960) findings in Chapter Three: the way in which the counselor participates and encourages others to participate, especially during early sessions, affects the amount and nature of members' participation later.

When a counselor notes an instance in which a client plays a helping role effectively, he may wish to take early note of it to encourage such behavior. He also may wish to help the client reveal the clues he used to detect another's real feelings. For example, in a first session with Job Corps girls, one girl noted from some rather subtle clues how another had been hurt and reflected the feeling accurately. The counselor responded as follows: "Jean, you sensed how Darlene felt and you helped her to say it. I get the feeling that you have helped to make this a safe place for Darlene to talk about this problem. I also sense that there is something else you want to say but I can't tell whether or not it is about your problem or Darlene's." Thus the counselor took note of Jean's helpfulness and tried to express his concern for her.

Structuring continues throughout the treatment period. Whenever anyone is unsure of what is expected, the members of the group clarify. Sometimes they need new operational guidelines; sometimes all that is needed is clarification of an earlier agreement. Effective structuring contributes to the therapeutic climate; overstructuring and rigid rules interfere with it. Though it is appropriate for the counselor to describe the conditions under which he has been best able to help clients within a group setting, he also should encourage clients to help define what they feel they need to work most effectively. He must be sensitive also to the possibility that members may not be communicating what they expect, or that they cannot really believe they can do what they have agreed to do in group counseling. These doubts must be detected and discussed before a therapeutic climate will emerge.

Summary

A counselor should define his role for those whom he serves, know whom he can help best by the various techniques he is qualified to use, and convey this information to those who make referrals to him.

A counselor should be free to accept for group counseling only those whom he is reasonably certain he can help in groups. Even those who volunteer should be expected to demonstrate commitment to talk openly about their problems, to change their behavior and attitudes, and to help others change. They should be expected also to help develop and maintain a therapeutic climate.

Good prognosis for growth is not sufficient for membership. The counselor also must consider each member's impact upon individuals as well as upon the total group.

The counselor needs certain information in order to choose the best possible combination of individuals for successful group counseling. Much of this information can be obtained in the intake interview. School counselors may obtain additional information from records and from conferences with colleagues and parents. Only occasionally will a school counselor need the kinds of diagnostic test data commonly used by psychotherapists.

Primary structuring is done before the first session with clients, further structuring as the need arises. Though the counselor's efforts to clarify expectations are important, the real structuring is done by the way he functions within the group—knowingly, or unknowingly, encouraging certain behaviors and discouraging others.

References

Allport, G. W. *Personality and Social Encounter*, Boston: The Beacon Press, 1960.

Bach, G. R. *Intensive Group Psychotherapy*, New York: The Ronald Press Company, 1954.

Beck, Dorothy F. "The Dynamics of Group Psychotherapy, as Seen by a Sociologist, Part II: Some Puzzling Questions on Leadership, Contextual Relations, and Outcomes," *Sociometry*, 1958, 21:180–197.

Broedel, J., M. Ohlsen, F. Proff and C. Southard "The Effects of Group Counseling on Gifted Adolescent Underachievers," *Journal of Counseling Psychology*, 1960, 7:163–170.

Daniels, M. "The Influence of the Sex of the Therapist and of the Co-Therapist Technique in Group Psychotherapy with Boys," *Dissertation Abstracts*, 1958, 18:1489.

Ewing, T. N., and W. M. Gilbert "Controlled Study of the Effects of Counseling on the Scholastic Achievements of Students of Superior Ability," *Journal of Counseling Psychology*, 1967, 14:235–239.

Fiedler, F. E. "An Experimental Approach to Preventative Psychotherapy," *Journal of Abnormal and Social Psychology*, 1949, 44: 386–393.

Freedman, M. B., and Blanche S. Sweet "Some Specific Features of Group Psychotherapy and Their Implications for Selection of Patients," *International Journal of Group Psychotherapy*, 1954, 4:355–368.

Ginott, H. G. "Play Group Therapy: A Theoretical Framework," *International Journal of Group Psychotherapy*, 1958, 8:410–418.

Joel, W., and D. Shapiro "Some Principles and Procedures for Group Psychotherapy," *Journal of Psychology*, 1950, 29:77–88.

Johnson, J. A. *Group Therapy: A Practical Approach*, New York: McGraw-Hill, Inc., 1963.

Lindt, H. "The Nature of Therapeutic Interaction of Patients in Groups," *International Journal of Group Psychotherapy*, 1958, 8:55–69.

Nash, E. H., J. D. Frank, L. H. Gliedman, S. D. Imber, and A. R. Stone "Some Factors Related to Patients Remaining in Group Psychotherapy," *International Journal of Group Psychotherapy*, 1957, 7:264–274.

Ohlsen, M. M. *Guidance Services in the Modern School,* New York: Harcourt, Brace & World, Inc., 1964.

Parloff, M. B. "Therapist-patient Relationships and Outcomes of Psychotherapy," *Journal of Consulting Psychology*, 1961, 25:29–38.

Peck, M. L., and R. H. Stewart "Current Practices in Selection Criteria for Group-Play Therapy," *Journal of Clinical Psychology*, 1964, 20: 146.

Powdermaker, Florence B., and J. D. Frank *Group Psychotherapy*, Cambridge, Mass.: Harvard University Press, 1953.

Psathas, G. "Phase, Movement and Equilibrium Tendencies in Interaction Process in Psychotherapy Groups," *Sociometry*, 1960, 23: 177–194.

Rickard, H. C. "Tailored Criteria of Change in Psychotherapy," *Journal of General Psychology*, 1965, 72:63–68.

Ryan, W. "Capacity for Mutual Dependencies and Involvement in Group Psychotherapy," *Dissertation Abstracts*, 1958, 19:1119.

Spielberger, C. D., H. Weitz, and J. P. Denny "Group Counseling and the Academic Performance of Anxious College Freshmen," *Journal of Counseling Psychology*, 1962, 9:195–204.

Staples, Ethel "The Influences of the Sex of the Therapist and of Co-Therapist Technique in Group Psychotherapy with Girls," *Dissertation Abstracts*, 1959, 19:2754.

Stranahan M., C. Schwartzman and E. Atkin "Group Treatment for Emotionally Disturbed and Potentially Delinquent Boys and Girls," *American Journal of Orthopsychiatry*, 1957, 27:518–527.

Wattenburg, W. W. "Who Needs Counseling?" *Personnel and Guidance Journal*, 1953, 32:202–205.

Chapter Six

Resistance

Failure to cooperate in the therapeutic process, or the blocking of another client's growth within the treatment group, is resistance. Clients may avoid the discussion of problems, the identification of alternative ways for solving these problems, the trying of new ways of behaving, or open assessment of failures they have experienced in trying to change their behavior, or they may fail to help develop and maintain a therapeutic climate within the treatment group.

Redl (1948) described resistance as an unavoidable reaction to change. He said that the part of a client's personality that counseling is designed to change tries to maintain itself. When, therefore, action to change the person appears likely to succeed, resistance occurs. Hence, a client experiences ambivalence—trying to change while resisting change.

A client may exhibit resistance in individual counseling by missing appointments, arriving late, postponing appointments, terminating the relationship, questioning whether or not he can be helped by the treatment, dwelling on his case history, growing preoccupied with side issues or symptoms, being unable to think of anything to talk about, acting anxious or confused to distract the counselor from hurtful therapeutic material, getting angry, acting out his impulses, requesting advice, or by being spontaneously cured (flight to health). All of these may be exhibited in counseling groups, too.

Bry (1951) described a number of additional ways in which resistance is exhibited in a treatment group: protective talking, selective silence or withdrawal from the interaction, and acting-out. Bach (1954) noted two others: advice giving and monopolizing. Other behaviors of clients that may indicate resistance are: questioning whether or not confidences are being kept, wondering whether or not the group is a safe place to discuss certain problems, requesting clarification on what is really expected of clients in a group, and having difficulty accepting responsibility for helping develop and maintain a therapeutic climate.

Ambivalence

When clients experience the procedures described in Chapter Five they enter the group with a reasonably good understanding of what to expect. Though they expect to be helped, they realize that they may have difficulty discussing certain problems. Sometimes they will even remember how it helped in the intake interview to tell the counselor why some topics were difficult to discuss. They also tend to remember how the counselor listened and tried to understand, and the care with which he seemed to select each client to insure that only those who were ready to profit from group counseling were admitted. All such experiences and memories tend to reduce resistance. Nevertheless, almost everyone exhibits resistance occasionally. Even when *he recognizes* that he wants to face a problem and deal with it, he may question whether or not: (1) the other clients will be able to accept him when they discover what he is really like; (2) he is willing to suffer as much as he may in order to solve the problem; (3) he may uncover still other problems of which he is at present unaware; and (4) he can achieve the goals that he and his counselor have set for him. Osborn (1949) noted that everyone has experienced such feelings: wanting and not wanting the things for which they have contracted.

The Counselor's Reaction to Resistance

Most of the time counselors can accept and cope with resistance. Furthermore, they have learned to recognize it and to use it to understand the resisting client and to identify therapeutically significant material, as well as to identify new goals for the resisting client.

At one time or another most counselors have had difficulty accepting the resisting client, detecting his feelings, and responding to those feelings. Occasionally the counselor who can accept his own real feelings will realize that he feels blocked, frustrated, unappreciated, and even angry. On such occasions he should try to determine to what extent a client's resistance is a function of his use of inappropriate techniques or of his own unresolved problems (countertransference). He may do this by carefully critiquing a recording of that session, preferably with a trusted colleague or supervisor (another reason for the type of supervision recommended in Chapter One). Goodman, Marks, and Rockberger (1964) concluded that when a therapist or counselor does not cope well with resistance within a group, the explanation may lie in counter-tranference distortion. To study this problem and to improve their general effectiveness they met together weekly for mutual supervision for two and a half years. The following quotation reveals how they functioned and tried to help each other:

> The focus shifted slowly, almost imperceptibly at first, from patient dynamics to exposing and exploring the irrational and distorted in our own perceptions of the therapeutic situation.
> It became apparent that not only were our distortions interfering with our role as group therapists but that each one of us had specific islands of sensitivity (repetitive familiar situations) which had not been brought to light or resolved in his personal and control analysis. We found that the setting of

peer group supervision permitted shades and nuances of emotional working through which contrasted with the authority-bound setting of the traditional supervisory experience.

The procedure in these sessions was for one of the therapists to choose for presentation and discussion the group which was not meeting his expectation for movement and in which he was encountering stiff resistance. The presenter would often present a tape recording of a session of his problem group, and his colleagues would question his interventions as well as the meaning of the interaction of group members. They would speak of the feeling they got as they listened to the session, and the presenting therapist would speak of what he saw as the resistance. The focus would then shift to some excess or lack of effective response in the presenter, a particular defensive attitude or position, and the feelings and reactions of his colleagues. . . . As we studied our countertransference to our groups, our patients, and each other, we became increasingly aware that these in turn induced reactions in our patients and led, at times, to seemingly impenetrable resistance phenomena within our therapy groups. . . . (pp. 335–336)

We would, therefore, hypothesize that the phenomenon of a therapy group in a state of resistance which the therapist recognizes but is unable to deal with is likely to be related integrally to a countertransference distortion of the therapist. The therapist becomes bound up in affects related to his personal past, which are inappropriate to his current situation, and he cannot act constructively. We have no doubt that many premature terminations of treatment are based on such phenomena.

We have found the peer supervisory group an excellent setting in which to bring into consciousness many of the binding images which interfere with our work. As was noted in the clinical examples, the peer supervisory group often mirrors the complex forces operative in the therapeutic group situation, and as such may be more immediately helpful than the didactic supervisory relationship, which is more paradigmatic of the individual treatment situation. (p. 343)

Inasmuch as a case has already been made for the counselor's understanding himself and the ways in which his own unresolved conflicts may interfere with his effectiveness as a counselor, for group counseling for the counselor, and for group supervision of the counselor by his peers, let it suffice here to agree with Goodman, Marks, and Rockberger that supervision by peers can increase effectiveness of even the experienced therapist. Countertransference will be discussed further in Chapter Seven.

Coping with Resistance

The methods described in Chapter Five for initiating group counseling and for selecting clients make membership in a counseling group safe, meaningful, and attractive. Giving clients responsibility for convincing the counselor that they are ready for group counseling, that they are committed to its purposes and to the achievement of their own individual goals, and that they will develop and maintain a therapeutic climate enables them to accept considerable responsibility for their own growth. Within such a climate, clients tend to perceive resistance as deviant behavior. Hence, the counselor need not fear within such groups the dangers of group cohesiveness described by Slavson (1957). Though the kind of group resistance described by Redl (1948) and Freedman and Sweet (1954) can be difficult, clients' acceptance of the therapeutic group norms described in Chapters Four and Five makes the task easier than it tends to be in most therapy groups, in which so much of the responsibility for coping with resistance is accepted by the therapist.

The counselor relates to the resisting client best when he tries to empathize with him, tries to capture his feelings, and tries to help him express his sincere desire to be helped while he is experiencing some ambivalence about accepting assistance and about behaving in a way that would enable him to be helped. To the extent that a counselor can reflect these feelings accurately in meaningful, concrete terms and help the resisting client express them during early contacts, while still feeling accepted and understood, he can teach the resisting client as well as the others to recognize, accept, and cope with such feelings.

By helping clients discover how the resisting client feels, and explaining how this phenomenon may be recognized in oneself and in others, the counselor prepares clients to cope with it—especially if he brings it up after resistance has first been effectively dealt with in the group. He also can reinforce effective behavior by taking note of instances in which a client detects and helps another express feelings of resistance, helps the resisting client by discussing simliar problems of his own, and reviews clients' responsibility for developing and maintaining a therapeutic climate. Group members also learn to reward a client for recognizing and coping with his own feelings of resistance.

When a resisting client discovers that most clients have similar feelings and that some even have similar problems, which they are willing to discuss and try to solve, he is enabled to discuss his own problems. Seeing fellow clients deal openly with their problems and change their behavior and attitudes during the normal course of treatment encourages even the resisting client to deal openly with his problems and to try to change his behavior. Bach (1954) describes the depth of this support as follows: "In giving of love and sympathy the group as a rule naturally goes much further in overt expressions than any other professional therapist would, could or should ever do. At such moments the group demonstrates a truly remarkable intensity in its expression of support." (p. 96)

When a client recognizes resistance in himself, or at least realizes that he needs to talk about something and cannot, he often requests an individual session with the counselor. To reap the full benefits from treatment in and by the group, the counselor should encourage such a client to discuss his reasons for such requests within his counseling group prior to the individual session. Several benefits follow: (1) Other clients are more likely to accept the client's need for individual attention without the usual "sibling" rivalry. (2) In helping the client discuss why he cannot discuss a certain topic, the counselor and the other clients provide the understanding and support that the client needs to deal with the topic within the group. (3) Finally, such discussion can be used to structure the relationship for the private session. Here the writer agrees wholeheartedly with Bach (1954) : that such individual sessions should be group-centered—getting the client ready to cope with his problems in the group. As long as the client is a member of a treatment group, he should look upon group counseling as his primary source of help. This approach also prevents the drainage problem described by Bach, in which clients save very private materials for the individual sessions, allowing the group sessions only the more superficial material. Perhaps this is why those counselors who have encouraged regular individual counseling to accompany group counseling have concluded that clients could not be expected to discuss very private material within the group setting.

As stated in Chapter Four, the counselor must accept responsibility for helping his clients recognize, cope with, and accept responsibility for dealing with the antitherapeutic forces as well as to use the therapeutic forces within their group. Hora (1958) illustrated how failure to accept this responsibility could destroy a group's effectiveness:

> It is the function of the therapist to reveal to the group the nature of the forces affecting it and to set an example of courage and understanding in refusing to yield to the unhealthy values emanating from the particular patient. For instance, one patient succeeded to paralyze an entire group by using his alcoholism as a guilt-inducing threat over members. At first he managed to squelch all expression of negative feelings toward him under the implied threat that he would go out, get drunk and get himself into trouble; then he expanded his threatening influence in such a manner as to prohibit expressions of feelings toward others. He did it by coming threateningly to the defense of anyone who was being criticized. Thus the group arrived at a stalemate where communication was strictly reduced to pretended concern over the welfare and safety of this one member. A seemingly hopeless uneasy tension developed. This oppressive cloud was lifted by the therapist when he exposed the forces which were responsible for the impasse. (p. 158)

Perhaps another example would have even more meaning for counselors: the case of a prospective school counselor participating in group counseling with other prospective counselors. Every time the counselor tried to reach for any client's feelings and reflect them during the first two sessions, this resisting client complained that this was not what he expected—that they were all being treated as sick patients rather than reasonably healthy persons who merely wanted to understand themselves a little better. When the counselor reflected this client's fear of becoming therapeutically involved and exposing his unresolved problems, helped the other clients understand the phenomenon of resistance, and explained how failure to deal with it would prevent all of them from getting the assistance for which they had contracted when they asked to join the group, they were able to cope with this particular client and assume their responsibility for helping him cope with his resistance. Perhaps at this point some readers will wonder: "Doesn't this approach focus too much attention on achieving insight?" Notice, though, that the counselor did not give a classical interpretation of resistance, nor did he try to help the client achieve insight. He merely conveyed that he could understand the client's fear to discuss openly the problems that bothered him, and helped the other clients empathize with the resisting client and help him learn to deal with his feelings of resistance.

Occasionally every client will be reluctant to talk. This is most apt to occur when clients have not been selected with sufficient care; or when some fail to begin at once to talk about problems that really bother them and consequently the others become suspicious of them; or when all or most clients are faced simultaneously with highly threatening materials. The last phenomenon Freedman and Sweet (1954) and Redl (1948) have labeled group resistance. When the counselor recognizes group resistance he should merely reflect this feeling and then cope with the phenomenon as suggested in the previous paragraph. Occasionally he may feel that he must ask the group whether they still want to try to get help in this group. Or he may ask the clients to review the problems that bother them and describe the kind of assistance that they would like from the group. Still another approach is to encourage members to point out to every other client the problems with which each should try to learn to cope. Very rarely a counselor may suggest that perhaps it would be helpful to repeat the intake interview, giving each a chance to reappraise the problems with which he would like assistance, his readiness to discuss them, and his commitment to change his behavior and attitudes. Usually when members are given such an opportunity, they come through convincingly or voluntarily withdraw. Should any client fail to demonstrate his readiness and fail to withdraw, perhaps the best solution is to discuss the problem with the entire group. If the group permits such a client to remain even on a temporary basis, they must convey precisely what they expect from him and their willingness to help him function as prescribed.

What in the early group sessions may appear to be resistance may actually be clients' reactions to inadequate structuring. From their research with out-patient World War II veterans Powdermaker and Frank (1953) concluded that when there is too little structure, intense competition develops among patients, and when there is too much structure, clients tend to become too inhibited and spend too much energy in trying to please the therapist. For coping with resistance they had the following recommendations for the therapist:

1. He can usually leave the leadership in this situation to the group, especially if there is a patient with initiative with whom the resistant patient can identify. In such a case the doctor can devote his efforts to facilitating the process of identification. Often this is best done by maintaining an interested silence. In this connection it may be mentioned that therapy is often facilitated if the doctor does not attempt to meet a challenge from a resistant patient but leaves it to the group.
2. In a newly formed group he should not attempt to get a withdrawn patient to talk about himself until others have set an example. In a mature group he need not be concerned about this, since others will have already done so.

3. He should be alert for situations in which members of the group express feelings which seem to be similar to those of the resistant patient, particularly hostile and fearful feelings about one another or the doctor.

4. He should seize the opportunity to take advantage of a response by the resistant patient to any occurrence in the immediate situation related to his feelings.

5. In a newly formed group explicit support of the resistant patient may be desirable and probably should be given by the doctor if the group fails to supply it. Essentially, support consists of taking the patient seriously and conveying the idea that an effort is being made to understand his problems. It may be indicated merely through withdrawal of pressure. In a mature group he need not mitigate attacks by other members on the resistant patient or offer overt support. . . .

In early meetings overt support seemed more necessary than in later ones, in which considerable criticism could be borne and might even be helpful. In later meetings the support was implicit in the patients' long-standing interest in one another. (p. 276)

Bry (1951) also agreed that the group can and will cope with a resisting member:

The first and most striking thing in handling of resistance in groups is that frequently resistance does not have to be "handled" at all, at least not by the therapist. The group is remarkably effective in dealing with this phenomenon. Early in the experience of each group considerable effort is directed toward demonstrating what resistance is and how to become sensitive to its appearance in others as well as oneself. The group members as well gradually develop ideas as to how to deal with resistance and how to use it productively. In cases of protective talking, sooner or later a group member usually gets sensitive to its resistance character and starts complaining about the "beating around the bush."

Similarly, the selective silence of a group member is certain to be eventually discovered and made the subject for special probing. Once discovered, a weak point can be relentlessly laid bare by a group. It is of course not enough merely to recognize manifestation of resistance. In cases of acute resistance it must be understood why it appears at a particular point and in a

specific form. The objective is to recognize and overcome resistance and then proceed with the task of understanding the nature
of the basic conflict. Considerable initiative is displayed by
group members also in the interpretation of acting out. Emphasis should be directed toward the nature of the basic anxieties
as well as toward the characteristic defense mechanism used.
The understanding of acting out, as observable in the relations
between group members, constitutes a very important portion
of the group's work. The emotions displayed in the process of
acting out, and the fact that they are immediately interpreted,
seem to enhance the therapeutic effectiveness of the handling
of resistance in the group situation.

There are situations in which the therapist has to take over.
This is very frequently necessary in the early stages of treatment. It is further required when resistance is particularly
complex or intensive. It is also necessary when resistance is
not recognized or not sufficiently understood by the group.
Among types of resistance frequently unrecognized by groups
are intellectualization and advice giving activities in which all
the members of the group may engage. . . .

There must obviously be a correlation between the depth of
interpreting resistance and the over-all treatment goals. It is
difficult to generalize on this issue. In psychoanalytically oriented type of group therapy the aim is to affect psychodynamic
processes to the extent necessary for eliminating major symptoms and for satisfactory social adjustment. . . . (pp. 112–113)

Bry's approach encourages more confrontation of the
resisting client by other clients than was suggested earlier.
Perhaps this is not as essential for reasonably healthy clients—
especially when they are taught to recognize feelings of resistance, accept them for what they are, and help the resisting
client express them.

Bry also recommends use of interpretation* in coping

*Because some writers do not distinguish between interpretation and
reflection, these terms are defined here. When the counselor or another
client explains to a client why he behaves or feels as he does at a given
time, it is interpretation, but when the counselor or a client observes
how a client feels and tries to mirror these feelings in order to help the
client express them or to check whether or not he is feeling with him, it
is reflection. For both, the respondent uses both nonverbal and verbal
behavior to determine what should be said. To reflect accurately, the

with resistance. There are several reasons for questioning this, especially for adolescents. Katz, Ohlsen, and Proff (1959) reported that the counselor's interpretations of their under-achieving adolescents' resisting behavior was perceived by clients as attack. This certainly supports Ackerman's (1955) conclusion that adolescents are vulnerable to criticism and others' judgment of their worth. Excepting perhaps the dependent client, most adolescents resent both the notion of external evaluation and the air of superiority often conveyed by interpretation. For the dependent client, interpretation tends to let him rely on others when instead he should be learning to accept more responsibility for helping himself. Finally, interpretation tends to encourage clients to intellec-tualize—to dwell unnecessarily on history and to spend too much psychic energy on the search for insight.

It is also questionable whether the counselor should encourage other clients to put the resisting client "on the hot seat." A few have even gone so far as to designate a given chair (such as the red chair) for the resisting client when his turn comes to face up to the problems that bother him and decide what he must do to change his behavior. In any event, clients will pressure the resisting client to talk when they want to help him and when they are not certain they can trust him until he has shared his problems with them. Rather than trying to force such a client to talk, the counselor should help the other clients express these feelings and help the resisting client to respond to them, so that they learn how to cope with each other. Whenever all or part of a session is focused on one client, the other clients tend to be less involved therapeuti-cally or to function only as the counselor's helpers. In order to profit fully from the therapeutic interaction within his group, every client must play two roles simultaneously—helper and client—listening very carefully to what other clients say,

---

respondent must empathize with the client being helped. A good inter-pretation requires this in addition to a good understanding of the dynamics that influence the client's behavior; it also often conveys superiority on the part of the interpreter.

helping the speaker express himself, allowing the speaker's discussion to uncover therapeutic material within him, and dealing with his own problems as he becomes aware of them.

Summary

Resistance is any behavior by a client that interferes with his own or another's growth. It is a natural phenomenon, which the counselor can minimize by informing clients what is needed to create a therapeutic climate and making them feel responsible for developing and maintaining one, by helping them recognize resistance, by explaining to them how failure to cope with it prevents them from obtaining help, and by showing them how to cope with it. When resistance is first exhibited in the group the counselor should try to guess how the resisting client feels and reflect these feelings. Immediately after his first successful experience in helping a client deal with this phenomenon, the counselor should describe it for the entire group, tell how it is often exhibited, and explain why it is important for the group to deal with it and how they may do so. The need to resist is further reduced when clients observe the increased acceptance of fellow clients as they deal openly with their problems, are stimulated by disclosure of others' problems, and discover how others have been helped.

Two techniques commonly used for coping with resistance are questionable: interpretation, and the encouraging of clients to put pressure on a resisting client. Interpretation tends to encourage intellectualization and to make clients dependent. When clients are put on the hot seat, the full therapeutic impact of the group is no longer felt continuously by every client.

The counselor should try to help every client recognize the therapeutic forces within the group and use them, recognize the antitherapeutic forces within the group and cope with them. Once clients understand and accept what is needed, they will define and maintain therapeutic group norms. Resisting behavior will tend to be perceived as deviant behavior within such groups.

References

Ackerman, N. W. "Group Psychotherapy with a Mixed Group of Adolescents," *International Journal of Group Psychotherapy*, 1955, 5:249–260.

Bach, G. R. *Intensive Group Psychotherapy*, New York: The Ronald Press Company, 1954.

Bry, Thea "Varieties of Resistance in Group Psychotherapy," *International Journal of Group Psychotherapy*, 1951, 1:106–114.

Freedman, M. B., and Blanche S. Sweet. "Some Specific Features of Group Psychotherapy and Their Implications for Selection of Patients," *International Journal of Group Psychotherapy*, 1954, 4:355–368.

Goodman, M., M. Marks, and H. Rockberger "Resistance in Group Psychotherapy Enhanced by Countertransference Reactions of the Therapist: A Peer Group Experience," *International Journal of Group Psychotherapy*, 1964, 14:332–343.

Hora, T. "Group Psychotherapy, Human Values and Mental Health," *International Journal of Group Psychotherapy*, 1958, 8:154–160.

Katz, Evelyn W., M. M. Ohlsen, and F. C. Proff "An Analysis through Use of Kinescopes of the Interpersonal Behavior of Adolescents in Group Counseling," *Journal of College Student Personnel*, 1959, 1:2–10.

Osborn, Hazel "Some Factors of Resistance Which Affect Group Participation," *The Group*, 1949, 2:2–4, 9–11.

Powdermaker, Florence B., and J. D. Frank *Group Psychotherapy*, Cambridge, Mass.: Harvard University Press, 1953.

Redl, F. "Resistance in Therapy Groups," *Human Relations*, 1948, 1:307–313.

Slavson, S. R. "Are There Group Dynamics in Therapy Groups?" *International Journal of Group Psychotherapy*, 1957, 7:131–154.

Chapter Seven

Transference

The counselor must understand the phenomenon of transference in order to detect therapeutic material and facilitate therapeutic interaction within a counseling group. Because various practitioners have defined transference so differently, we shall review some common definitions and then define the term as it is used in this text. We go on to consider the implications of transference for the understanding of human behavior in general, its use in facilitating change in clients, and its influence on the counselor's effectiveness (countertransference).

What Is Transference?

Freud first used the term *transference* to label a common reaction of patients to their therapists. According to English and English (1958) this phenomenon can best be described as a displacement of affect from one object to another; it is the process whereby a patient shifts affects applicable for a significant other onto the analyst.

Wolf (1963) pictured such a patient projecting unconsciously and inappropriately onto another the very traits that kept him from relating effectively to some significant other. He described transference as an unreasonable reaction that may be exhibited by some affective disturbance such as mild anxiety, irritability, depression, and fearfulness. Because the patient is unable to control his response despite its drawbacks, Wolf characterized the transference response as excessive, well beyond what one would expect from the provoking circumstances.

Glatzer (1965) portrayed transference as symptomatic of the conflict between id, ego, and superego. Like English and English she described transference as an unconscious attempt to imbue current relationships with old attitudes that are inappropriate for those present. She also pointed out that positive transference may be a cover-up for negative feelings for significant others. She said that deeply neurotic patients are unable to love tenderly because their unconscious phantasies are so centered around the oedipal and preoedipal figures that they feel guilty about these fantasies. Their transference love objects are both loved and feared. A therapeutic group enables them to work through these feelings so that they can learn to give and accept mature love.

From Bach's (1957) frame of reference, transference is a particular type of interpersonal contact in which unfulfilled regressive needs seek to fulfill themselves with objects realistically unsuited for these activated infantile motivations. Unlike the therapist in individual treatment, group members react when they are bombarded with transference demands: "In groups this exchange is so vivid that it is very difficult for the therapist alone to distinguish between unreal projections and justified reactions, between healthy self-assertions and the acting out of infantile wishes." (p. 67)

As Bach indicated, a client may try to cope with some unfulfilled needs by using a member of his group as a transference object. He may express love, hate, or anger; may relive hurtful experiences; may try to cope with conflict; or may use the relatively safe climate of the therapeutic relationship to explain what he would like from the relationship and what he is willing to give to it. Within such an emotional climate, and as a consequence of the contagious influence of other clients' dealing effectively with similar content, defenses begin to weaken. Hence, reasonably healthy clients often discover that they are using others to resolve their own problems.

The classic analytic explanation of transference can account for only part of the interaction. Much of the interaction within a counseling group is reaction to reality. Clients solicit reactions from other members and give them honest feedback. They learn to express both positive and negative feelings for the members of their group and develop improved skills for coping with conflict. From Lerner's (1964) research one may conclude that schizophrenic youth failed to learn this from their families during the process of growing up. He found that both normal youth and disturbed youth experienced conflict within their families, but that normal youth came from families in which conflict was faced and resolved, whereas disturbed youth came from families in which conflict was ignored or denied.

The present writer sees transference as the client's assigning to another the role of a significant person in the client's life and then relating to that person as though he actually were that significant other. The significant other need not be someone from the past but may be someone in the client's present life—a fellow worker, a supervisor, a teacher, a parent, a child, a lover, or a mate. Many factors in group situations tend to focus interaction on the present rather than the past. For when clients are encouraged to empathize with each other, to express and cope with their feelings for each other, to help each other change their attitudes and behaviors, and to generalize to significant relationships outside of their counseling group, their interaction tends to focus on the present. Even those who use classic analytic methods in group treatment have noticed this tendency to focus on the here and now, especially in adolescent groups. Adolescents' struggle for independence, their concern about relationships with peers, and their search for identity focus attention on the present. Their concern about the future distracts their attention from the past. Perhaps this explains why some classic analysts have questioned whether adolescents are capable of establishing a transference relationship.

Bach (1957) said that group members set each other up to activate and to release wishes and fantasies. They do not necessarily limit themselves to re-experiencing earlier experiences; they also entice each other into dealing with their here-and-now unfulfilled needs.

There are many and varied transference objects within a treatment group; the range depends, at least in part, on the counselor's criteria for selecting clients. Freedman and Sweet (1954) noted that transference also tends to be experienced differently than in individual therapy because of the multiplicity of transference objects and because transference objects do not regulate their reactions as does the therapist. In the group, too, the therapist is observed relating to others and thereby becomes less of a "blank screen."

Because patients do react to each other, Durkin (1964) concluded that transference must be analyzed in piecemeal fashion in groups, rather than systematically as a therapist would do it:

> The repeated interruptions which inevitably occurred as one member or another brought his ideas, his feelings, his problems, or his interpretation to the others, could not be avoided without sacrificing full member participation. The effect was kaleidoscopic. To avoid it, the therapist would have had to conduct a leader-centered group in which he made all the interpretations and did not give the members a chance to come to grips on their own with whatever problem was brought up. . . . (p. 149)

When the counselor encourages clients to take considerable responsibility for developing a therapeutic climate within their treatment group, for improving their *own* mental health, and for helping fellow clients change their behavior and attitudes, even classic interpretation of transference will be repeatedly interrupted, as Durkin indicated. Such interruptions discourage intellectualization and encourage clients to express their real feelings for each other. By reacting openly and honestly, they learn to express positive feelings as well as negative ones, to recognize conflict, and to cope directly with it rather than trying to ignore it or deny it. The support and the pressure they sense from their group members, and the new human-relations skills they have learned and practiced within the group, encourage them to apply what they have learned in living with significant others outside the group.

Implications for Other Relationships

Previous experiences with significant others may influence the way individuals react to some persons anywhere. Under the right circumstances anyone may be motivated to assign someone the role of a significant other and react to him as though he were that person. This probably accounts for persons' liking some new acquaintance immediately and disliking others. These individuals may actually exhibit behavior that reminds a person of some significant other. Bach (1957) found that certain types of individuals in his treatment groups tended to be assigned certain roles as transference objects on the basis of their physical appearance and mannerisms.

Inasmuch as persons tend to fulfill the roles to which they are assigned, both in treatment groups and in daily living, they often need assistance in coping with this problem—especially when they cannot accept or fulfill such roles. Adolescents, for example, often complain that peers, parents, teachers, and even employers expect them to do things that are inappropriate for them. Though they do not recognize this as transference, and it may not be transference, they want help with the problem. The kind of voluntary discussion groups and leadership training groups described by Ohlsen (1964) can help them communicate why the expectations are unreasonable for them, what they are really like, and what they would like from the relationships. Such group experiences also can sensitize them to their impact on others and teach them improved ways for relating to these significant others. T groups also have been used extensively for these purposes.

Eliciting Transference

A counselor consciously structures for treatment on the basis of his professional preparation, his own professional experiences, and research evidence. Very likely, and perhaps unconsciously, he reinforces certain behaviors and discourages other behaviors. The nature and extent of the transference elicited in his groups seems to depend on the following questions: Does he believe he knows what most of the clients should do to improve their adjustment? To what extent can he encourage them to decide what they should do? How do dependent clients make him feel? Is it important for him to impress his clients with his insightful interpretations? Does he believe that most clients must understand why they behaved as they have in the past before they can change their behavior? Does he encourage clients to use him, or other members of the group, as transference objects? Does he encourage his clients to express their feelings for each other, to try to cope directly with the conflicts that arise, and, where appropriate, to generalize to significant others outside the treatment group? To what extent does he encourage them to focus discussion on their present problems and specific changes in their behavior? Does he encourage his clients to focus on early childhood experiences, or rather to deal only with the part of their history that has relevance for their current problems?

In sum, the counselor's needs, values, and expectations help determine the extent and nature of transference reactions within the treatment group—not only the extent to which the counselor is the primary stimulus for transference, but the degree to which other members become transference objects.

Patterson (1959) concluded that ambiguity evokes projection and transference. He observed that the more unstructured or ambiguous a situation is, the more clients are inclined to project. He likened ambiguity in counseling to projective testing in which responses are influenced by internal motivations, attitudes, and unresolved problems. He also noted how classic analytic methods elicit transference:

> The analytic rule of free association—"tell me everything
> that comes to your mind"—carries no restrictions. The analyst
> is silent for long periods, giving the impression of a blank
> screen. In the orthodox use of the couch, he is out of view of
> the patient and therefore not present as a reality in the visual
> field of the patient. These conditions maximize the opportunity
> for projection on the part of the patient, for the development
> of irrational or unrealistic perceptions—in other words, for the
> development of transference. (p. 201)

Can a counselor ever be a blank screen, especially when
he functions in a group? Clients observe how he reacts to
others as well as how he attempts to help them. They recognize
that he is a real person with his own feelings, values, needs,
and expectations. Where the counselor sits and what he does,
as well as his words, determine what clients expect from him.
If he sits in an open circle of chairs, occupies a chair like the
clients, and encourages clients to react to him as well as to
fellow clients, he will be perceived more as a true member
than if he maintains his distance by sitting behind a desk and
enhances his status by assuming the primary responsibility
for helping individuals deal with transference. On the other
hand, even a group-centered counselor is someone special
whose words and actions are valued more than those of other
members. Clients do, and should, expect him to describe treatment conditions within which clients seem to be most effectively helped. The roles he plays determine the degree to
which he makes clients dependent upon him and himself a
primary transference object.

Because of his many and varied contacts with students
outside of the counseling relationship, and because he also is
expected to provide leadership for discussion groups and leadership training groups in addition to group counseling, the
school counselor certainly is not seen as a blank screen. Students do get to know him as a person, and they can be confused
about what they should expect from him in such different
groups. Nevertheless, he can still be effective, provided that

he does not have responsibility for evaluating or disciplining them and that he takes special care to distinguish clearly the purpose for which each group is organized and how it differs from other groups in which counselors function as leaders.

Can a counselor ever be completely objective? Probably not, but counseling can increase his awareness of his own needs, values, expectations of clients and of himself, and his unresolved problems; help him understand how these factors influence his effectiveness as a counselor; and help him learn to function more effectively. Goodman, Marks, and Rockberger (1964) made a strong case for cooperative supervision among colleagues on the job to minimize interference by these elements with the counselor's effectiveness.

Transference: A Treatment Vehicle

Classic analysis encourages transference with the therapist, and to a lesser degree with the other members of the group, and makes interpretation of transference a central factor in treatment. Glatzer (1965) succinctly describes this process as follows: "As the patient repeats his infantile relationships in his relationship to the analyst, his buried feelings emerge and become accessible to interpretation. The repetition of the infantile conflicts under controlled analytic conditions enables the maturing ego to re-evaluate and handle more objectively the early repressed conflicts." (p. 167)

Fried (1965) said that psychoanalytic group psychotherapy tries to improve patients' emotional-mental functioning by helping them to recognize the unsuitability of archaic emotions transferred indiscriminately and automatically onto present-day figures who do not warrant them. Patients also come to understand the nature of their defenses and the ways in which they try to manage their emotional turmoil. Notice Fried's emphasis on helping patients work through their transferred feelings.

It is important to note that there exists a rather pronounced tradition among group therapists to select as the focus of their attention among transferred emotions, defenses, and transferred objects the third category, namely, the transference objects. I question the usefulness of this particular emphasis upon transference objects since I believe that the recognition of the transference object is of limited dynamic value. Understanding of the emotions that are being transferred, and particularly of the defenses that are being used as part and parcel of an emotional-mental approach that has become so firmly entrenched as to constitute an essential core of personality and character, is of highest dynamic importance. While it is often vividly clear and amusing to see how, given the cast of a therapy group, a person will focus on a certain member as though he or she were, say, a domineering intolerant older sibling, and it is tempting to point this out, such recognition of transference object is of lesser value than understanding of the transferred emotions and defenses against them. If someone discovers that he falsely equates an older woman in the group with his mother, he will find this interesting, but, in and of itself, such insight will not prompt new reactions and actions inside or outside the group. It is more important that the patient find out what emotions he transfers to the transference objects and what defenses and adaptations he uses in dealing with these emotions. And, above all, the patient must genuinely discover that both the old emotions and the defenses and adaptations can be replaced by truly up-to-date reactions. This last step is the one that clears the road for new behavior. (pp. 49–50)

Undoubtedly many patients have been successfully treated by such methods, especially when the therapist focuses upon the transferred feelings rather than the transference objects. Furthermore, this may be the best way to treat some neurotics and psychotics. Nevertheless, wherever possible, the counselor should try to avoid certain problems that are associated with classical treatment of transference:

1. excessive dependency
2. unnecessary intellectualization
3. extension of the treatment period
4. acting out
5. threat to transference objects

Whenever a client seeks treatment, he experiences *dependency*. Counselor responses that encourage transference also encourage dependency. Patterson (1959) observed: "Transference, then, develops in a situation where the therapist is a superior, authoritative figure, and the client is made to feel inferior and childlike. A dependence of the client on the therapist naturally results. A threatening and insecure situation fosters regression and leads to defensiveness (resistance), which encourages projection and misperception of the actual situation." (p. 204)

With less ambiguity, less use of interpretation, more focus on the present, greater effort to empathize and to understand the client as he is, and the expectation that he will act independently, much of this dependency can be avoided. When the counselor believes in the client's ability to solve his problems, expects him to take responsibility for doing so, expects his fellow clients to help him without letting him lean on them, is able to identify dependency feelings (help fellow clients identify these feelings) and help him cope with his dependency feelings, a client is less inclined to become dependent. Group members also can encourage the dependent client to learn new and more independent ways of behaving, reinforce independent behavior, provide support and assistance in analyzing the failure he experiences when he takes independent action, and encourage him to try again to be independent.

Use of interpretation encourages *unproductive intellectualization* and hence tends to *lengthen the treatment period unnecessarily*. Some clients react to interpretation as though they were attacked. Others change their behavior without achieving insight (Chapter Two).

Clients often find it easier to discuss their past, to discover crucial elements that shaped their behavior, and to understand the sources of their behavior than to identify improved ways of behaving and put them into practice. As a matter of fact, persons often enter group treatment knowing that they should do many things differently, and knowing why, but lacking the self-confidence and the courage to try to behave differently. These qualities must be developed during treatment. Acceptance, support, and pressure from group members can encourage such a client to experiment with new behaviors and help him convey his new self to significant others. Others' confidence in his ability to change and his observation of good models also motivate change. Though the counselor may allow clients to search for and share insights, he should not encourage it. Instead he should help clients discuss the problems that bother them and their doubts about their ability to change their behavior, encourage them to explore what they can do to resolve their problems, to take action, and, when they fail, to appraise their action.

When transference is elicited, clients are more apt to *act out* impulses toward the transference object (for example, attack verbally or even physically a teacher who has been assigned the role of a hurtful authority figure). If they believe it appropriate within the safety of their group to assign a fellow client the role of a significant other and respond to him spontaneously as though he were that other, some clients may act irresponsibly and justify it as experimentation with new behaviors. Obviously, when transference is dealt with adequately, such tendencies to act out can be recognized and dealt with before the client pursues them (see Chapter Nine).

Acting out does reveal therapeutic material that can be dealt with afterwards; nevertheless, it should be prevented *whenever possible*. Such efforts protect the transference object from being hurt and the client himself from the subsequent guilt and natural consequences. If these complications are avoided, it is also easier to help the acting-out client express his feelings for the transference object, discover new ways of relating to him, and even practice these in role playing.

Finally, some counselors are concerned about the impact of transference on the *transference object*. Being treated as though he is someone else may be disturbing if it uncovers problems for the transference object. At the moment he may be confused or hurt or frightened, but he certainly can cope with these feelings, and the problems uncovered, in a sensitive, understanding, and accepting group. When the counselor discovers that the transference object has difficulty accepting the role he has been assigned, he tries to reflect the client's feelings with a comment such as: "You're confused. You can't understand why he responded to you as he did—it doesn't seem to make sense; his responses don't seem to be appropriate for what you have done and feel." In other words, the counselor helps the persons involved deal with their feelings for each other without even labeling the phenomenon as transference. When the counselor does open up discussion to help the transference object cope with the feelings projected on him, he merely alerts him to what is happening. In the instance above he might add: "It's almost like he has assigned you someone else's role—treating you as though you were that other person." This helps the transference object accept the projecting client's feelings toward him and makes it easier for him to play temporarily the assigned role. In order to encourage generalization beyond the treatment group, and to avoid intellectualization, the counselor may follow with a response such as: "Perhaps it would help if he could tell you of whom you remind him, so that we can set up a role-playing situation in which you can play the part and help him work out his relationship with that person. Naturally, we want to help him apply what he learns here to improve his relationship with this other person outside our group." Since the next chapter is devoted to use of role playing in treatment groups, we note here simply that this approach focuses on the transferred emotions, on the learning of new human-relations skills, and on generalization outside the treatment group rather than intellectual discussion of the transference object.

Transference will be exhibited in group treatment even when the counselor does not specifically encourage it. On such occasions the counselor should help clients express their feelings for each other, and when conflict arises to face up to it and deal with it. Unfortunately, too many clients are inclined to deny or ignore conflict rather than to cope with it directly. Many also need to learn to express and accept others' positive feelings for them. They do not perceive and accept positive reactions in their social field. Even reasonably healthy clients who try to learn to live more richly with significant others experience some of the deprivation of neurotics. To more fully actualize themselves they must learn to recognize and enjoy positive reactions as well as to cope with their problems.

Transference problems can be treated without formal recognition or interpretation of the underlying transference dynamics. The clients' learning to cope with each other within the counseling group usually generalizes outside the group. Although this should not be forced, the counselor should use the therapeutic forces within the group to encourage clients to apply outside the group what they learned from counseling—to help them expect to behave differently outside their counseling group as well as within it.

Countertransference

When the counselor assigns a client the role of a significant other and treats him as though he were that person, the counselor is exhibiting countertransference. Goodman, Marks, and Rockberger (1964) reported that countertransference distortions were the counselor's *main deterrents* to effective handling of resistance within a treatment group. Because interaction within a treatment group does uncover unfulfilled needs and unresolved problems for the counselor, he must be able to recognize countertransference and disengage himself. Whenever he suspects countertransference he should critique a recording of the session, preferably with a trusted colleague or respected supervisor (see Chapter One).

Nonetheless, a counselor must learn to recognize feelings that suggest countertransference. Korner (1950) listed the following as countertransference reactions: thoughts wandering away from the interaction; having difficulty focusing attention on a client's communication; experiencing lack of sensitivity toward a client; suddenly having difficulty comprehending what a client is trying to convey; sudden appearance of thoughts that are unrelated to what a client is saying; feeling at a loss what to do next to stimulate more productive interaction; discovering that many of one's clients discuss similar problems; and feeling too protective of certain clients. Korner concluded that counselors tend to recognize, and perhaps cope with, negative feelings toward a client better than excessive positive feelings.

Cohen (1952) described the following feelings of a therapist for a patient as warning signals of countertransference: unreasoning dislike, inability to feel with him, overemotional reaction to his troubles, excessive liking for him, dreading the treatment period with him, undue concern about him between sessions, defensiveness, argumentativeness, indifference, inattentiveness, provocativeness, impatience, and feeling angrily sympathetic with him.

Korner's and Cohen's warning signals can be used by a counselor to detect countertransference. Whenever he notices any of them, he should study a recording of the counseling session to analyze the nature of his participation, identify his own emotional needs exhibited in counseling sessions, and appraise his management of resistance, transference, and countertransference.

As clients become increasingly aware of the phenomenon of transference, they notice when the counselor assigns a role out of his own life to clients. If he can accept their reactions to him, they can help him recognize countertransference. When, however, they recognize that he has special feelings for a client, they tend to react to these feelings. He must help them express these feelings toward him as they would toward any other group member. He must also try to be open to his own feelings and to assess their impact on his relationships with his clients. Occasionally, as will be illustrated later, the counselor must deal with feelings for a client that distract him from his therapeutic role.

Some counselors and therapists contend that the counselor should be a real member of the group, presenting his own problems and seeking solutions like any other member. Such an approach may be effective, and research evidence may eventually support it—at least for some counselors and therapists—but the writer prefers Korner's model, which calls for recognition and disengagement. The treatment hour belongs to the clients; usually they have paid for it, and hence the counselor should not expect to use it for his own growth and development. Even though clients should be encouraged to help fellow clients while they are obtaining help for themselves, the counselor should try to use all of his psychic energy in helping his clients. Though he must try to be open to his own feelings as he tries to help others, rarely need he express them or try to deal with his problems in the treatment group.

Occasionally the counselor finds his feelings toward a client so distracting that he must clear the air in order to make the rest of the treatment hour productive. Bob's behavior in the parent group illustrates such a case. These parents sought help with their underachieving, hostile, ninth- and tenth-grade children. Bob had convinced the counselor that he should be admitted to the group even though his wife had refused to attend. The men were factory workers and skilled craftsmen; only one (Chuck, who later dropped out) had attended college. During the first eight sessions all except Bob had openly discussed their problems. Bob had severely criticized the others for wanting their children to do well academically so that they could go to college. He belittled the value of education and resented his college-professor wife's ambition for their son, an only child. In spite of these attitudes he often requested the counselor to advise the others: "Tell them what to do and insist that they do it." At the beginning of the ninth session two of the women and one of the men shared some success experiences. Then Chuck said, "I can't seem to get my kid to do good school work. He just doesn't seem to give a damn. He is doing the same thing I did when I was in high school. I don't mind working two jobs to get ahead enough money to send him to college, but it sure as hell gripes me that he doesn't have the good sense to see the good of it." When the counselor said, "You'd like for him to have something better than you have had," Bob said, "So you think that college is great too— that college graduates are better than the rest of us—that you are better than I am. If you are so damn good why don't you tell Chuck what to do." After a pause of a minute or two (during which he tried to formulate what to say) the counselor said, "I guess that you don't think that we try to understand how you feel—that we put you on the spot like your wife does." This evoked Bob's attack on counseling and his second threat to quit the group, and for the first time the others were not bullied by him. They told him off.

After a rough 15-minute interchange, the counselor responded to Bob as follows: "I can understand why the others responded to you as they just did. In fact, I am pleased to see that they are strong enough not to be bullied by you any more, but I would like for you to stay if you are willing to try to talk about the things that really bother you—if you are willing to accept responsibility for working on your problem. I'd like for all of us to try to capture how you feel, help you express these feelings, and figure out what you can do. It has been difficult for me to like you, but I'll try. It has been difficult for me to help you too. When I try to guess how you feel and to help you express your feelings, you deny them. When I try to help others discuss their feelings, you criticize them for having these feelings. Little wonder that they attack you."

Here the counselor was discussing his own feelings, and hence for that moment was a client, but he quickly got out of the role. What he said cleared the air for himself so that he could focus better on his client's needs. It also let Bob know that the counselor wanted him to stay, it structured relationships, and it provided new material for discussion. After a brief discussion of their feelings for Bob and his for them, the group asked Bob to try to discuss what really bothered him. Had they dwelt on the counselor's feelings for clients, he would have indicated that the time was for them—that he discussed his feelings for them only when he felt that he must to clear the air and maintain his effectiveness.

The case above illustrates one way a counselor can cope with a distracting client. Korner recommended that when a counselor recognizes countertransference, he proceed cautiously the rest of that treatment session—that he limit his interpretations and reflections and that he resist the temptation to push the client. Finally, he urged the counselor to consult with associates concerning that particular session. If a counselor records every treatment session, he can preserve the raw data for critical analysis whenever countertransference is suspected. Students in training should video-record the session that follows the suspect one to pick up subtle nonverbal clues that may be influencing the relationship.

Frequently, when the counselor detects countertransference in groups he can merely sit back for a moment and listen to the interaction until he tunes in again. Sometimes it is necessary for him to ask the group to review what occurred during the period in which he was distracted by countertransference. Occasionally he may need to admit that he was distracted and to request a review of the interaction. Such behaviors enable him to disengage himself from the countertransference object and tune into the interaction so that he can function more effectively for the rest of the counseling session. Careful study of the recording helps him prepare to cope with the problem better.

Summary

An individual is exhibiting transference when he assigns another the role of a significant other and treats him as though he were that significant other. Transference occurs even within normal interactions in nontherapeutic relationships. The counselor's perception of the treatment process, his role in it, his response to transference, his own needs, his expectations for his clients, his criteria for selecting members of a treatment group, and the needs of his clients determine the extent to which the counselor becomes the primary transference object, and the extent to which members use each other as transference objects.

Those counselors and therapists who use transference as a primary vehicle for treatment do many things to induce it. Although undoubtedly many patients have been treated successfully by this method, the writer does not recommend it for his clients because it makes them unnecessarily dependent, encourages intellectualization, extends the length of the treatment process, precipitates acting out, and possibly could hurt or confuse the transference object. Anyway, the classic analytic explanation of transference can account for only part of such interaction. Much of the interaction within a counseling group is reaction to reality. What a client says and does precipitates genuine reaction from another—not transference or countertransference.

Instead of inducing transference and interpreting it, the counselor should encourage clients to empathize with each other, to discuss problems openly, to seek and try out solutions, and to change behavior and attitudes. Clients tend then to face up to the conflicts that arise within their counseling group. The counselor should encourage clients to deal with their feelings for each other, without labeling as transference even the obvious instance, helping the transference object to accept the way he is being used or to cope with frustration he may experience. A counselor also may call attention to transference to set the stage for dealing with significant others through use of role playing.

When a counselor assigns the role of a significant other from his own life to a client and treats him as though he were that person, the counselor is exhibiting countertransference. Such distortions interfere with the counselor's effectiveness. Clues that may help a counselor recognize this condition are reviewed in the text. After recognition, he must find a way to disengage himself from the countertransference object. Often he need only tune back into the interaction to pick up its therapeutic trend. Sometimes he will have to ask the group to review the interaction so that he can pick it up. Whenever he is suspicious of countertransference he should review the recording of that counseling session, searching for evidence of countertransference and its impact on clients.

References

Bach, G. R. *Intensive Group Psychotherapy*, New York: The Ronald Press Company, 1954.

Bach, G. R. "Observations on Transference and Object Relations in the Light of Group Dynamics," *The International Journal of Group Psychotherapy*, 1957, 7:64–76.

Bradford, L. P. "Membership and the Learning Process," Chapter 7 in *T-Group Theory and Laboratory Method*, New York: John Wiley & Sons, Inc., 1964.

Cohen, Mabel B. "Countertransference and Anxiety," *Psychiatry*, 1952, 15:231–243.

Durkin, Helen E. *The Group in Depth*, New York: International Universities Press, Inc., 1964.

English, H. B., and Ava C. English *A Comprehensive Dictionary of Psychological and Psychoanalytical Terms*, New York: Longmans, Green & Co., Ltd., 1958.

Freedman, M. B., and Blanche S. Sweet "Some Specific Features of Group Psychotherapy and Their Implications for Selection of Patients," *The International Journal of Group Psychotherapy*, 1954, 4:355–368.

Fried, Edrita "Some Aspects of Group Dynamics and the Analysis of Transference and Defenses," *The International Journal of Group Psychotherapy*, 1965, 15:44–56.

Glatzer, Henriette T. "Aspects of Transference in Group Psychotherapy," *The International Journal of Group Psychotherapy*, 1965, 15:167–176.

Goodman, M., M. Marks, and H. Rockberger "Resistance in Group Psychotherapy Enhanced by the Countertransference Reactions of the Therapist," *The International Journal of Group Psychotherapy*, 1964, 14:332–343.

Korner, I. J. "Ego Involvement and the Process of Disengagement," *Journal of Consulting Psychology*, 1950, 14:206–209.

Lerner, P. M. *Resolution of Intrafamilial Conflict in Families of Schizophrenic Patients*, a doctoral dissertation, University of Illinois, 1964.

Ohlsen, M. M. "Voluntary Discussion Groups," pp. 323–329, and "A

Leadership Training Program," pp. 380–385, in *Guidance Services in the Modern School*, New York: Harcourt, Brace & World, Inc., 1964.

Patterson, C. H. *Counseling and Psychotherapy:* Theory and Practice, New York: Harper & Row, Publishers, 1959.

Wolf, A. "The Psychoanalysis of Groups," in M. Rosenbaum and M. Berger, *Group Psychotherapy and Group Function*, New York: Basic Books, Inc., 1963.

Chapter Eight

Role Playing:
A Group-Counseling Technique

Role playing enables clients to convey feelings and information otherwise difficult to communicate, to disclose feelings they may not have admitted harboring, to experiment with and practice new ways of behaving, to assume and to experiment with new developmental roles, to obtain feedback with reference to specific behaviors, and to see themselves as others see them. It can be used by a counselor without a stage or additional professional personnel, and it should serve specific purposes to enhance group counseling, rather than being the primary treatment method. When clients can discuss their problems frankly and openly, discover new and better ways of behaving, and develop the self-confidence and the commitment to apply what they have learned in everyday living without further practice in their counseling groups, then role playing is not necessary; dealing with the problems verbally is more economical.

The newcomer to the field is often introduced to role playing under two other common titles: sociodrama and psychodrama. When, for example, role playing is used in the classroom by an elementary teacher to help a child cope with a bully or by an employment counselor to help his clients practice job interviews, it is usually called sociodrama because its purpose is to help someone with a common social problem. When role playing is used in counseling or psychotherapy, it is usually called psychodrama. Moreno (1946, 1952, 1963, 1964) has contributed more than anyone else to the application of these techniques in treatment groups. His work dates back to his use of role playing in 1911, even before he developed his here-and-now encounter treatment in Vienna in 1922.

Role Playing's Contributions to the Therapeutic Process

Role playing increases *spontaneity* and thus reduces *resistance*. Moreno's publications on treatment of a wide range of patients over a half century support this notion. Riessman (1964) reported that males from the lower socioeconomic classes were more responsive to role playing than to the talking-out treatment. Borgatta (1954) found that role playing within a discussion group encourages participation by group members who previously had not entered in. In an earlier paper (1951) he concluded that role playing reduced the tension and relaxed the silent member sufficiently so that he could participate. From his experience in training foremen, French (1946) concluded that role playing stimulated participation, involvement, and identification. Lippitt and Hubbell (1956) concluded from their review of the literature that role playing facilitated expression of feelings and attitudes. Katz, Ohlsen, and Proff (1959) also found that role playing facilitated spontaneous expression of feelings by gifted, under-achieving ninth graders.

Viewing psychodrama as a projective technique, Drabkova (1966) found that it revealed children's problems and motives more directly than did individual treatment techniques. Besides increasing spontaneity, role playing seems also to increase *involvement*. Perhaps it also lifts the interaction from an intellectual plane to *reality*. Preparation for and enactment of role playing with a client's problems focuses on the here and now and encourages him to apply what he has learned.

Role playing may be used to facilitate communication when (1) a client is fumbling for words, trying to describe a problem and the persons involved; (2) a client is trying to clarify his relationship with an important other for himself as well as for fellow clients; or (3) a client is touched by another's problem that appears to have special significance for him, but he is not quite ready to accept it as his own. A counselor may reflect such feelings as follows: "I am not sure that I am following you. If you are willing to do so, perhaps it would be helpful to role-play this situation. Tell us who is involved and select from our volunteers those whom you would like to play the various roles." Often it helps if the client who has the problem plays the role of the person with whom he has greatest difficulty describing his relationship, then plays his own role. Usually it also helps to play back the recording of the role playing, enlisting all the clients' assistance in examining the relationships involved and searching for improved ways of relating. Play-back and discussion of recordings, especially video recordings, helps a client *see himself* more clearly as others see him, including some of the subtle nonverbal behavior that seems to influence his relationship with significant others.

Boring and Deabler (1951) were among the first to recognize the significance of critiquing recorded role-played sessions:

> The role player in the situation does not always retain a memory of the significant spontaneous verbalizations he has made; he loses much of the scene as he plays it, and without a play-back of it, he retains only a general impression of the situation as a whole. In the play-back, he is brought face to face with himself in a dynamic lifelike situation, and often for the first time, he sees himself more nearly as he is seen by others. . . . (p. 374)

Many counselors have observed that when a client plays the role of a significant other he empathizes with that significant other. Counselors also have tended to agree that fellow clients become more accepting and empathic after they have seen one of their group cope with his problems in a role-played scene. Lippitt (1947) reported that when a client plays another's role he experiences how that other person feels. Moreno (1947) found that when children exchange roles with one another they experience one another's problems and concerns. Greenberg (1964), Mann and Mann (1958), and Shaftel (1967) suggested that taking another's role increases one's feeling for that other person and acceptance of him.

When a client really *tries to project himself* into another's role and to see life through his eyes, he can perceive better the other person's feelings within the relationship. And when he observes another playing his own role, he will see himself differently. But what happens when a client takes the role of another without *trying to perceive the relationship through the other's eyes?* For example, a father plays the role of his son just to prove to himself and his fellow clients how his son ought to behave to resolve their conflict. Does such an experience merely reinforce his perception of how his son should feel and behave, making him less empathic in trying to resolve the conflict? This is very unlikely. When he behaves in this way, the other clients tend to question the authenticity of his role playing: "Is that the way your son really reacted and behaved when you tried to talk to him about this matter? If he behaved like that, why weren't you able to resolve the problem with him?" If lack of authenticity is not picked up by fellow clients during role playing, it can be picked up during the critiquing of the role-played session. As he observes himself playing a significant other's role, even such a client tends to become more empathic and to see himself in their relationship more accurately.

Most agree that role playing increases *self-understanding*. Self-acceptance also tends to be enhanced by the *other* clients' reactions, their genuine acceptance of the primary role player (the one for whom the role-played scene was planned). Increased self-understanding has been supported by Drabkova

(1966), Fonte (1954), Lippitt and Hubbell (1956), Head (1962), and Moreno (1966).

Chapter Seven made the point that role playing could help clients cope with transference in group counseling. However, the counselor should not assume that all strong feelings for others in the group result from transference, nor should role playing be used to keep clients from dealing with their feelings for each other here and now. When they have expressed their feelings for each other and tried to cope with their relationship problems, a counselor may use role playing to help them examine the implications of these learnings for relationships outside of their counseling group—to enhance the chances for generalization.

When a counselor decides that calling transference by its name would help the transference object to accept the role assigned him in order to help the role-assigning client, and that role-playing the problem situation would enable the role-assigning client to cope best with his problem, he asks the latter to describe the situation and the primary persons involved, and to select his cast for role-playing the scene in accordance with the guidelines given later in this chapter. After the role playing, he may wish to tell the clients how to recognize transference and how to cope with it in the future. Usually, when transference objects understand the phenomenon of transference, they can more readily accept the roles that fellow clients assign to them in attempting to resolve their problems. The risk is that clients may waste time in intellectualizing about transference objects: Who reminds whom of whom?

Finally, role playing gives a client an opportunity to experiment with new ways of behaving and to obtain feedback from fellow clients. It also gives him a chance *to practice* a social skill, an approach for coping with a difficult situation, or a method for relating to an important other in his life. As they mature, children and youth are frequently called upon to assume new roles. Role playing can be used to help them to relate in new ways to important others such as parents, teachers, employers, and friends of the opposite sex as they assume these new roles.

Introducing Role Playing

How should a counselor introduce role playing? For many elementary-school children this will not be a new technique. They are accustomed to their teacher's use of it to help them cope with everyday problems [see, for example, Wells (1962)]. Increasingly others have experienced it in group guidance activities, leadership training, and T groups.

A counselor should introduce the idea of role playing when he describes group counseling for prospective clients. Role playing itself can be introduced in many situations that arise naturally within counseling groups. For example, an under-achieving ninth grader was complaining about how unfairly he had been treated by an English teacher, who failed to notice how he had changed his behavior. The counselor responded: "Jim, I guess it's pretty discouraging when you really try to get your assignments in on time and she doesn't even notice how you have changed. I also seem to pick up the feeling that you don't know how to tell her that bawling you out in front of everyone really discouraged you—made you feel like giving up even when you wanted to meet her expectations. If you like, maybe we can help you practice talking to her. First we must know who was really involved and how they behaved so you can select the persons to play these roles." After Jim described what happened and who did or said something, the counselor asked the clients to volunteer for the roles. First Jim played the teacher's part, then his own role. Even before he played his own role he said, "Now I can see a couple of things I have been doing that 'tick' her off."

Nevertheless, Jim was still reluctant to discuss his problem with his teacher. A couple of the students suggested that the counselor go with Jim to see the teacher, and the counselor said, "I guess you think he needs someone to protect him, and perhaps to make the teacher feel a little ashamed for the way she has treated Jim." Most of the clients agreed, but they also saw that it might start trouble between the teacher and the counselor, and the teacher might make it even tougher on Jim. Eventually Jim decided to try to talk to her by himself. It was a rough experience, but he made his point without "spouting off," and the relationship between Jim and his teacher did improve ever so slowly (his fellow clients offered support and encouragement, which Jim needed to reinforce the change). After Jim reported to the group on his conference with the teacher, the counselor took the opportunity to explain how clients could detect other situations for which role playing would be appropriate, and he suggested guidelines to increase its effectiveness.

Guidelines for Role Playing

Whenever any member of a group discovers a situation suited to role playing, he should state why he feels it would be appropriate. However, he also should recognize the requirements that the person whose problem suggested role playing (the primary role player and/or director) sees value in using it, elects to use it, and can select role players from volunteers (clients who he feels can play the essential roles).

The primary role player should describe the persons involved and how he thinks they feel. Every member of the group should be encouraged to ask questions in order to obtain the best possible picture of the situation and those involved in it. Regardless of the role he plays, the primary role player and/or director achieves increased understanding of the situation and learns new relationship skills as he casts, directs, and plays roles. Sometimes the purposes for role-playing a scene are fulfilled even before the role playing is begun.

After the primary role player has described the situation and the primary characters involved, clients are encouraged to volunteer for various roles. Even reticent clients who have difficulty participating will often volunteer. When roles are left unfilled, clients are encouraged by the counselor to suggest persons for these roles. If no one volunteers, members usually permit the director (the client whose problem suggested role playing) to complete the casting. Those who work with children may wish to encourage role players to use puppets or dolls to speak and act for them. Some children seem to find it easier to respond through puppets (or dolls) than to try to play roles of specific persons.

Role players should be helped to perceive role playing as an impromptu play, in which everyone makes up whatever lines convey best how his character feels. Everyone should feel that once he accepts his character's role and is briefed for it, he is on his own. Even though he may have been given his character's exact words, he should not be concerned about remembering and repeating them. Instead, he should try to feel as he believes his character feels and to express his character's feelings as best he can, using his own words.

The counselor also encourages his clients to use soliloquy whenever they believe that their characters will speak and behave differently from the way they really feel. For example, a nonconforming eleventh-grade client, who was trying to learn to conform and accept certain limits, took the role of a boy much like himself. When he was put on the spot by a fellow student, he said: "Look, lay off, can't you see I'm trying to get along with Mr. Smith?" Then he turned his head to the audience, cupped his hand to the side of his mouth, and said in soliloquy, "That bastard is pushing me again. He can't stand to see me get along and stay out of trouble. I'd like to bash him in the mouth." The soliloquy not only helped the boy to convey his feelings, but it helped the entire group to empathize with him and enabled fellow clients to give him support while he was learning to live his new role.

Just before a scene the counselor should assess whether all the players understand their roles. Anyone who has questions or wants help in playing his role should be encouraged to speak. While playing the scene every actor should feel free to stop whenever he feels unable to proceed, either because he has run out of material or because he is faced with behavior that he cannot act out. When he lacks material, he may use soliloquy to request it. When he cannot act out the behavior before him, he may wish to recess the interaction to enlist members' assistance. Such freedom makes the actors more secure in their roles; very likely it also increases their openness and spontaneity.

The counselor assists the director, especially in preparing persons for their roles and in helping them put into words what they think their characters feel. Even here the counselor does not take the authoritarian role usually associated with the dramatic director. Instead he merely helps the director clarify a situation or a relationship and helps a player state a feeling.

Sometimes the counselor is asked to play a role. The role in which he is cast (perhaps that of an authority figure for the primary actor) often affects his relationship with certain clients long after the scene has ended. Although these problems can be worked out, they tend to distract clients from some of the benefits achieved in role playing. The counselor can prevent these problems by declining to play roles.

When someone (other than the director) terminates the role playing, he should first be given opportunity to request assistance or information or to react to whatever caused him to stop; then other actors and, finally, the audience should be given their chance to react to the interaction, to give feedback, or merely to ask questions for clarification. Usually the director stops the role playing when he has obtained the assistance he wants, or when he wants to restructure, or when he merely wishes to react to what has occurred. Here again the counselor should help clients focus on the feelings involved and on learning new ways of behaving.

How may the director benefit from discussion of the role-played scene? First, he has a chance to reveal his feelings about what happened during the role playing, to comment on whatever he may have discovered about himself and/or the relationships, and to consider the possible benefit of replaying the scene—possibly giving himself another role and soliciting new volunteers. From the comments of others he obtains new perceptions of the relationships and of his own function in the situation, feedback on how he behaved, and suggestions on how he could try to behave differently.

Other role players reap benefits, too: evoking others' reactions, experiencing new roles, and practicing approaches for coping with new or difficult situations (usually they volunteer for roles that have special meaning for them, though they are not always conscious of this fact). They also get feedback on the way they played their roles and the way they tried to cope with the problems with which their character was confronted. They should have an opportunity to express how they felt in their roles, how they felt about playing these particular roles, and what they learned from the experience. Sometimes such experiences enable them to solve problems without ever claiming them as their own. A more common reaction is for a client to see the relevance of the role for himself and to discuss the related problem with new openness.

Least benefited are the members of the audience. Even they, however, tend to become deeply involved in reacting to the scene. Some volunteer for roles when scenes are replayed. Usually those in the audience profit to the extent that they can and do become involved. Moreno (1966) stressed the importance of involving everyone present—looking upon everyone as a potential role player—and of giving everyone an encounter with his real self and his problems.

Standard Roles

Some counselors use standard roles, encouraging group members to take various roles commonly encountered in everyday life. Boring and Deabler (1951) developed twelve standard roles which they used in treating groups of from 12 to 16 veterans: mother-son (small boy), father-son (small boy), father-mother-son (small boy), siblings (two brothers), boy-girl (adolescent boy), mother-son (adult), father-son (adult), father-mother-son (adult), husband-wife (cold supper), neighbors in conflict, job-seeker versus personnel man, and childhood sex attitudes and experiences. ". . . These basic situations allow the patient to be introduced to and to participate in more or less general roles which also prepare him for participation later in more personally structured ones related to his own conflict areas." (p. 373) They recommend, besides the group therapist, that two other persons play the auxiliary male and female roles. Though there is value in this approach, and though the writer sometimes uses a similar one in group guidance for adolescents, and he teaches elementary teachers to use it for sociodrama in the classroom, nonetheless, in group counseling he prefers to use material from his clients' own lives.

Harth (1966) used a variation of this standard-role notion to treat failing lower-class third graders. He had them play the roles of various school personnel, so that they might change their attitudes toward school and better appreciate the attitudes of school personnel. His clients did improve their classroom behavior, but he failed to obtain significant changes in attitudes. Perhaps his tests were not sensitive enough to detect the attitude changes that occurred. However, he concluded that the students were not able to change their attitudes because they were unable to express their true feelings in these sociodramatic experiences.

Here are some everyday situations a counselor may use to help elementary-school teachers recognize the value of role playing in the classroom and implement its use: a child tells a friend or a teacher or a parent that he is too dumb to learn to read or to do arithmetic; a child tells someone that he is afraid he is going to fail and he doesn't know what to do about it; a child is upset when his mother leaves him at school, and he does not know how to discuss it with his mother or teacher; a child is confronted by a bully and does not know what to do; a child knows someone whom he likes and does not know how to become a friend; and a child is grieving for the loss of a relative, friend, or pet and wants to talk to someone.

Role playing has its place in group guidance, home-room discussion groups and student forums, and leadership training groups; here students recognize the value of scenes such as: asking for a date, carrying on a conversation on a date, conducting a club meeting, presenting a speech to the student council, talking to a teacher about a grade, requesting help with school work, interviewing for a job, and interviewing for college admission. Students also see quickly how they can use role playing to resolve common problems with parents such as restrictions on dating, use of car, and their role in deciding their choice of career or college.

Summary

Role playing can be used for specific purposes to increase the effectiveness of group counseling, but it should not be the sole treatment method for groups. When problems can be handled satisfactorily by discussion, role playing is not needed.

Role playing can help clients express themselves more spontaneously, improve communication, increase their involvement in the therapeutic interaction, increase feelings of empathy for others, increase understanding and acceptance of themselves and of others, experiment with new ways of behaving, experiment with new roles, and practice specific behaviors.

When the counselor describes a new service such as group counseling, he should describe role playing as one of the ways of helping clients in groups.

When the counselor first observes a good situation for using role playing he should explain how it can be used; help the client whose problem revealed the need for it to describe the situation and the primary characters involved, select role players, and brief them; and help clients react to what they learned. After clients have discussed their experiences, he should explain how they can tell when to use it again and for what purposes.

References

Borgatta, E. "An Analysis of Three Levels of Response: An Approach to Some Relationships among Dimensions of Personality," *Sociometry*, 1951, 14:267–315.

Borgatta, E. "An Analysis of Social Interaction and Sociometric Perception," *Sociometry*, 1954, 17:7–32.

Boring, R. O., and M. L. Deabler "A Simplified Psychodramatic Approach in Group Therapy," *Journal of Clinical Psychology*, 1951, 7:371–375.

Drabkova, H. "Experiences Resulting from Clinical Use of Psychodrama with Children," *Group Psychotherapy*, 1966, 19:32–36.

Fonte, N. "Research: A New Strength for Family Living," *Marriage and Family*, 1954, 16:13–20.

French, J. "Role Playing as a Method of Training Foremen," in J. L. Moreno (ed.), *Group Psychotherapy*, New York: Beacon House, 1946, 172–187.

Greenberg, I. "Audience in Action through Psychodrama," *Group Psychotherapy*, 1964, 17:104–122.

Harth, R. "Changing Attitudes toward Schools, Classroom Behavior, and Reaction to Frustration of Emotionally Disturbed Children through Role Playing," *Exceptional Children*, 1966, 33:119–120.

Head, W. A. "Sociodrama and Group Discussion with Institutionalized Delinquent Adolescents," *Mental Hygiene*, 1962, 46:127–135.

Katz, Evelyn W., M. M. Ohlsen, and F. C. Proff "An Analysis through Use of Kinescopes of the Interpersonal Behavior of Adolescents in Group Counseling," *Journal of College Student Personnel*, 1959, 1:2–10.

Lippitt, Rosemary "Psychodrama in the Home," *Sociatry*, 1947, 1:148–167.

Lippitt, Rosemary, and Ann Hubbell "Role Playing for Personnel and Guidance Workers," *Group Psychotherapy*, 1956, 9:89–114.

Mann, J. H., and Carola H. Mann "The Effect of Role Playing Experience on Self-ratings of Personal Adjustment," *Group Psychotherapy*, 1958, 11:27–32.

Moreno, Florence "Psychodrama in the Neighborhood," *Sociatry*, 1947, 1:168–178.

Moreno, J. L. "Psychodrama and Group Psychotherapy," *Sociometry*, 1946, 9:249–253.

Moreno, J. L. "Psychodramatic Production Techniques," *Group Psychotherapy*, 1952, 4:243–273.

Moreno, J. L. "The Actual Trends in Group Psychotherapy," *Group Psychotherapy*, 1963, 16:117–131.

Moreno, J. L. "The Third Psychiatric Revolution and the Scope of Psychodrama," *Group Psychotherapy*, 1964, 17:149–171.

Moreno, J. L. "The Roots of Psychodrama," *Group Psychotherapy*, 1966, 19:140–145.

Riessman, F. "Role Playing and the Lower Socio-Economic Group," *Group Psychotherapy*, 1964, 17:36–48.

Shaftel, Fannie, with assistance of G. Shaftel *Role Playing for Social Values:* Decision Making in Social Studies, Englewood Cliffs, N.J.: Prentice-Hall, Inc., 1967.

Wells, Cecilia G. "Psychodrama and Creative Counseling in the Elementary School," *Group Psychotherapy*, 1962, 15:244–252.

Chapter Nine

Difficult Clients

This chapter discusses ways of coping with typical clients who have been difficult for beginning counselors to manage within a group. These types of clients were identified by the writer while supervising counselors as they encountered their first group. The counselors had completed a practicum in individual counseling. All except the doctoral candidates in clinical psychology had had some counseling experience in schools or in rehabilitation centers.

The clients to be discussed here are: the resister, the advice-giver, the silent and/or withdrawn one, the submissive and/or other-controlled one, the anxious one, the griever, the scapegoat, the hostile one, the acting-out client, the socializer, and the monopolizer. Obviously these are not distinct, discrete types, but beginning counselors usually do react to such characteristics differently and hence they are discussed separately.

To work effectively with any difficult client, a counselor must try to answer such questions as: (1) How does he make me feel? (2) What is his impact upon me? (3) What danger signals have I noticed that may indicate countertransference? (4) Is he using me as a transference object? (5) What is his impact on the other clients? and (6) How can I cope with any antitherapeutic influence he may have upon the other clients?

To respond to such a client therapeutically, a counselor must try to discover: (1) What is unique about him? (2) How does he feel? (3) What unfulfilled needs does his behavior suggest? (4) What are reasonable treatment goals for him? and (5) How can I respond to him therapeutically and help the other clients to do so, too?

In order to involve the other clients in treating a difficult client, a counselor must search for answers to questions such as: (1) What is his impact on the other clients? (2) How does he make them feel? (3) What feelings does he have in common with other clients? (4) How can I respond to these feelings, and help those who share them respond to him? and (5) How can I help the other clients detect how he feels, make it safe to discuss these feelings, and encourage him to take steps to change his behavior?

The Resister

The resister is dealt with in Chapter Six, hence he will not be discussed here. Perhaps, however, two points should be reviewed for emphasis: (1) the counselor must be open to his own genuine feelings lest he feel blocked, frustrated, or unappreciated and not recognize it; and (2) he must try to capture and to help the resisting client discuss the feelings that are keeping him from facing his problems openly and dealing with them.

The Advice-Giver

Who is he? What unfulfilled needs does he exhibit? How does he feel? Bach (1954) reported that giving advice fulfills some important unmet—and perhaps unconscious—needs for the advice-giver. From Freud's (1933) work he noted an underlying sadism in the overzealous person's wish to heal another. Powdermaker and Frank (1953) presented three other reasons for advice-giving in the treatment group: (1) to divert attention away from one's own problems; (2) to exhibit superiority to the doctor ("I can help him better than you can") ; and (3) to conceal contempt and hostility for the one seeking assistance. Other reasons for advice-giving that evolve from resistance are (1) the advice-giver's inability to let another face and try to cope with painful material and (2) his efforts to cover up his own dependency feelings by telling others what to do. Some genuinely believe that this is the way to help their fellow clients. Others use advice-giving to solicit feedback for their coping behavior.

As Bach noted, clients do come to see the folly of advice-giving but they cannot give it up easily. They also discover that it reveals more about the advice-giver than it does about the advisee. Mere interpretation of the advice-giver's behavior is not sufficient, however; in fact, it tends to make him feel attacked, and more defensive. Hence, his fellow clients should be helped to discover his real feelings and to make it safe for him to discuss them. For example, the counselor may respond to the advice-giver as follows: "I guess you think he feels pretty uncomfortable when he discusses that topic and you don't want to see him suffer any more if you can prevent it. Hence, you suggested something specific that he can do so he won't have to discuss it any further." The latter part of the counselor's response includes an interpretation, but its primary aim is to help the advice-giver discuss his fears about the uncovering of hurtful material and discover how the one whom he tried to protect responds to his behavior, and to encourage other clients to respond to the apparent therapeutic material revealed by the advice-giving.

Even when the advice-giver has learned to deal with the problems that motivate him to give advice, he can easily be seduced into giving advice by a dependent advice-seeker. Such a client usually appears to be so helpless, and to be faced with a problem that requires such immediate attention, that the advice-giver tells him what to do. On such occasions the counselor is tempted to point out that the advice-giver was seduced. Usually one obtains better results by reflecting the feelings of the advice-giver and the helpless one. "[To the adviser:] His needing help right now really touched you so deeply that you suggested some things he could do. [to the advice-seeker as part of the same response:] When you feel so helpless you like to have someone like him let you know that he cares enough to tell you what you should do." Such a response gets both clients' feelings out in the open where they can be dealt with. After the advice-giver has begun to cope with this problem, he often learns to express his hostile feelings toward the advice-seeker who seduces him, and he can admit that he resents being used. Then he can help the dependent one learn how to take responsibility and to act more independently.

Bach's explanation of advice-giving has relevance for the counselor, too—especially for the beginning counselor who has recently left the classroom in which he was the expert. His prior experiences as evaluator and disciplinarian, coupled with his limited repertoire of well-integrated treatment skills, tempt him to advise clients. Though he himself finds it difficult to avoid giving advice to the advice-seeker, he often has difficulty in accepting parallel action by the advice-giver. He is inclined to attack the advice-giver with a confronting interpretation, rather than to try to understand him and help him deal with these feelings as suggested above.

The Dependent One

Most dependent clients feel relatively inadequate. Some feel inadequate in most situations, others in only a few. Within these situations they lack the confidence both to make decisions and to act upon them. Dependent clients have had their dependent behavior reinforced by persons who needed to have someone dependent upon them or by important others such as parents and teachers who did not bother to teach them, during the normal process of growing up, how to behave independently. Hence, these clients require opportunities to learn and practice independent behaviors. They also need the understanding and support that a group of peers can provide when they approach independent action and retreat from it, and when they try it, seem to fail, and must re-evaluate what they tried before they can develop the courage to try again. As a consequence of such experiences, the confidence others show in them, and observations of how others have learned to behave more independently, dependent clients can learn to behave more independently. A good model is more powerful than advice. They also profit from expressing their dependency feelings. Few of them, however, require exploration of the reasons for their dependency; such historical discussions, though interesting, rarely increase clients' motivation to change their behavior.

On the other hand, dependent clients are not easily helped. They have learned many effective ways of manipulating others into doing things for them: for example, (1) by appearing so helpless that they convince other clients and the counselor that at least for the present some specific advice or assistance is essential; (2) by getting themselves into situations in which they seem to lack any coping resources; (3) by appealing to the strength, wisdom, and maturity of others and thereby seducing others into taking responsibility for them. Rarely do they recognize how others feel when they realize that they have been used. They have not discovered why some friends and acquaintances have avoided them or how those who cannot escape from them must resent them. Role playing can be used to bring out these feelings and to help the dependent one practice new relationship skills. When the counselor detects and reflects these feelings in the used ones and helps them express them, he not only helps them deal with the dependent client but he also provides feedback to the dependent client. This helps the dependent client understand his relationships with others and motivates him to learn new ways of relating to them. Such discussions also help the used ones to recognize and to cope with dependent clients outside the counseling group.

The Submissive and/or Other-Controlled One

This type of client was described by Grater (1958) in his paper "When Counseling Success Is Failure." This client treasures others' approval so much that he discusses whatever others seem to like or tries to do what others want him to do. Consequently, he is often used by others and he resents it, but he is afraid to express the resentment because he questions his own worth—doubts that he can win others' love and acceptance except by letting them use him.

This client is very sensitive to others' needs. If, for example, other members like to talk about sex problems, he discusses sex problems, even though he recognizes that he should try to face and cope with submissiveness. In individual treatment he often elicits countertransference. Usually, when counseling ends, he is picked by fellow clients and the counselor as one of those who has been helped most. He seems to talk very openly about his problems, and he makes others feel close to him because he seems to have problems in common with most if not all of them. Actually he is often helped with all of his problems except the one with which he needs help most—being controlled by others.

In order to help this client most readily, the counselor must convey in the intake interview that his own task is to listen and to help the client reveal those problems with which *he wants help most*. The counselor must be very wary of giving any nonverbal or verbal clues about topics that he likes to have his clients discuss. Focusing on the clients' feelings, he must even be cautious in clarifying them lest he contaminate the clients' responses. Once the client reveals the need to learn to cope with being other-controlled, the counselor must help him get ready to tell fellow clients about it at the first group session. When he reveals this problem in his counseling group, the counselor must try to convey to others how readily this problem can be overlooked and openly enlist their assistance in watching for chances to help the client deal with it.

Unfortunately, some other-directed clients who seek help from the group do not recognize that submissiveness is among their problems. Sometimes it can be picked up anyway in the intake interview. At other times it can be brought to the surface by a carefully timed reflection, especially when the client is dealing with his problems of trying to please an important other, such as a spouse or a parent, or when the counselor notes that he has just been used by another client in his group. In any case, helping him recognize and express his feelings of doubt about his worth and resentment about being used gets these feelings out where others can help him deal with them, enables them to express their feelings toward him concerning his worth, and encourages him to learn and practice new relationship skills.

The Silent and/or Withdrawn One

The silent one and the withdrawn one may be one and the same; on the other hand, they may be two who perceive themselves very differently and have very different reasons for remaining silent. Hence, a counselor must observe the silent one very carefully to detect how he feels about himself.

Some clients have learned to become deeply involved in interacting with others with a minimum of talking. When others express their feelings or deal with their problems, they convey empathy and support; they experience feelings with others, learn from others, and adapt what they learn to solve their own problems. Others serve as their mouthpiece. Usually these silent ones *openly reveal their problems early*, so they are not looked upon with suspicion. Some clients who fall in this category recognize that their school performance or their proficiency at work is underrated. Hence, even though they can be helped within their counseling group with minimum verbal participation, they recognize that they must improve their verbal-interaction skills in order to gain the recognition they deserve.

Another infrequent verbal participator within a counseling group is the deliberate, slow-moving person who takes his time to figure out how he feels and what he wants to say. He also may be reluctant to interrupt others to express himself. If the counselor watches him carefully, he will note that repeatedly he nearly gets the floor and then loses it to another. Merely observing that once again he has lost out is usually sufficient to sensitize other clients to his need for assistance in capturing the speaker's role. He also may need to learn either to express himself more effectively or to cope with resistance.

The withdrawn one tends to have a more negative self-image than either of the silent ones described above. He tends to be less confident that he can be helped by counseling and that he can say anything that really will help others. Carefully timed reflection conveys empathy and helps him reveal his problems. When he tries to express his feelings, he discovers that the other members really care and that they want to help him change. Furthermore, he discovers that they can be very patient in helping him face his problems.

Most counselors want every client to interact verbally, and some, especially former teachers, are made to feel uncomfortable by the silent one. They are tempted to call upon him as they did in class recitations. This tends to put him on the spot. Fellow clients also tend to put him on the spot because they are suspicious of him. Helping him discuss precisely how he feels not only increases his readiness for change, but it increases others' acceptance of him. Participating in such interaction also provides him the practice he needs in the socializing skills.

The Anxious One

Chapter Four made the point that some tension seems to be essential to motivate changed behavior. Tension is not the same as anxiety. Tension is energy within one's system that requires discharge, and there is usually some pleasure in discharging it. A person experiences tension when he meets obstacles in achieving goals, when he is unable to satisfy some need, and when he anticipates some exciting or challenging event—for example, when he waits in the wings to go on stage to perform, when he waits for an athletic contest to begin, and when he prepares for and waits for an examination to begin.

In the last example one would expect the tension to be discharged by the completion of the examination. A student should, however, experience a *minimum of anxiety* when he functions well. When he doubts his ability to achieve success or worries about the outcome to an extent that interferes with his preparation or with his performance during the examination, his state becomes one of debilitating anxiety. Thus, tension is a stimulus for action, whereas anxiety tends to interfere with effective action. When clients recognize the need for counseling, the pain and inefficiency associated with anxiety may motivate them to change.

The anxious one is worried, fearful, apprehensive, or upset. He shows his anxiety in a counseling group when he tries to discuss some painful experience, or when he tries to cope with some difficult situation in which he fears failure or other unhappy consequences. Sometimes the other members, including the counselor, are afraid that he will talk too freely —that he will reveal more than he can cope with. Some of his fellow clients may become upset, fearing that if they help him talk so openly, they will be expected to do likewise. Under these circumstances, especially during the first few sessions, clients and sometimes even inexperienced counselors reassure the anxious one. Though laymen often do this to support him, the underlying attitude conveyed may be rejection, lack of empathy and compassion for him, or doubt concerning his ability to cope with his problems, or lack of confidence in the treatment process. Thus, the feelings of the reassurer as well as the anxious one must be detected and reflected to get them out in the open where they can be dealt with.

Careful selection of clients can minimize this difficulty. When a counselor selects only those clients whom he believes that he can help in a group (see Chapter Five), he can react to an anxious client with greater confidence. It also is important for clients to know that they were selected with care.

When they realize that their fellow clients are considered good treatment risks, their group becomes more attractive and they can respond more spontaneously to each other. Members' confidence in the anxious one, their willingness to try to understand him, and their ability to help him express his feelings provide genuine support. When he weeps, others try to empathize with him and to understand him. They help him talk and are patient, but do not try to interfere with his weeping or to comfort him with shallow reassurances. When he becomes somewhat disorganized they help him clarify what he feels, expect him to try to express himself clearly, and expect him to learn new ways of coping with his problems. Clients should be helped to accept the notion that these things happen when they obtain assistance. Talland and Clark (1954) found that their patients were helped most when they discussed their most painful topics.

Finally, are clients likely to uncover material with which they cannot cope? This rarely happens in counseling groups. However, some clients can be severely challenged when they are confronted with probing questions or penetrating interpretations. Actually they feel safer in the type of counseling group described in this volume than they do in everyday interaction at home, at school, or at work, where they may be confronted with hurtful nagging or where they may be asked why they behaved as they did in a given situation. Though clients face and relive hurtful events, and they are pressured to change their behavior and attitudes, members also provide genuine support. Even when another uncovers painful material with a penetrating reflection, he is trying to reach the anxious one in a nonauthoritarian manner rather than to confront him with his maladaptive behavior; he is trying to empathize with the anxious one, to convey confidence in his ability to solve his problems, and to provide support while the anxious one learns to behave differently. From observation of the counselor, clients learn to provide such genuine support while helping each other change behavior.

Some readers may wonder, nonetheless, what they can do when they believe a client is revealing too much in the first

session or two; they are concerned that the client may regret
what he revealed, or that he may talk too freely outside the
counseling group. When a counselor begins to feel uncomfortable with such a client he should continue to listen and try
to assess whether he is uncomfortable about the client or about
himself (see Chapter Seven). If he suspects that the client
may continue to reveal his private thoughts and feelings outside the counseling group and get hurt by it, the counselor
is obligated to clarify expectations—differentiating between
what is appropriate behavior in a counseling group and what
is appropriate elsewhere. If he feels that the anxious client
regrets something that he has revealed, the counselor should
reflect these feelings so that others can react, and where necessary review and/or formulate new guidelines for their group.
When doubts about a particular member are involved, the
counselor, and the other members too, should help the anxious
one state his doubts and work out his relationship with the
person involved.

Sometimes the counselor or some fellow client cannot
follow what the anxious one is saying. He may be talking too
fast or incoherently. By making a clarification response the
counselor conveys that he is interested and wants to help,
while encouraging the anxious one to try to make sense:
"Pardon my interruption, but I'm afraid I did not understand
what you are trying to convey. I'm not sure whether you tried
to speak to your Latin teacher, or whether you are afraid to
speak to her or you don't think it will do any good." A similar
response can be made when the client is unloading too fast and
the counselor feels that slowing him down could help other
members follow the interaction: "I'm having difficulty keeping up with you—trying to understand everything you are
telling us. Apparently, a number of things are upsetting you.
Perhaps we could understand you better if you could select
one or two problems with which you would like help first and
go over them a little more slowly."

When the counselor is uncomfortable, he should consider
critiquing the recorded session with another counselor with
whom he feels comfortable. From such sessions he can learn

new ways of dealing with such critical incidents and determine whether or not countertransference was involved. If counter-transference is evident, they should discuss what evoked it and how the counselor may cope with it. In any case, the counselor must assess what he can do to help the anxious one deal with relevant material; enlist other clients' support and assistance; help them deal with any threatening material the anxious one uncovers in them; and help the anxious one generalize to his important others outside the counseling group.

The Griever

How does he feel? Why does he grieve? Clients seem to grieve for a number of reasons. Most experience loneliness and hopelessness for the future. Many feel helpless. Often, after a long illness of a loved one, the response to his death may be relief—followed by feelings of guilt. Many also feel guilt and self-condemnation because they wish they had treated the deceased better or differently, or because they wonder whether everything possible had been done to save his life. On the other hand, if he really rejected the deceased, a griever may at first feel relief and possibly even pleasure, but a guilt reaction may follow. Some counselors and therapists believe that the princi-pal feeling is one of self-pity.

Children often experience feelings like those described above when a much-loved neighbor, friend, or relative moves away. They also experience real grief over loss of a pet.

When someone denies the loss or is not helped to grieve, related problems may be exhibited years later. This is what happened to Frances, a fifty-year-old widow who sought treat-ment in a group of counselors. In her intake interview she said she needed help in coping with a grieving sister. Her sister's husband had been dead a year, but her sister still refused to go out with their friends and relatives, often cried herself to sleep, would not return to work, and seemed to be completely helpless. In response to another client's reflection Frances admitted reluctantly that she resented her sister very much.

Later in the same session she also expressed some resentment toward an old neighbor and friend who had recently lost his wife. Early in the next session she cried and discussed the death of her own husband. Though she had lost her husband five years earlier, she had not worked through her own grief until it was uncovered in the group. Once she had dealt with her grief, she was able to help her sister get the treatment she needed and to cope with her old friend's affection for her.

Lindemann (1944) studied psychoneurotic patients who lost a relative during treatment; the relatives of patients who died while hospitalized; disaster victims from the Coconut Grove fire and their relatives; and the relatives of servicemen. For acute grief he reported a common syndrome:

> . . . sensations of somatic distress occurring in waves lasting from twenty minutes to an hour at a time, a feeling of tightness in the throat, choking with shortness of breath, need for sighing, and an empty feeling in the abdomen, lack of muscular power, and an intense subjective distress described as tension or mental pain. The patient soon learns that these waves of discomfort can be precipitated by visits, by mentioning the deceased, and by receiving sympathy. There is a tendency to avoid the syndrome at any cost, to refuse visits lest they should precipitate the reaction, and to keep deliberately from thought all references to the deceased. (p. 141)

He also found that reaction to grief could be delayed, and that morbid grief reactions represented distortion of normal grief. These distorted reactions included (a) overactivity, (b) acquisition of symptoms of the deceased, (c) a recognized medical disease, (d) alteration in relationships to friends and relatives (patient is irritable, does not want to be bothered, and gradually isolates himself), (e) hostility toward specific persons, (f) efforts to hide hostility, giving appearance of schizophrenia, (g) a lasting loss of social interaction, (h) actions detrimental to his own social and economic existence (he behaves in foolish ways that damage friendships, and he wastes financial resources or permits himself to be cheated out of them by unscrupulous persons), and (i) agitated depression (his grief is exhibited with insomnia, feelings of worthlessness, bitter self-accusation, and self-punishment—he may become dangerously suicidal).

Unknowingly, his friends and relatives often keep the griever from facing reality and dealing with grief. Rather than letting him discuss his real feelings and weep, they block his grieving with empty reassurances. They may even be so stupid as to suggest that he will soon forget—that time heals all wounds. Even the suggestion that he will soon forget is perceived by him as an attack: it seems to challenge the sincerity of his love for the deceased, when in fact he feels his loss so keenly that the whole future looks bleak. Until they learn to react more therapeutically, even fellow clients also tend to respond in these nonhelpful ways.

What the griever needs to know is that friends and relatives care about him—that though they cannot understand fully how much his loss hurts, they want to help him express his grief and to discover the strength to deal with it. Furthermore, they provide real support when they show confidence in his ability to cope with it by helping him express it, rather than deny or conceal it. Even though he may prefer to withdraw, they patiently involve him appropriately in their relationships. They also help him to move back into other meaningful social relationships and to re-establish himself in his work. With such considerate responses they may be given opportunities to protect him from leeches who would take advantage of him during his grieving period.

Lindemann describes this grief work as follows:

> The duration of a grief reaction seems to depend upon the success with which a person does the grief work, namely, emancipation from the bondage to the deceased, readjustment to the environment in which the deceased is missing, and the formation of new relationships. One of the big obstacles to this work seems to be the fact that many patients try to avoid the intense distress connected with the grief experience and to avoid the expression of emotion necessary for it. The men victims after the Coconut Grove fire appeared in the early psychiatric interviews to be in a state of tension with tightened facial musculature, unable to relax for fear they might "break down."

It required considerable persuasion to yield to the grief process
before they were willing to accept the discomfort of bereave-
ment. . . . They became willing to accept the grief process and
to embark on a program of dealing in memory with the
deceased person. As soon as this became possible there seemed
to be a rapid relief of tension and the subsequent interviews
were rather animated conversations in which the deceased was
idealized and in which misgivings about the future adjustment
were worked through. (p. 143)

To illustrate how a patient moved out into the stream of
life and developed a future for herself, Lindemann described
the case of a forty-year-old widow: ". . . She then showed a
marked drive for activity, making plans for supporting herself
and her little girl, mapping out the preliminary steps for
resuming her old profession as secretary, and making efforts
to secure help from the occupational therapy department in
reviewing her knowledge of French." (p. 143) For some persons like this griever counseling includes assistance in choosing
a vocation.

Group counseling provides opportunities for many to
grieve who did not seek counseling for that purpose. It is not
uncommon when one client does his grief work to find that it
uncovers the need for grieving in most of the other clients.
They also learn how to function as more effective laymen in
helping friends and relatives do their grief work.

Often adults do not realize that most children experience
grief. They fail to notice how deeply a child feels about the
loss of a pet or how much he misses that friend or relative
who moved away. He also worries about what may happen to
loved ones. Beginning elementary-school counselors are often
surprised about the number of children who seek assistance
with grieving problems—especially when they are telling children about group counseling and mention grieving as an
example. They also have been impressed with the sensitive
way in which children can help each other learn to cope with
grief in groups. When a school counselor helps important

others such as parents and teachers discover how the griever feels and teaches them how to respond, they can help the child resolve many of his grieving problems. Counselors also can use seminars and discussion groups to help teachers and parents work through their own grieving problems and prepare themselves to help children and youth cope with such problems more effectively. Counselors might also conduct small discussion groups in churches to help members as well as the clergy understand better the phenomenon of grieving so that they may help others grieve and recognize those who need intensive treatment to cope with grieving.

The Scapegoat

The scapegoat is the focus of displaced aggression. Some masochistic persons set themselves up for this role. They derive pleasure from being insulted, offended, or mistreated. Others permit it in order to have relationships with others; they doubt their ability to be genuinely loved and accepted, and they would rather be a scapegoat than have no relationships at all. Some others are naive: they lack the social skills to cope with those who hurt them. Scapegoating is a common phenomenon, which can be observed even in a group of animals. In counseling groups one often finds a scapegoat who is the victim of jokes, is teased, is confronted with probing questions or hurtful interpretations, or is kept on the "hot seat." When these occur in a counseling group, the scapegoat may be victimized by a sadistic person who pretends to be trying to help.

Since the disadvantages of putting someone on the "hot seat" and treating one client at a time have already been discussed in Chapter Six, it will suffice to state here that such methods tend to encourage clients to use the scapegoat as an object for their displaced aggressions. Instead, when a counselor observes a client being used as a scapegoat, he should reflect the feelings that he feels the scapegoat is experiencing.

Usually he has feelings of hurt plus some of the others described above. Such a reflection enables the hurt one to express how he feels and rallies support and understanding from the others. It also helps the hurter discover his impact on others and encourages him to search for new ways of relating to others. Sometimes when he has hurt others, the hurter will experience the role of scapegoat. Then his feelings of hurt also must be reflected. However, this is not sufficient. Members of the group should expect, and assist, both the scapegoat and the hurter to learn new ways of relating to others. Careful structuring may be needed here, lest clients become so afraid of hurting someone that they lose their spontaneity, or for fear of hurting them they grow reluctant to put pressure on each other to learn new ways of relating. Structuring and related discussion helps them distinguish between sadistic hurting and helping one another deal with hurtful material during the course of getting help.

The Socializer

The socializer is the one who wants to extend the counseling relationships into social relationships outside the group. He wants his fellow clients and the counselor to be his best friends. He so thoroughly enjoys *the quality* of his relationships with the members of his counseling group that he may wish to substitute these relationships for those with his important others. Rather than allowing this to happen, the members of his counseling group should help him perceive the counseling group for what it is—a temporary relationship in which he learns to cope with his problems and with his important others so that he can build new relationships with others outside his counseling group. Failure to deal openly with this problem often leads high school and college youth to resist termination of their counseling group. It also encourages clients to socialize with fellow clients during counseling.

Some counselors question the extent to which a counselor can or should control socializing of members outside of the counseling group. As a consequence of his experiences in treating more disturbed patients, Bach (1954) discussed this controversial point as follows:

> Clinical management of the natural tendency of emotionally disturbed patients to socialize with and to seek further support from each other outside the official clinical meetings is a controversial point among group therapists. Most group therapists accept their patients' socializing needs, but few make it an official part of the clinical program as we do. Classically oriented psychoanalysts see in socializing outside the therapeutic setting only obstruction to the therapeutic process. . . . (p. 114)

Bach encourages his patients to socialize. He feels that it relieves some of the tensions that build up during group sessions and enables clients to discover that in spite of their problems they can relate effectively to each other socially. Furthermore, he believes that they do reveal things about themselves within the relaxed social atmosphere that they may not reveal in the treatment group. He also expects his patients to bring back into their group the new material revealed during socializing. He believes that their custom of sharing and communicating all interpersonal interaction that occurred during the socializing tends to prevent misuse of acting out.

Nevertheless, there are at least four reasons for discouraging socializing: (1) it increases chances for confidences to be broken; (2) it tends to increase acting out; (3) it encourages clients to become dependent upon fellow clients for meaningful relationships, when instead they should learn to relate to their significant others; and (4) it enables them to escape from their responsibility for coping with resistance *within their treatment sessions.* Furthermore, socializing seems to increase drainage—the revelation of private material in social sessions rather than in the therapy session.

The Acting-Out Client

Acting out may be expressed as transference: a client may inappropriately express toward a group member feelings that he has for some important other person. Obviously, too, clients may act out with others outside their treatment group. Acting out also may be resistance—a substitute for remembering and coping with the problem within one's counseling group.

Ziferstein and Grotjahn (1957) described a patient for whom acting out was resistance. Escaping from the pain of remembering and dealing with relevant material, she fled to the pleasure of her sexual acting out:

> As long as this deep oral longing is not understood, interpreted, worked through, and integrated, it will lead to acting out. It would appear, then, that not only in the case of acting-out characters, but also in the case of acting out in the course of therapy, the basic cause of acting is the patient's repressed orality, and that acting out is essentially a defensive maneuver against orality. . . .
>
> Acting out is a form of activity whereby a patient unconsciously discharges repressed, warded-off impulses and relieves inner tension. Instead of remembering certain traumatic and therefore repressed experiences, the patient relives them. However, the patient is unaware of this fact, and to him his actions seem appropriate to his present situation. . . .
>
> There are people in whom the tendency to act out is prominent throughout life. These are the "acting-out" characters, who are frequently found to be oral individuals, with low tolerance for frustration or postponement of gratification, and with defects in superego and ego formulation. . . .
>
> Acting out is only a temporary, and not a satisfactory, solution. This analytic handling of acting out, as of any resistance, is prompt interpretation. With the help of interpretation, "acting out" is changed into "working through."
>
> Acting out may involve the patient in realistic troubles, sometimes of a serious nature. This may complicate the treatment if the therapist reacts with anxiety and tries to restrain the patient, by exercising his authority rather than by understanding and interpreting. The patient may then take advan-

tage of the therapist's anxiety and punish him by further acting
out, or he may react as to a forbidding parent with castration
fear or submissive compliance. The result may be a chaotic
situation, aggravated in part by the countertransference of the
therapist and the other group members. Most important: the
therapist and the group may vicariously enjoy the patient's
acting out and unconsciously encourage him, perhaps rationa-
lizing it with the idea that it's good for the patient to develop
the courage to gratify impulses, test reality, learn in the school
of life, etc. etc. In this situation the therapist and the group
members are behaving like parents of delinquent children
[Johnson and Szurek (1952)] who unwittingly encourage
their children to act out the parents' own repressed impulses.
(pp. 81–83)

This type of encouragement to act out occurs also in
groups of reasonably healthy clients. Two examples are described here. The first was an attractive college freshman who
joined a group of college undergraduates for assistance in
relating to peers. At the first session she revealed that she had
been married and divorced the previous summer. From her
description of her husband he seemed to have considerable sex
appeal, but they experienced poor sexual adjustment and she
left him after a few weeks. She also discussed a man whom
she was dating and with whom she was tempted to have inter-
course. During this discussion she solicited sympathy from the
group, cleverly, but subtly, attracted special attention from
two of the men, and seemed to appeal for her group to condone
her acting out. Though the members offered verbal objections
to her having an affair, they did condone it by their nonverbal
behavior and their laughter. A well-timed reflection by the
counselor, concerning her desire to have this behavior condoned and members' willingness to enjoy it vicariously, alerted
everyone to what was going on so that they all could state
openly what they felt. Consequently, they refused either to
condone or reject her wish to act out; they conveyed that she
must decide what was right for her and accept responsibility
for her own behavior.

An eleventh-grade boy (Ralph) told the members of his

high school counseling group about the way his unreasonable
father nagged him. Ralph had been very open in discussing
some other problems and had been very helpful to the others
during the six previous sessions. Everyone, including the counselor, grew obviously angry with Ralph's father. When Ralph
concluded that he would "smash him in the mouth" the next
time his father nagged him, they obviously supported the idea,
and no one picked up these feelings and helped the members
deal with them. Consequently, no one was surprised when
Ralph did have a fight with his father.

Wolf [in a panel discussion by Durkin, Glatzer, Kadis,
Wolf, and Hulse (1958)] stated that acting out is always
destructive and irrational but that it can be used therapeutically. In Ralph's case the counselor did use the acting out
therapeutically, but had he detected what was going on earlier,
he could have helped Ralph deal with these feelings without
hurting either himself or his father as he did.

". . . Acting out is a dramatic means of discovering per-
sistent problems and then discovering the means to deal with
them." (Wolf, p. 92). In the same panel discussion Glatzer
said:

> A therapist must not be involved in encouraging this blind,
> irrational behavior or in overstressing its possible benefits
> as abreaction any more than he would encourage resistance in
> any other form, instead of analyzing it. . . . What is needed,
> then, is not the opportunity to act out, to solidify the unwilling-
> ness to learn, but to stimulate understanding of its motivation
> and inappropriate quality so that it becomes ego-alien. Acting
> out seems to me like the hard core of resistance, and like all
> resistance it must be repeatedly worked through in order to
> attain what Fenichel (1945) describes as "the union with ego
> of what was previously warded off by it." . . .
> I don't think that an extended period of acting out makes
> it fuller or richer. It is still blind, driving behavior and it seems
> to me, nothing therapeutic is gained by permitting it to continue
> unanalyzed. Constant interpretation as soon as the therapist
> becomes aware that his patient is acting out and understands
> what he is doing (and this often gives the patient sufficient
> time to act out) tends to promote insight into his destructive
> behavior and seems to minimize its frequency. I cannot see why

acting out should be permitted to remain unanalyzed any longer than it takes the therapist time to recognize it and see its significance. . . .

One of the advantages of immediate handling of acting out in the group situation is that a spontaneous interpretation of acting out in a fresh setting seems to have a more dynamic effect. Permitting a patient to act out, make a fool or nuisance of himself, when the therapist is aware of what is going on, may constitute a greater narcissistic injury to the patient than early interpretation and help to further encapsulate his repressed memories. . . . (pp. 93–94)

The writer agrees with most of the excellent ideas quoted above:

1. A patient should be helped to recognize the phenomenon of acting out as early as possible.
2. Whenever possible it should be prevented by prompt action.
3. The acting-out patient should discover early that it is a kind of activity in which he or others can be hurt. (Whereas the authors quoted above would accomplish this by a well-timed interpretation, the writer would use reflection—for the reasons stated in Chapter Six. As suggested in Chapter Six, he would teach clients to recognize and cope with this phenomenon just as they do other forms of resistance.)
4. When acting out does occur, it can be used therapeutically within the group.

A counselor should not accept the notion that acting out is inevitable. Of course, it may happen sometimes, but much of it can be prevented. Perhaps it is more easily prevented with less disturbed clients than those of the authors quoted above. A carefully timed reflection brings the material into the open where it can be dealt with. The client tempted to act out is helped to understand his motivations better, learn new and better ways of solving his problems, and discover how fellow clients react to his irresponsible behavior. His fellow clients, in turn, often discover how they encourage and condone such behavior. Sometimes they discover that an acting-out client takes advantage of his being in treatment, using it to justify things he has wanted to do but ordinarily would not do. When the one who is or may be hurt as a consequence of a client's acting out is a member of the counseling group, or someone plays the part of the hurt one in re-enacting the scene, the counselor can reflect the hurt one's feelings and help both the hurt one and the hurter deal with the resulting problems. If, however, the counselor does this merely to shame the acting-out client, his response will be seen for what it is.

In any case, role playing (see Chapter Eight) can be used effectively to deal with acting out and to prevent it. Involving the one who is tempted to act out in describing the tempting setting, in selecting the role players from his counseling group, assigning them appropriate roles, acting out the scene, and listening to the reactions to the role playing provides him with rich feedback. Role playing also can give him practice in coping with such situations.

Although acting out can uncover repressed material to be dealt with in the treatment group, the counselor should try to prevent it whenever possible in order to protect those who may be hurt. Note also Glatzer's point that allowing a client to act out can further encapsulate repressed material—thus making it *less accessible to treatment*. Moreover, it is easier to help a client express and cope with his feelings for a transference object (or the real person) before he acts them out than it is to deal with the shame and embarrassment, as well as the underlying motivations for acting out, afterward.

The Hostile Client

What is known about the hostile client? How does he feel? What makes him hostile? Usually he has been hurt, let down, or abandoned by someone whose love and acceptance he needs. When he has given up, he no longer expects to be accepted or loved. He tends to be demanding, brutal, sullen, and defiant. It is difficult for others to prove to him that they want even to try to understand him. Whereas the aggressive person often steps upon others in moving toward his goal, it is an accident; the really hostile one, however, is often distracted from his goal in order to step upon someone. Those who try to help these clients must recognize that though both may appear to be hostile, they feel differently, hence they must be responded to differently. Counselors also must try to distinguish the acting-out client, who behaves in a hostile manner in order to avoid discussion of his problem, from the one who is really hostile.

When adolescents are pressured into counseling against their will, they appear to be hostile and they find it difficult to accept counseling. Even when they seem to cooperate, they often feel resentful, feeling that they do not need help themselves or that the important others who pushed them into counseling need it more than they do. Their counselor and fellow clients must discover and help them express such feelings before they can deal with problems that they really accept as their own.

Another type of client appears to be hostile when he actually feels inadequate or lacks the human-relations skills to cope with some specific situations. Frequently he is "badgered" by a teacher, a parent, or an employer or by a peer who is an intellectual bully, and he strikes back because he is overwhelmed or cornered. Like the trapped animal he would run away if he could, but he is caught and forced to fight. He needs to learn a wider repertoire of human relationships and verbal skills in order to express and deal with these feelings.

These so-called hostile clients tend to be especially threatening to beginning counselors who were formerly teachers. They are not used to allowing their students to express hostility. When it was expressed in their classrooms, they were caught in the power struggle, and they tend to perceive the expression of such feelings as defiance of them.

When the beginning counselor discovers: (1) that the client is not attacking him as a person but as a transference object; (2) how these various types of clients feel and how much each needs the group's aid; and (3) that a hostile client tends to reveal much therapeutically significant material about himself to which the counselor can respond, the counselor learns to relate to the hostile client and to empathize with him.

Difficult as it is for the hostile client to accept other members' efforts to empathize with him, this is what he needs. When they respond to him with genuine warmth, trying to understand how he feels and to help him express these feelings, and conveying their willingness to help him cope with these feelings, their confidence in his ability to change, and their expectation that he will change, he may doubt their sincerity but he tries to change. Previously he has learned to expect and to deal with hostility. When he does not get it, he looks for it anyway. Though he may be surprised, he does not feel like attacking them. Furthermore, he discovers that the members of his counseling group can really detect how he feels, and gradually he learns to detect and respond to others' feelings. This new way of relating to others becomes increasingly attractive as he learns to play their game—trying to understand them and to help them as well as to accept assistance from them.

The Monopolist

The first difficult client discussed was the resister. Most group therapists agree that the monopolist is a resister. Most of them also agree that he is a poor risk for group treatment.

A number of characteristics of the monopolist seem to make him a poor bet. Bach (1954) said that the monopolist's effort to rule the roost in a group is a defensive overreaction to neurotically feared attack or isolation from the group. The monopolist does seem to be a self-centered recognition-seeker who tries to maintain a place for himself in the center of the stage. As others enter the limelight he tries to upstage them. Some believe that he wants to prove that he is superior to everyone, including the counselor. He is certainly skilled in capturing and holding the speaker's role. Hence, he is able to focus discussion *on his preferred topics* and to divert attention from the topics he dislikes. In many ways he exhibits the traits of the pampered child. Most believe that he becomes highly threatened whenever anyone moves in to compete with him for the limelight—that he really feels very inadequate and maybe even unloved. Perhaps he fears isolation because he perceives himself either as having little to offer or as having inadequate relationship skills.

Perhaps some monopolists do not really believe that most of their associates have anything significant to say. Even among those who ask to join counseling groups, admitting dissatisfaction with their human-relations skills, high school and college counselors can expect to find some intellectual snobs. Many are bright and have some good ideas, but they often fail to differentiate between topics in which they are proficient and those of which they have only very superficial knowledge. In other words, various monopolists may feel very differently and for very different reasons. Hence, those who are able to reach and treat them must be able to identify and help each express the feelings he is experiencing. Most monopolists also need to learn and practice new relationship skills. All need *feedback from respected others* on how they affect others.

Perhaps the group is the best place to help the monopolist —difficult as it can be. At least among the younger, less disturbed who are treated in an educational setting, many can be helped in groups—especially when they are selected with care and they are assigned to groups with others whom they admire and who are strong enough to capture their attention and give them feedback. Often it helps to place such a student in a group with older, more mature students. It also helps to explore with him in the intake interview whether he can be sensitive to others' feelings, share time with others, and help others discuss openly what bothers them, as well as *discuss openly what really bothers him about himself.*

Bach's recommendation that the monopolist be accepted for group treatment on a probationary basis has merit. This is most effective when other members realize why the monopolist is accepted on a probationary basis, when he talks openly about why he needs their help, when they are helped to provide honest feedback the first time he tries to monopolize, and when he sincerely tries to accept and use the feedback they give him. He tends to be *shocked and hurt to learn how others react* to his monopolizing. When, for example, the counselor noticed that the other members were reacting to Frank negatively, the counselor said, "You get angry with Frank when he takes over. I guess it is pretty difficult for you to believe that he really wants to change and that he is really interested in what you want to discuss." When he exhibited shock to their frank response, they told him what they expected from him. Among other things they set a time limit on any single comment, reviewed with him what he wanted to work on, and, with the counselor's help, agreed on some things they could do to reinforce nonmonopolizing behavior. Though he found that it was difficult to live up to their expectations, he responded to the group pressure. He did not want to be perceived as a deviant in a group of peers whom he respected and admired. Most such clients also tend to be impressed with their fellow clients' sincere desire to help them. Furthermore, learning to listen to others and trying to help them tends to be highly satisfying and reinforcing, at least for the adolescent monopolizer.

Although Powdermaker and Frank (1953) found that ignoring, rebuffing, and questioning the monopolist were not effective, they did discover ways that fellow patients could help him (and in general these techniques support those described above):

> The common feature of successful techniques was that they made the patient aware of the meaning of his behavior with respect to his relations to the group at the time. It seemed helpful under different circumstances to hold the patient to a detailed examination of a single situation in his daily life that was relevant to the group situation, to examine with him his feelings about the immediate group at the point when he started to monopolize, and to call attention to the development of dissatisfaction on the part of the group and of the monopolist with the behavior. (p. 194)

Summary

When they begin group counseling, even experienced counselors can profit markedly from the assistance of an understanding supervisor or trusted colleague. With such assistance a counselor can discover those clients with whom he has difficulty coping effectively. Careful analysis of recorded counseling sessions enables the counselor to discover, with the assistance of such a person, the impact that these clients have on him, his impact upon them, and more effective techniques for coping with them.

A counselor must understand why certain clients are difficult for him, what their impact is on him and how he may cope with it, what these clients' unique feelings are and how to respond to them, and how he can involve other clients in helping each. This chapter has stressed the advantages of having other clients as well as the counselor try to identify and reflect each client's unique feelings in order to help each face up to his problems and to motivate each to search for his own best solutions. It is also important that clients develop the interpersonal skills to apply outside of the counseling group what they have learned to apply within it.

References

Bach, G. R. *Intensive Group Psychotherapy*, New York: The Ronald Press Company, 1954.

Durkin, Helen E., Henriette T. Glatzer, Asya L. Kadis, A. Wolf, and W. C. Hulse "Acting Out in Group Psychotherapy," *American Journal of Psychotherapy*, 1958, 12:87–105.

Fenichel, O. *The Psychoanalytic Theory of Neurosis*, New York: W. W. Norton & Company, Inc., 1945.

Freud, S. *New Introductory Lectures*, New York: W. W. Norton & Company, Inc., 1933.

Grater, H. A. "When Counseling Success Is Failure," *Personnel and Guidance Journal*, 1958, 37:233–235.

Johnson, A. M., and S. A. Szurek "The Genesis of Anti-Social Acting Out in Children and Adults," *Psychiatric Quarterly*, 1952, 21:323–343.

Lindemann, E. "Symptomatology and Management of Acute Grief," *American Journal of Psychiatry*, 1944, 101:141–148.

Powdermaker, Florence B., and J. D. Frank *Group Psychotherapy*, Cambridge, Mass.: Harvard University Press, 1953.

Talland, G. A., and D. H. Clark "Evaluation of Topics in Therapy Discussion Groups," *Journal of Clinical Psychology*, 1954, 10:131–137.

Ziferstein, I., and M. Grotjahn "Group Dynamics of Acting Out in Analytic Group Psychotherapy," *International Journal of Group Psychotherapy*, 1957, 7:77–85.

Chapter Ten

Counseling Adolescents in Groups

Most of the ideas so far presented apply to the counseling of adolescents as well as adults. In fact, the case material for Chapter Five dealt primarily with adolescents. Nevertheless, some special attention must be given to the adolescents. Why do they react as they do to adults' efforts to help them? Why does group counseling seem to be particularly appropriate for them? What are reasonable treatment goals for them? How may they be assisted by cooperative efforts of their important others? Some attention also will be given here to techniques other than group counseling that can help adolescents cope with the various forces in their lives, to recognize and use their own resources for self-actualization, and to further their normal development toward maturity.

Goals for Adolescents

Most of the adolescent's problems arise because important others fail to understand his unique needs and cannot help him fulfill these needs during the normal process of growing up. The literature on adolescent development is reviewed briefly here to help the counselor recall the adolescent's needs, recapture some of his feelings and empathize with him, and translate these needs into general goals. However, for the reasons stated in Chapter Two, no general goals are adequate. Best results are obtained when the client is encouraged to help develop specific goals in behavioral terms to meet his unique needs.

Ausubel (1954) concluded that adolescence is rigorous testing for the adequacy of the personality structure laid down in the childhood years. Though personality defects appear to be more glaring during this period, they tend to be only transitory disturbances. Even when personality defects are more basic, these maturing experiences merely aggravate the condition: "The actual terminal point for the appearance of most serious personality disorder is after, rather than during adolescence." (p. 511)

Unlike Hall (1904), who described adolescence as a period of storm and stress, Hurloch (1967) cited Gesell, Ilg, and Ames' (1956) findings to support the notion that it could better be described as a period of heightened emotionality. Many do tend to be irritable, to get excited more easily than adults do, and to explode more frequently than adults do because they lack the repertoire of human-relations skills to cope with significant others' confrontations and expectations. Hurloch concluded that except for those who experienced markedly deviant sexual development, most learned to cope with the problems they met as adolescents [Caplan (1956), Dunbar (1958), Frank and Frank (1955), and Jones and Bayley (1950)]: "During adolescence, those who deviate markedly from the norm for sexual maturing for their sex group are the ones most likely to experience heightened emotionality of a severe and prolonged type. This is not because of the maturing itself but because of the many personal and social problems deviant sexual maturing brings." (p. 77)

Hurloch cited Ayer and Corman's (1952) research to illustrate how the adolescent's view of himself as a participating member of society emerges during this period. His interest in national and world affairs is fostered in high school and college as well as by all the communication media. He thinks more deeply about challenging social problems than most adults realize. With his knowledge and his idealism he tends to become disappointed, disillusioned, and cynical with adults' complacency [Neidt and Fritz (1950)]. He cannot understand why adults do not appreciate his sincere desire to change things that obviously need to be changed. He thrives on genuine participation and on achieving changes by his own efforts. He also thrives on praise for real accomplishments.

Kirkpatrick (1952) discovered that adolescents are quick to spot an adult phony. They see their elders for what they are. Though adolescents can be difficult at times, and adults often wonder whether they will ever find themselves, Kirkpatrick concluded that most do, and without any permanent scars.

Garrison (1965) concluded from his review of the research literature that much of adolescents' anger response results from frustration of some goal-seeking activity. Youth are often pressured to work for others' goals, or feel that they are not permitted to make decisions that are rightfully theirs, or are expected to have aspirations that are inappropriate for them. Adolescents also tend to get angry when they are cornered or put on the spot. When they lack the verbal or social skills to cope with a bully, they strike back as the cornered wild animal does.

Ackerman (1955) reported several other characteristics of adolescents that influence their behavior in treatment groups. He concluded that the most striking aspect is their yearning to complete their incomplete selves. They feel compelled to accommodate to the rigorous requirements for full adult responsibilities: "During this phase, one observes their extraordinary sensitiveness to other persons' judgments of their worth, their constant concern with proving adequacy, their profound sense of vulnerability to criticism and attack from without. They are caught between the twin horns of conformity and defiance. It is small wonder that they show such trigger-edge irritability." (p. 249)

Ackerman also noted their conflict with authority and

their problems in developing relationships with the opposite sex. He reported that nowhere is their rawness and their need to prove themselves more vivid than in the relationship between the sexes. Each is acutely aware of the other and is highly sensitive to the other, but lacks the confident movements of the more experienced, mature adult.

The adolescent is seeking identity. He is trying to determine who he is, what he would like to do, and what he can do, and to develop the will and the self-confidence to do it. He is trying to learn to face his problems and to develop the skills for solving them. He also is struggling for independence from such important others as parents and teachers. However, there are times when he feels very dependent on them. With his increasing intellectual maturity, his struggle for independence, and his change in referent group from family to peers, he tends to question many of the previously accepted guidelines for his behavior—especially those stressed by his parents and his church. Peers' acceptance is highly valued.

Some adolescents are forced to rebel to achieve independence. For many the problem is that no one has ever really tried either to teach them independence or to involve them meaningfully in solving the problems they have recognized in their homes, schools, churches, and neighborhoods. Hence they become reactive; they fight for what they perceive to be their rights and try to call attention to social problems with demonstrations, strikes, riots, and youth gang activities (see Chapter Four). Though they rebel to avoid conformity, the rebellious tend to conform more than the conformist. The difference is that they are controlled by peers rather than by their significant adults and these adults' values and traditions. Sometimes they are used by unprincipled demagogues (who may be about their age, but more likely are young adults who pretend to understand them in order to use them).

When rebellion has no purpose except to fight conformity or to revolt against the establishment and all the traditions of the past, it is a neurotic reaction to authority. Healthy rebellion arises out of love for something—a recognition that something must be changed and a commitment to change that which is wrong. Healthy rebellers have goals. They recognize some specific changes that they believe must be made to improve their institutions. Furthermore, they want to be involved in defining the changes that need to be made; they are willing to learn how to make the changes; and they are willing to work hard to achieve these essential changes. They are willing to accept assistance from understanding adults who will listen to them, respect their ideas, and help them develop their resources for achieving their desired changes. They also are willing to accept sensitive adults' ideas and to cooperate with them to achieve their mutual objectives, but they react very negatively to adults who only pretend to cooperate and really want to manipulate or use them.

Unfortunately, many adults seem to assume that rebellion is necessary—that this is the way adolescents achieve their independence—and hence that adults must learn to tolerate it. When significant adults learn to empathize with adolescents, to listen to them when they want to discuss problems, to respect their ideas for resolving problems, to enlist their cooperation in solving problems, to involve them in developing meaningful limits (and to change and redefine them as they mature), and to expect them to maintain these limits, many of the heartaches and conflicts with which adolescents are confronted in growing up can be avoided. Adolescents can accept from understanding adults information and assistance in learning the skills they need in order to meet their increasing responsibilities. They also can accept their own dependency—even while they are trying to learn to be independent. For example, they see the value of reasonable limits, and they try to accept responsibility for maintaining them, but they also feel more secure when they know that their parents are strong enough to enforce these limits when they themselves are not able to do so.

What is required of significant adults to foster independence, to provide information, and to teach the essential human-relations skills is herculean. Even parents who know what they should do tend to assert their authority, demand respect, and get caught up in a power struggle. They criticize and blame the adolescent when he needs encouragement—when, in fact, encouragement pays off much better than discouragement [Dinkmeyer and Dreikurs (1963)]. The adolescent needs to know that his significant others believe in him and that they are willing to help him meet his responsibilities. Bernard (1957) also observed that adolescents must earn security and that they tend to earn it with intellectual, social, and physical skills: "The love of others, their protection and guidance, are important to the extent that they serve as encouragement to building of such skills on the part of the individual." (p. 313) The ways in which significant others can be taught to provide this quality of assistance are discussed later in this chapter.

Adolescents' needs can be summarized as general goals for group counseling as follows:

1. Search for identity and meaningful goals.
2. Increased understanding of himself and of his special interests, abilities, and aptitudes.
3. Adequate information about his environment and the choices available to him.
4. Improved skills in assimilating and appraising information about himself, important others such as friends or possible employers, and opportunities available to him.
5. Added confidence in his ability to face his problems and solve them.
6. Increased sensitivity to others' needs and improved skills in helping them satisfy their needs.
7. Improved communication skills—learning to convey real feelings directly, and with consideration for others' feelings.
8. Improved social skills.
9. Learning to practice independent behavior.
10. Learning to cope with authority figures.
11. Learning to participate in developing and maintaining limits on his own behavior.
12. Improved understanding and ability to cope with physical and emotional changes associated with maturation.
13. Improved skills in learning to live roles associated with maturation.

Group Counseling Meets Adolescents' Needs

Described below, for each of the needs listed above, are some ways in which group counseling can contribute to its fulfillment, as well as some ways in which other services can supplement group counseling.

Search for identity is a central theme for the adolescent. He wants to know who he is, what he can become. This is reinforced by our emphasis on individual success, by parents' ambitions for their children, and by the school's expectations that students will make at least tentative plans for vocations and education beyond high school. Most adolescents know many things about themselves and they know that they are important to some people. At the same time they have many doubts about themselves—often more than they think most other adolescents have, and certainly more than the adults they know and admire had when they were adolescents. For some these feelings can be dispelled by good reading material on adolescent psychology and by voluntary discussion groups, but neither of these can provide the warm, accepting atmosphere that a college freshman portrayed in describing her group-counseling experiences as a high school senior (five girls and a young male counselor) :

> As the weeks passed, I learned to talk about more facets of me and to make more daring decisions. The relationship I had with the girls was unique because, for one, I could talk about the real me with no fear of being attacked. . . .
>
> We all talked about our abilities to express emotion, about our role as women in a working world, and about our work as students. I was more concerned than other girls about my role as a career woman. I wanted a career and a home. . . .
>
> We all found ourselves growing up in the group. . . . We had gained self-confidence regarding social situations and our abilities to achieve our goals. We were more sure of accomplishing our goals because we had learned to set realistic goals. Our confidence in social situations was inspired by the open, honest relationship we had in the group. Finally, we had taken on some decision-making responsibility in the group; we were

treated like adults there, so we wanted to act like adults. [L.
Ohlsen (1966), pp. 401–402]

Within such a group (especially with both boys and girls
present) an adolescent discovers that he is someone special.
He also discovers that other teenagers whom he admires and
respects have problems, some perhaps more serious than his
own. Furthermore, in spite of his faults, they really accept him
and they are committed to help him learn to relate to important others outside the counseling group as well as to richly
relate to him within their group. Experiencing such genuine
acceptance strengthens his ego—gives him the self-confidence
and the courage to face up to his problems and to solve them.

Increased self-understanding should have begun prior to
adolescence. Very early in life understanding parents and
teachers should have helped him discover what he has a right
to expect from himself. Even when this has been done well,
the adolescent tends to face many questions about his interests, abilities, and aptitudes that will require thorough self-
appraisal with the individual assistance of a competent
counselor, and often some special testing, carefully interpreted
by a counselor for the individual. Possessing this kind of
information, the adolescent is better able to explore his real
self with fellow clients, sharing his positive feelings about his
strengths, explaining why he cannot accept and use certain
strengths, and revealing his areas of doubt—wondering to
what extent his weaknesses will block certain plans. His fellow
clients' ability to empathize and to accept him provides the
support he needs to face up to his weaknesses—then to correct
them if he can do so with reasonable effort or to accept them
and to adapt his plans accordingly.

Obtaining adequate information about his options and
environment is a problem for everyone, but especially for
adolescents. Who should go to college? What does one need
to know to choose a college? How can one get ready for
scholarship and admission testing programs? What can one
do to increase his chances for getting off to a good start in

college? What problems do young people meet on their first job? How may they cope better with them? How does one get a job? How can one make the most of his opportunities in high school? How can one best meet a girl (or boy) whom he would like to date? How can one decide when he is really in love?

Though adolescents may sometimes appear to be flippant, they are seriously concerned to learn more about their opportunities and to improve their understanding of their environment. Many of them are naïve and they know it, and they are embarrassed about it. Many of their questions can be answered by directed reading—especially when they are given an opportunity to discuss and clarify what they learned in small voluntary discussion groups or in counseling groups where they feel it is safe to ask their questions and say what they think. Within the safe atmosphere of a counseling group, they also *enhance their own self-respect by helping others.* Rarely do today's adolescents feel as genuinely needed and appreciated as they do in counseling groups. (They also can experience this feeling of genuine worth when their family council openly deals with its problems and the parents exhibit genuine respect for their children's needs and ideas.)

Improved skill in assimilating and appraising information about one's opportunities can be acquired in the ways just discussed. However, one must also learn where to find validating information and how to make decisions. When an adolescent fails, he can profit from the assistance of fellow clients in appraising his decisions and actions and in planning for new ones. Failure alone teaches the adolescent nothing except how one can be hurt, but with the assistance of accepting others (especially peers) he can discover why he failed and how he may attack the problem again, discuss openly how he was hurt, why he may be reluctant to try again, and discover why he must try again. Where the problem involves new or threatening relationships, he can even practice his new approaches by role-playing the encounter.

Understanding teachers also can do much to help youth assimilate and appraise information. They can look for and take note of instances in which youth displayed good judgment in class discussion and in written work. They also can try to limit their discouraging behavior, trying to help youth learn from their mistakes rather than merely criticizing them. Conscientious teachers appreciate the assistance of accepting counselors in learning to play this supportive role more effectively. Techniques that a counselor can use to do this are discussed later.

Added confidence in his ability to face and solve his problems develops in a counseling group. When an adolescent discovers that other teenagers have problems, are willing to deal openly with their problems, and can solve them, he develops more confidence in himself and the treatment process. Good models have a tremendous impact on adolescents and can teach them how to relate openly and to help others. Ackerman (1955) found that adolescents catch on quickly to the notion of reaching behind mere talk to respond to genuine feelings. They learn how to pick up the real feelings revealed by such nonverbal behavior as body posturing, facial expressions, and motor behavior. Ackerman also found that he could foster the use of these nonverbal cues by sharing his bases for his interpretations.

Improved sensitivity to others' needs and improved skills for helping others are developed in a counseling group in the ways discussed above.

Adolescents also learn, in the ways just discussed, to *communicate* their real feelings and needs. A family conference can be used effectively to further this process. If, even after role-playing a scene in a counseling group, the adolescent does not feel adequate to face and deal with a family conflict, the counselor can arrange a family conference (or one for only him and his parents) in which the adolescent is given an opportunity to reveal how he has been hurt in the home, how he feels about them (and usually he feels much more positive toward them than he has let them know), and what he would like from them (and usually his most important wants are much more acceptable than they realized). During such a family conference the counselor helps the *other mem-*

bers listen to the adolescent—helps him express himself. The counselor also helps the adolescent listen to his family as they discuss their feelings for him, thereby increasing his sensitivity to others' needs. Finally, he helps them to agree at least on some tentative solutions. Often he helps them establish a family council, providing them with a technique for dealing with family problems and for helping adolescents improve communication skills. Such a structure also enables adolescents to help parents function more effectively as parents, accepting and fulfilling their roles as models for their children. *Improved communication* is also engendered by consultation with parents and teachers.

Improved relationship skills learned in such meaningful groups as family councils, classroom discussions, voluntary discussion groups, and counseling groups can be used to *improve social skills*. Ohlsen (1964) described meaningful social programs and extraclass activities that can be developed in schools to provide social experiences and leadership training for youth.

Independent behavior can be studied, practiced, and reinforced in a counseling group. Adolescents discover there that their ideas are respected, that they as well as others do foolish things in trying to achieve independence, and that their fellow clients can provide helpful feedback and suggestions for improving their behavior. They also learn, by role playing as well as talking, to *convey to authority figures what they want* and why they feel justified in their expectations.

Important as these experiences are for adolescents, perhaps even more can be accomplished in separate discussion groups for parents and teachers. Parents and teachers can better accept adolescents and their responsibilities for them when they discover for themselves, not only from reading but also from observing adolescents and talking frankly with them, (1) what really bothers the adolescents with whom they are involved; (2) how they feel and how much they really want acceptance, understanding, and assistance in coping with their new selves; (3) how much they appreciate assistance in developing independence in preference to fighting for it; (4)

what it means to adolescents to be respected, to have their ideas seriously considered and at least sometimes accepted; (5) the extent to which they will try to get along with authority figures who try to empathize with them; (6) the extent to which they use important adults as models—copying bad characteristics as well as good ones. However, it still will not be easy for adults to help adolescents learn to be independent, because most of the adults' models have used authoritarian approaches in trying to cope with adolescents. Beleaguered adults will recognize and appreciate a consultant's assistance.

The rationale has already been presented for giving adolescents an opportunity *to participate in developing and maintaining limits for their own behavior.* Obviously, it helps teach them to accept the responsibilities that accompany increased independence. Equally crucial are the experiences that develop meaningful values and reasonable expectations and provide good models. When important others failed to provide such essential positive influence, Gadpaille (1959) noted from his experiences in treating delinquent adolescents that:

> The great majority of such adolescents I have interviewed came from such disrupted and rejecting homes that they were never able to feel that their needs could or would be fulfilled by their parents. There was no real benefit to be gained by "being good" and conforming to the demands of their parents, and the resentment of this state of affairs spread to include all authority. The only way to get what they wanted was to take it by force, considering only themselves. Since this learned pattern is associated with considerable pleasure impulse gratification, they become fixated in it.
>
> It should be stressed here that the delinquent population from which the observations of this communication are drawn is, I think, a typical one. Most of these adolescents were not the products of criminal subcultural groups or of rigid, punitive societies. They were primarily products of homes in which social values were, at least, verbally stressed, but were stressed without adequate parental reward for adherence to those values. (p. 277)

These important others who should have helped these adolescents develop meaningful values and served as models for them in their daily lives were phonies, and hence adolescents rejected both the people and their values. Adolescents need models who try to live the values they preach. However, youths' models need not be perfect. In fact, many good models have their greatest impact when they discuss with adolescents the significance of their values for themselves, the problems they are facing in trying to be the kind of adults they would like to be, and enlist the adolescents' assistance in reinforcing the behavior they are trying to learn to practice. Significant others also must possess the ego strength to enforce the limits that adolescents have helped to define. Unfortunately, many authority figures do not possess the ego strength, the knowledge of adolescents, the human-relations skills, and the confidence in their adolescents to fulfill these roles. Many are afraid to do what is necessary lest the adolescent challenge their authority or reject them and their love.

Within an effective counseling group, adolescents discover fellow clients who are good models. They also discover their peers' models and how models have shaped these fellow clients' behavior. (Good books, especially biographies, also can provide powerful models for youth. Once they discover the value of such models, they often suggest relevant books for each other.) They observe their peers' search for reasonable compatibility between real selves and ideal selves; they help others change their attitudes and behaviors; and they help them learn to convey their new selves to important others outside their counseling group. Eventually they conclude that they can achieve these goals, too. Observing others solve their problems increases the adolescent's confidence in his ability to solve his own problems.

Improved understanding and ability to cope with physical and emotional changes is achieved in group counseling for the very reasons stated above. In this meaningful relationship with admired and trusted peers adolescents can learn to discuss their new feelings, how to cope with these feelings and others' expectations of them (for example, what a date expects). They discover that they can talk about their concern about their size, personal grooming, condition of skin, appetite, health, sexual development, social development, and attractiveness to the opposite sex.

Counselors also can enhance normal development by preparing teachers and parents to answer adolescents' questions. In discussion groups a counselor can help teachers and parents discuss, and role-play coping with, such communication problems as (1) their own discomfort and embarrassment with their adolescent's questions; (2) their sensitivity to his emotional readiness for the information; (3) their intelligent use of good reading material to answer his questions and to open up topics for discussion; (4) their good sense to stop when they have answered his questions to his satisfaction; (5) their ability to accept his questions seriously—no matter how naïve or irrelevant they may find them; (6) their ability to answer *his* questions for him *now* rather than answer the related questions that they wished someone had answered for them; (7) their own maturity to recognize and admit when they lack adequate information to answer his questions; and (8) their ability to recognize and help him discuss the feelings behind his questions, and when appropriate to refer him for assistance that they are not able to give.

Improving skills to learn and live new roles ties in directly with the previous paragraphs. Fulfilling this need also relates directly to the adolescent's search for identity, increased understanding of himself, and improved social skills. To discover that others are struggling with similar problems makes his own more acceptable; seeing others learn to cope with their problems is encouraging; and helping them increases his respect for himself. Thus group counseling is especially appropriate for adolescents. It enables them to satisfy some of their strongest needs, especially in providing real assistance to peers while obtaining assistance from them.

Special Considerations for Counseling Adolescents in Groups

Like the difficult clients described in Chapter Nine, adolescents require the counselor's understanding. He must try to detect and reflect each adolescent's *unique feelings*. To be helped by group counseling the adolescent must discover that it is safe for him to discuss how he really feels, that others care enough to help him face and resolve his problems, that they expect him to change, that they will give him an opportunity to practice new ways of behaving, and will help him evaluate his successes and failures at trying new behaviors.

Berman (1954) concluded that the counselor's own feelings about himself determine to a large extent whether the above goals can be achieved in a group:

> I should like to stress again that the ability of the therapist to understand the patient is determined to a considerable extent by how well or how poorly he understands himself. The presence in the therapist of a blind spot related to his own adolescence may handicap him in the performance of his professional services. Such a scotoma will cause him to be aloof, timid, hostile or lacking in empathy for the adolescent. It will be the therapist's trust or mistrust of the adolescent, his fears and dislikes, and his positive feelings which will strongly determine how well or how poorly the therapy is managed.

> Adolescent patients most often find themselves in a most uncomfortable situation. Almost invariably they are brought to therapy against their will. They are made to feel that they are culprits and that whatever the difficulty is, the problem of doing something about it rests solely with them. Adolescent patients are defensive, frightened, disorganized, bewildered and suspicious. Whether they are passive and seemingly compliant or overtly hostile, they enter treatment with misgivings. So it is with caution that they permit the therapist to become an ally, as a possessor of knowledge in living which they are eager to have and as an understanding person who can help them formulate more constructive values which meet their particular needs. (p. 241)

Obviously Berman described adolescent patients who were forced to accept psychotherapy. Nevertheless, when conflict does arise between an adolescent and an authority figure, adults assume too readily that it was the adolescent's fault. Adolescents know what really happened, and they do not expect adults to be perfect, but they do expect them to try to be honest and fair. Perhaps this is why they are so sensitive to others', especially adults', criticisms. Consequently those who offer group counseling to adolescents must try to convey that group counseling is offered to them because the counselor believes that *they can be helped*—not because they have done something wrong and therefore it is their responsibility to learn to adapt to some specific situation. Unless the school counselor is very careful, he can portray himself as defending the authority figures in the school or home and thus markedly reduce his chances of helping youth.

As reported in Chapter Five, every client should be selected for group counseling with care. Adolescents, in particular, want to know precisely what they are getting into, what will be expected from them, for whom the group is planned, and what they can expect to get from it. When a school counselor describes group counseling for adolescents, he should give examples of problems which his clients have discussed in groups. Such presentations clarify what is expected, convey that the groups are designed for normal youths who are struggling with normal problems they faced in growing up, help them discover the relevance of group counseling for them, and encourage them to ask their questions in order to clarify expectations. The counselor also should describe the intake interview and its purposes. Careful discussion of all these items helps to structure the group counseling, to increase readiness for it, and to increase commitment for it. This approach also conveys respect for the adolescent's ability to appraise a service, to decide for himself whether he can profit from it, and to accept responsibility for developing and maintaining a therapeutic climate in his treatment group. Thus, it tends to counteract the negative feelings adolescents have felt when dragged into treatment in other settings.

The impact of an attractive group for changed behavior was discussed in Chapter Four. Given the adolescent's peer orientation, this is even more significant for adolescent groups. The techniques for selecting clients described in Chapter Five increase the attractiveness of counseling groups.

The fact that everyone who requests admission cannot be admitted increases the attractiveness of group counseling. Furthermore, expecting them to demonstrate their own readiness for group counseling (including their ability to talk openly about what bothers them) challenges adolescents in a positive way. To them it seems to convey: "We want you. Are you ready? Can you make the necessary commitment to convince yourself as well as me?"

The writer tends to be more active, especially in early sessions, with junior and senior high school groups than with college students or adults. Though they appreciate the opportunity to define their expectations and to take an active role in developing and in maintaining a therapeutic climate, younger people seem to have less tolerance for ambiguity than college students and adults. They do not want to be told what to do, but they want help in deciding what decisions they must make to function effectively. They also learn best from a good model. They learn from observing the counselor's behavior how to help others. As they improve their skills in helping others, the counselor can gradually reduce his activity.

Because adolescents are very sensitive to others' judgments of their worth, they tend to perceive the counselor's use of interpretation as attack [Katz, Ohlsen, and Proff (1959)]. On the other hand, their interests in reaching behind mere talk to uncover genuine feelings make subtle reflections, and even use of interpretation by clients, attractive to adolescents. Adolescents' interpretation of behavior seems to enable them to help fellow clients recognize the consequences of their inappropriate behavior and to nudge them to take action. They perceive interpretation by fellow clients as a cooperative effort to help each achieve increased understanding of himself rather than as an expert's demonstration of his superior knowledge. Finally, adolescents are less inclined than adults to dwell on

history and to use interpretation as a basis for intellectualizing, thus avoiding affective material. Hence, *clients'* limited
use of interpretation may be more acceptable for adolescents
than for adults.

Katz, Ohlsen, and Proff (1959) reported that role playing
was notably effective for adolescents. It facilitates spontaneous expression of feelings. As reported in Chapter Eight,
it also helps adolescents communicate ideas and feelings and
gives them a chance to practice human-relations skills required
for specific situations. Head (1962) said that: "The appropriate use of sociodrama is particularly indicated for helping the
adolescent increase his knowledge, understanding, and insights
into his own behavior. These insights and understandings are
achieved through identification with roles, real or fancied, of
persons portrayed in actual conflict situations." (p. 128)

Head also concluded that the adolescent reveals his perception of himself through his choice of roles and his portrayal
of the roles he plays in sociodrama.

Finally, adolescents need assistance in conveying their
new selves to important others and in helping these important
others learn to live with their new selves. Broedel, Ohlsen,
Proff, and Southard (1960) found that it is not sufficient to
help adolescents change their attitudes and behavior. Adolescents also must be helped to convey their new selves to important others; to share with important others the frustrations
that they experience in learning to apply outside their counseling groups what they learned in these groups; and to state
clearly what they need from important others to establish new
ways of living. With their clients' knowledge and approval,
school counselors can further this process through feedback to
individual teachers and parents.

Voluntary Guidance Groups

Secondary school and college students who have not recognized the need for group counseling often will elect to participate in voluntary discussion groups. At least they can be

provided information that they recognize they need and be given a chance to discuss its implications for them. As with the introduction of group counseling, best results are achieved when the leader describes the nature of such discussion groups, their objectives, what is expected of participants, and how members select their own topics. Here are some examples of discussion topics:

1. How do I go about getting the job I would like most?
2. What are some of the common problems young people meet on their first job? How may they be avoided? How can one cope with them?
3. How can I decide whether I should go to work or to college?
4. How should I choose a college?
5. How can I evaluate chances for scholarships, loans, and other financial aid?
6. What can I do to increase my chances for getting off to a good start in college?
7. What do my parents have a right to expect from me? What should I expect from them?
8. What are the advantages and disadvantages of going steady?
9. How does group counseling differ from these discussion groups? How can one decide whether or not to join a counseling group?

Usually the school counselor takes the initiative to organize such discussion groups. Eventually he should prepare teachers to accept responsibility for such groups so that he can devote his time to counseling.

Varied techniques have been used to involve students in these discussion groups. After several successful trial discussions for which students have suggested topics, a leader may ask the participants to suggest the names of students and faculty, from whom he selects an advisory committee for a given school building or a college residence hall. This advisory committee is charged with soliciting discussion topics from available participants, selecting discussion leaders from the students, and suggesting stimuli to kick off discussions.

These are student-centered discussions. Students suggest the topics and the persons to present ideas. A student-faculty committee represents them in planning and coordinating their discussions.

Teacher Discussion Groups

Increasingly school counselors are learning to function as consultants to teachers and parents as well as to counsel children. Their goal is to help these significant others further normal development. Most parents and teachers do care about youth, but many get so bogged down in their efforts to control them that they fail to exhibit their caring, to involve them in developing meaningful working relationships, and to encourage them.

Though obviously some individual consultation is necessary, much can be accomplished in teacher and parent discussion groups. Effective teacher discussion groups have certain common elements: (1) they are planned for those who want assistance; (2) those who want assistance are encouraged to help plan the sessions designed for them; (3) participation is voluntary; and (4) their leader is a nonevaluator. Thus, the group becomes a safe place in which teachers can admit their mistakes, share their ideas, and ask their questions. For the counselor to function effectively as a human-relations or psychological consultant to teachers, his role should be so defined that he can qualify as a nonevaluative discussion leader. Obviously, such a leader also must have the necessary professional knowledge and skills to help teachers better understand adolescents, to facilitate their sharing appropriate information in child-study sessions [or in guidance-committee meetings, Ohlsen (1964)], to diagnose learning and behavior problems, and to share ideas on how to deal with specific students and how to use behavior-modification techniques.

For example, a counselor met recently with a group of fifteen senior high school teachers who were concerned about helping their students meet their responsibilities for integrating transported Negro students into their all-white school. Everyone recognized that there are no "pat" answers, but everyone accepted for the group believed that by working together and sharing both their problems and their suggestions they could help all the students cooperate in making the experiment work.

In another school a counselor organized an informal seminar on adolescent psychology for from fifteen to twenty teachers. As in the seminar described above everyone sat in a circle; they listened, they shared information and ideas, and they learned to help others as well as to receive help for themselves. In that sense they behaved like the members of a counseling group. In another sense they differed from a counseling group: they talked about the problems they met as teachers rather than about their own personal problems. The group also was too large to be a very effective counseling group. Even for such discussion groups perhaps the number should be limited to fifteen. Before the close of each session they were given several suggested readings that might help them prepare for the next discussion topics, and to a degree this made this seminar similar to Powell's (1948) seminars on great books. These teachers searched for ideas that would help them understand adolescents better, relate to them more effectively, and help each integrate and apply what he learned.

Hertzman (1959) has conducted some very interesting but quite different seminars. His seminars were designed to improve teachers' mental-hygiene skills in the classroom. Workentin (1955) combined formal instruction in therapeutic methods with therapy:

> The teacher cannot avoid contributing to the affective learning of students. His very position before a class makes the teacher a recapitulation of other parental figures, whose attitudes are inadvertently learned by students; yet the social responsibility for such affective learning may not always be consciously acknowledged by the teacher. Students are even more likely to be quite unaware of the unacknowledged therapeutic parent-child relationship. All concerned will readily deal openly with intellectual needs, but often remain silent regarding

emotional needs. In the present experiment this was changed to place conscious emphasis on feelings, attitudes, and motivation. The purpose was to determine the value of directly therapeutic approach by the teacher. (p. 79)

Group psychotherapy with grade school teachers and medical students, conducted one hour per week for two school years, was possible with very satisfactory results. The response of the groups was positive and encouraging. In both experiments, follow-up contacts made two and three years later indicated that growth which was encouraged by the group sessions was continuing.

In the preliminary work with teachers, the therapist was primarily helping the group to permit themselves to consider their feelings about their work and themselves. There was a loosening of rigid teaching attitudes. Teachers were helped to take their feelings seriously as related to children, co-workers, and parents. The developing respect in the teacher for herself as a person then in turn resulted in more concern for the emotional development of her pupils. However, the changes seen in the teachers were not of a deep personality reintegration. The therapist had simply helped the teacher to use more adequately and with less fear some capacities already present. (p. 82)

When such therapy sessions are provided on a voluntary basis for the members of a school staff by an outside consultant, good results can be expected. For example, a college counselor provided such treatment for a group of school principals. His clients had earned doctorates recently and they were frustrated by their own failure to apply what they had learned in graduate education. As one of them said, "Now I know many new ways of handling my administrative problems better than I did, but I behave as a principal much as I did before completing my doctorate." Before starting the counseling group the counselor screened every prospective client very carefully to make certain that everyone was committed to talk about his problems, to change his own behavior, and to help others change their behavior. Everyone admitted perceived the rest as trustworthy. Within this safe environment they faced up to the problems that they met on the job and changed their behavior. This one academic year of intensive treatment really helped these administrators develop and apply functioning leadership skills.

For both of the latter two examples outside consultants were employed to provide intensive treatment. Generally this is a good policy for such treatment; a counselor should not provide counseling for his colleagues. Relevant American Psychological Association (1953) ethical standards on this matter are:

> Psychologists should not enter into clinical relationships with members of their own family, with intimate friends, or with persons so close that their welfare might be jeopardized by the dual relationship.
>
> 1. In the case of associates, students, and acquaintances, the psychologist has the responsibility of assessing the difficulties which ensue in establishing a clinical relationship and to refuse assistance if there is a possibility of harm to the client.
> 2. If there is a tentative decision to work with a person with whom the psychologist has other relationships, the nature of the situation and the possible difficulties should be carefully explained and the decision left to the person involved.
> 3. The principle does not bear upon supervisory relationships in the training of therapists. (p. 52)

Parents' Groups

Parent discussion groups like the first two teacher seminars described above have been used to help parents to better understand their children, to learn more effective child-rearing methods, and to find encouragement and support to apply what they learn. When parents accept responsibility for changing their behavior and participate in planning such seminars, the experience is more productive than are formal lecture courses.

Such books as *Children: A Challenge* [Dreikurs and Soltz (1964)] and *Between Parent and Teenager* [Ginott (1969)] have often been used for parent discussion groups. Such books can provide ideas in child-rearing practices, but the therapeutic forces of the group are needed to enable parents to apply these ideas. The format described above for teacher seminars seems to work well: four or five couples sit in a circle with the leader, sharing their ideas and developing the courage and self-confidence to behave differently. From their reading each couple usually identifies some specific child-rearing behaviors they wish to change, decide what each can do to help his spouse change, and decide on some specific reinforcers they can use to enhance changed behavior. Within such a setting the leader is less tempted to become the expert—the one who tells parents what to do. The more responsibility parents accept for their own learning and for changing their behavior, the greater the chances are that they will use what they learn to live more effectively with each other and their children.

Group counseling for parents also can be used effectively. Because some parents are reluctant to discuss their problems openly in front of their spouses and deal with their real feelings for each other, some counselors have tended to separate couples for group counseling. Though having both spouses in the same group can sometimes be difficult, it tends to yield best results. To profit most from the experience, however, each should be helped to discuss what worries and upsets him about himself rather than to merely gripe about his spouse. As the husband talks, the wife should be reinforced to respond to his comments empathically. She should be encouraged to function as the counselor's helper, trying to capture her mate's feelings and help him express his feelings, and he should do the same when she talks about herself. Such experiences enable each to empathize better with the other. With such an atmosphere they also learn to face conflict and to deal with it. According to Lerner's (1964) findings this is crucial for their children's adjustment as well as their own improved relationships.

Recently therapists have used a variety of approaches for family group counseling. Just a few examples of this technique will be described briefly.

Bowen (1961) arranged for the members of a patient's

family to live in the hospital and to be treated with the patient. He found that individuals behave quite differently outside their families than within them. He also found that parents of hospitalized patients held many strong opposing views. In particular they disagreed most strongly on the management of the patient. Bowen's goal was to help members of the family to define, discuss, and solve their own problems.

Guerney (1964) provided training for small groups of parents to prepare them to conduct play-therapy sessions at home for their children while being treated in their weekly sessions with other parents:

> Parent groups consist of mothers and fathers, about equally divided, who are not spouses. Because of the unique problems presented by the approach, flexibility of the group therapist's approach is necessary. Instructional techniques are used, including demonstration play sessions conducted by the therapist, and role-playing techniques. But when exploration of parental feelings and attitudes is involved in the instruction and later discussions, the group therapist is relatively client centered. Intensive probing and interpretation are generally not used.
>
> The manner in which the child play sessions are to be conducted is intended first to break the child's perception or misperception of the parents' feelings, attitudes, or behavior toward him. Second, they are intended to allow the child to communicate thoughts, needs, and feelings to his parents which he has previously kept from them, and often from his own awareness. . . . Third, they are intended to bring the child—via incorporation of newly perceived attitudes on the part of his parents—a greater feeling of self-respect, self-worth, and self-confidence. (p. 305)

Obviously Guerney's technique was designed for parents of young children, but it can be readily adapted for use with parents of adolescents. Instead of teaching parents to do play therapy, perhaps a counselor should help parents learn to listen, to communicate better how they really feel, and to develop better methods for dealing with family problems—such as a family council.

Freeman, Klein, Riehman, Lukoff, and Heisey (1963) described a sociologically oriented group technique for families. Its purpose is to provide the family with insight at the social level of external reality. It promotes, facilitates, and guides communication. The counselor tries to help the members of a family systematically improve their problem-solving skills:

> The focus is on the social process and the reciprocal relationships of the members as demonstrated by their social functioning. Emphasis on the external group interactions rather than the individual internalized conflicts is achieved by coordinating group process about a common group problem, the goal being group solution of the problem. Repeated goal-confrontation encouraged by the counselor aims at a conscious alternation of the interactions, and therefore problem solving. (p. 169)

Dreikurs, Corsini, Lowe, and Sonstegard (1959) divide each session into five phases: counseling with parents, counseling with children, reports by playroom director and important others such as teachers, interpretation of the purposes of behavior, and recommendations to parents. They have found that families can learn from others by observing others being counseled and by helping them interact with each other. The counselor also helps the members of a family learn to develop a genuine feeling of belonging and to cooperate in solving their own problems as a family unit in their own family council.

Fullmer and Bernard (1964) have developed another type of Adlerian family group consultation for helping members of a family understand interpersonal relationships such as parent-parent, parent-child, child-child, child-teacher, child-other significant adult, and so on. They try to see the entire family at once along with several other families. The focus is on the here and now—helping the members of the family adapt to their life situation in constructive ways.

> The counselor shuns authoritarian advice giving and concentrates mainly on clarifying statements and situations and

on guiding group members toward more emotional involvement in the counseling process. The counselor will find that he can diagnose these problems better if he pays attention to the non-verbal behavior of the family. (p. 225)

Although the writer agrees with these family group treatment authorities that an individual's problems often develop within his family and that the members of a family must learn to solve these problems, he does not encourage long-term family treatment. Instead, he helps members of a family learn to face and deal with their conflicts, to express their real feelings for each other (positive as well as negative), and to provide encouragement for each other. He tries to help them discover how they hurt each other with the self-righteous, nagging, and discouraging behaviors, how they can encourage each other, and how they can reinforce encouraging behaviors. In other words, he tries to help them develop within their families genuine feelings of acceptance, belonging, and respect, and he tries to improve their communication with each other.

When one or more members require more help than can be provided within a reasonably short time (say, eight weeks), then he tries to help the members of the family understand why this additional treatment is needed and what they can do to reinforce changed behavior during treatment and afterward. Often the counselor must arrange for this client who is treated outside the family to meet with the family to help him convey how he has changed, what he would like from them as he is now, and what they may expect from him. The counselor also may wish to encourage the other members of the family to discuss how they can reinforce his new behaviors and attitudes. Adolescents can be counseled effectively in groups without involving their significant others, but many adolescents' problems can be prevented by helping their significant others, and the gains achieved can be better reinforced and maintained with the cooperation and assistance of significant others.

Summary

Adolescents' domination by peers, their need to help others, and their suspicion of adults' desire to control them makes group counseling more attractive to them than individual counseling. The safe, accepting climate of a counseling group enhances the adolescent's understanding of himself and his environment; the development of his ego strength, his skills in appraising information and alternatives available to him, and a broader repertoire of social and human-relations skills; his search for identity and life goals, his awareness of others' needs and expectations, his efforts to improve his communication skills, his independence of action, his awareness of new role expectations, and his confidence and skills to live these new roles.

Most of the ideas presented in the first nine chapters apply to counseling adolescents as well as to adults. Nevertheless, counselors who work successfully with adolescents must be sensitive to and take account of some essential differences. For example, adolescents are very sensitive to adults' criticism of them, and they resent adults' demands on them to adjust when they experience conflict with adults—the assumption that they, rather than the adults, require treatment. Furthermore, when a counselor invites an adolescent to join a counseling group, he must convey his concern for the adolescent—that he is not being approached because he has done something wrong and that he is not obligated to change his behavior to satisfy the needs of an important other. The necessity to convince the counselor that he has something to talk about, that he will talk about it, that he will change his behavior, and that he will try to help others as well as himself really appeals to adolescents. Careful screening of clients increases the attractiveness of the group for all clients, but has special appeal to adolescents.

Those who counsel adolescents in groups should be aware that: (1) they should expect to participate more in counseling adolescents, especially during the first few sessions; (2) they may wish to teach adolescents to use interpretation with each other; (3) role playing encourages adolescents to communicate their ideas and feelings, to experiment with new roles, and to practice new ways of behaving; and (4) adolescents often need assistance in conveying their new selves to important others. Other group techniques also may be used to teach new skills and to provide adolescents with essential information.

Many of the adolescent's problems result from important others' failure to try to empathize with him, to understand his unique needs, and to help him fulfill these needs during the process of maturation. School counselors can help to prevent many of the adolescent's problems by serving as consultants to important others, such as the adolescent's parents and teachers. Though individual consultations will be needed, much can be accomplished in parent and teacher groups. The text describes briefly some group techniques that can be used to help teachers and parents.

References

Ackerman, N. W. "Group Psychotherapy with a Mixed Group of Adolescents," *International Journal of Group Psychotherapy*, 1955, 5:249–260.

Ausubel, D. P. *Theory and Problems of Adolescent Development*, New York: Grune & Stratton, Inc., 1954.

Ayer, F. L., and B. R. Corman "Laboratory Practices Develop Citizenship Concepts of High School Students," *Social Education*, 1952, 16:215–216.

Berman, S. "Psychotherapeutic Techniques with Adolescents," *American Journal of Orthopsychiatry*, 1954, 24:238–244.

Bernard, H. W. *Adolescent Development in American Culture*, New York: Harcourt, Brace & World, Inc., 1957.

Bowen, M. "Family Psychotherapy," *American Journal of Orthopsychiatry*, 1961, 31:40–60.

Broedel, J., M. Ohlsen, F. Proff, and C. Southard "The Effects of Group Counseling on Gifted Underachieving Adolescents," *Journal of Counseling Psychology*, 1960, 7:163–170.

Caplan, H. "The Role of Deviant Maturation in the Pathogenesis of Anxiety," *American Journal of Orthopsychiatry*, 1956, 26:94–107.

Dinkmeyer, D., and R. Dreikurs *Encouraging Children To Learn:* The Encouraging Process, Englewood Cliffs, N.J.: Prentice-Hall, Inc., 1963.

Dreikurs, R., R. Corsini, R. Lowe, and M. Sonstegard *Adlerian Family Counseling,* Eugene, Ore.: University of Oregon Press, 1959.

Dreikurs, R., and Vicki Soltz *Children: A Challenge,* New York: Duell, Sloan, & Pearce-Meredith Press, 1964.

Dunbar, F. "Homeostasis during Puberty," *American Journal of Psychiatry,* 1958, 114:673–682.

Ethical Standards of Psychologists, Washington, D.C.: American Psychological Association, 1953.

Freeman, V. J., A. F. Klein, Lynne M. Riehman, I. F. Lukoff, and Virginia E. Heisey "Family Group Counseling as Differentiated from Other Family Therapies," *International Journal of Group Psychotherapy,* 1963, 13:167–175.

Frank, L. K., and M. H. Frank *Your Adolescent, at Home and in School,* New York: The Viking Press, Inc., 1956.

Fullmer, D. W., and H. W. Bernard *Counseling: Content and Process,* Chicago: Science Research Associates, Inc., 1964.

Gadpaille, W. J. "Observations on the Sequence of Resistances in Groups of Adolescent Delinquents," *International Journal of Group Psychotherapy,* 1959, 9:275–286.

Garrison, K. C. *Psychology of Adolescence,* Englewood Cliffs, N.J.: Prentice-Hall, Inc., 1965.

Gesell, A., F. L. Ilg, and L. B. Ames *Youth: The Years from Ten to Sixteen,* New York: Harper & Row, Publishers, 1956.

Ginott, H. G. *Between Parent and Teenager,* New York: The Macmillan Company, 1969.

Guerney, B. "Filial Therapy: Description and Rationale," *Journal of Counseling Psychology,* 1964, 28:304–310.

Hall, G. S. *Adolescence,* New York: Appleton-Century-Crofts, 1904.

Head, W. A. "Sociodrama and Group Discussion with Institutionalized Delinquent Adolescents," *Mental Hygiene,* 1962, 46:127–135.

Hertzman, J. "Dynamic Group Experiences for Teachers and Students in the Classroom," *International Journal of Group Psychotherapy,* 1959, 9:99–109.

Hurloch, Elizabeth B. *Adolescent Development,* New York: McGraw-Hill, Inc., 1967.

Jones, M. C., and N. Bayley "Physical Maturing among Boys as Related to Behavior," *Journal of Educational Psychology,* 1950, 41:129–148.

Katz, Evelyn W., M. M. Ohlsen, and F. C. Proff "An Analysis through Use of Kinescopes of the Interpersonal Behavior of Adolescents in Group Counseling," *Journal of College Student Personnel,* 1959, 1:2–10.

Kirkpatrick, M. E. "The Mental Hygiene of Adolescence in the Anglo-American Culture," *Mental Hygiene*, 1952, 36:394–403.

Lerner, P. M. *Resolution of Family Conflict in Families of Schizophrenic Patients*, a doctoral dissertation, University of Illinois, 1964.

Neidt, C. O., and M. F. Fritz "Relation of Cynicism to Certain Student Characteristics," *Educational and Psychological Measurement*, 1950, 10:712–718.

Ohlsen, Linda "A Student's Perception of Group Counseling," *Clearing House*, 1966, 40:401–403.

Ohlsen, M. M. "Social and Leadership Development," Chapter 13 in *Guidance Services in the Modern School*, New York: Harcourt, Brace & World, Inc., 1964.

Powell, J. W. "The Dynamics of Group Formation," *Psychiatry*, 1948, 11:117–124.

Workentin, J. "An Experience in Teaching Psychotherapy by Means of Group Therapy," *Progressive Education*, 1955, 32:79–82.

Chapter Eleven

Counseling Children in Groups

This chapter discusses the development of a therapeutic relationship with children, techniques for improving communication with them, and ways of adapting group counseling techniques for children. It also discusses techniques for facilitating their normal development.

Most such group counseling is being done in the elementary schools. Besides counseling children, the elementary-school counselor consults teachers and parents to enable them to do their part in facilitating normal development. Two recent reports suggest that he can focus on these helping relations and avoid many of the clerical and administrative duties that absorb so much of the secondary-school counselor's time [ACES Sub-Committee Report on the Preparation of Elementary School Counselors (1967) and Ohlsen (1967)].

Developing a Relationship with Children

When a school employs an elementary-school counselor, its principal should invite him to describe his professional services to the faculty and answer their questions. Teachers can do many things to help the counselor develop a counseling relationship with children. Besides trying to understand his services and encouraging children to use them, they can invite him into their classrooms to describe counseling, to explain the *unique nature* of the pupil-counselor relationship, to give some examples of common problems that children have discussed with him, and to tell how they can arrange to see him. Under these conditions a counselor can convey to children that they are expected to discuss the problems that bother them and to learn new ways of behaving—that the counselor's office is where they can work on the things that bother them. Within this kind of atmosphere children do seek help—even from trainees who are assigned to cooperating schools for practicum [Ohlsen (1967)]. Furthermore, children often seek the counselor's assistance with problems before either their parents or teachers recognize that they need professional help. Such an arrangement enables children to obtain assistance early, and thereby prevents the development of serious problems later. A counselor also helps children with developmental tasks. Sometimes children can be encouraged by a counselor to discuss these developmental problems within their classroom, and thereby reach children who had not requested counseling.

Mayer (1967) also found that children as young as kindergarten and first grade do seek counseling on their own and apparently profit from a counseling relationship. He also concluded that the most important single source of information about a child is the child himself. McCandless and Young (1966) agreed that there is no substitute for the information that can be gained about a child by observing him and interviewing him. To understand a child an adult must understand how the child perceives his world, his own behavior, and his problems.

Perhaps elementary-school children trust counselors more quickly than do either adolescents or adults, but counselors tend to have more difficulty communicating with them than they do with older clients. Kaczkowski (1965) contended that children's limited vocabulary accounts for a large part of this difficulty. Often a child does not know the best word to express a feeling or to describe a relationship, or he knows only a single meaning for a word that has many meanings, and the counselor responds to one of the other meanings. Though the writer agrees with Ginott (1958) that children should not be forced to verbalize, a counselor can teach those who wish to do so the words that enable them to do it. On the other hand, Ginott made another relevant point: adults should not try to give children verbal insight. Neither should counselors over-look the fact that play is one of the natural ways for children to express themselves.

Moustakes (1959) strongly endorsed play techniques. He contended that a child is more apt to participate in play activi-ties on a mutual basis than when he is forced to rely entirely on verbal interchange. He described the client-counselor rela-tionship in play therapy as follows:

> Perhaps the most important aspect of the play therapy experience for the normal child is the concentrated relationship with the therapist. In the busy life of children the opportunity rarely exists to be alone for one hour with an adult once or twice a week. Furthermore, it is rare for a child to have a relationship in which he is the center of the experience, where he can express his feelings and be understood as a person, where the adult is fully understanding of the child, watching, listening, making statements of recognition, and being present in a deeply human sense.
>
> Play therapy is a form of preventive mental hygiene for normal children. It is a way for them to grow in their own self-acceptance and respect, a way to explore feelings and atti-tudes and temporary tensions and conflicts that cannot be expressed easily and safely in school or at home. Often threat-ening feelings and disturbing experiences can be worked through in three or four sessions. (pp. 43–44)

The parent and teacher discussion groups described in Chapter Ten are designed to help parents and teachers learn to give this kind of individual attention to children—even if only for short periods of time. They can learn to enjoy children more and to provide them with markedly improved relation-ships. Guerney's (1964) approach was designed to train parents of emotionally disturbed children to conduct play sessions with their children. Perhaps this method and other play techniques can be adapted for use with normal children in the family council.

Play techniques can be used effectively by counselors to help children convey what bothers them, to communicate feelings and reactions that are difficult for them to express verbally, and to discover new ways of relating to significant others. They also can be used to help them reveal material that is difficult for them to express directly in face-to-face relationships. For example, some children can talk freely about a problem with the counselor or another client on a play telephone (or do so when pretending to be talking to a trusted friend on a telephone). They also can use puppets and dolls to show how their families live together and relate to each other.

Sometimes, however, when they are thrust into a playroom with a wide range of play materials, they can waste most of the treatment time. They may be overwhelmed with the choice of media, or not be able to make choices, or not realize how to use counseling time. Sometimes they are distracted from their therapeutic tasks. Although the way in which children behave under these circumstances can be very revealing, its therapeutic productiveness can be increased by appropriate structuring—by the counselor's conveying to his client why they are using the playroom for a *work* session, how this kind of work differs from regular play, and how they may be able to select material to enable them to deal with their problems. Thus the counselor himself must recognize the difference between playing with children in the playroom and using play materials to facilitate communication and improved adjustment. Though there are times when a counselor may wish to encourage free play, much treatment time can be saved by helping clients select the play material that each requires to deal with his problems in the counselor's office.

Normal children talk to their counselors about a variety of problems: coping with new situations or developmental tasks; school phobias; doubts about their ability to succeed in their school subjects—especially reading and arithmetic; other learning problems; relations with important adults such as parents and teachers; relations with peers; and grieving. Some young children have had so little experience relating to persons outside their immediate family that they misinterpret others' efforts to relate to them. For example, some expect all adults who seem to accept them to treat them as their mothers do. Group counseling can help them to recognize individual differences and to relate to different individuals differently—to broaden their repertoire of human-relations skills and to adapt these skills to an ever-enlarging environment.

When elementary-school pupils ask to join a counseling group, an intake interview is scheduled as suggested in Chapter Five. Since only a few sessions are required ordinarily to help normal children, not all who request group counseling or are referred for it are assigned to counseling groups. Though they may demonstrate readiness for group counseling, the counselor may not assign some to a group because he decides that they can be helped adequately in a few individual sessions. For these children the intake interview becomes the first of several individual treatment sessions. For others the counselor may use several individual sessions to get a child ready for group counseling.

Children who profit most from group counseling are those who have something to talk about, are committed to talk about it, are committed to try to change their behavior, and are interested in helping others change their behavior. The counselor also should include in children's groups some who want to learn to express themselves, to learn to relate to others more genuinely, and to practice relationship skills—for example, the shy child who has difficulty participating in class discussion and the one who wants help in making friends. Rarely is it advisable to include in a single group only one type of client, such as behavior problems or gifted underachievers. Usually underachievers can be treated most effectively with other children who can accept their own ability and are concerned about learning how to do better than they are doing.

Those who develop an effective relationship with children

convey genuine respect for them and their ideas; believe in their ability to express themselves verbally; are able to help them express themselves when they have difficulty without feeling condescending toward them; are patient with them; and are able to listen with undivided attention. Ohlsen's (1967) recent experiences supervising NDEA enrollees convinced him that children can communicate with counselors much better than he realized that they could. These findings are supported by the ACES Sub-Committee's study of a select group of outstanding elementary-school counselors on job behavior [Ohlsen (1968a)].

Adapting Group Techniques for Children

Best results are obtained when both pupils and their parents understand what is expected in group counseling and accept these conditions. Sonstegard (1961) obtained significant results with gifted underachieving children when he also counseled their parents and teachers in groups. Whereas this may be desirable, it is not always feasible or even necessary. However, Ohlsen and Gazda (1965) concluded that best results are obtained when there are regular consultations with clients' parents and teachers. A counselor can convey to teachers and parents the information they need to better understand their children's behavior and attitudes, help them better accept their children, and teach them to reinforce the desired behavior without breaking confidences. When the counselor explains to the children why he needs to consult with their parents and teachers, they usually approve of the idea. They would like their parents and teachers to understand them better and to help them change their behavior. Though Ohlsen and Gazda realized that they did not do sufficient consultation, their clients expressed the need for the increased acceptance and understanding that can result from it. A fifth-grade underachieving boy expressed himself as follows: "We are just kids and don't count for much; even our dogs are treated better than we are." Such a child needs the help of his counselor to express these feelings to his parents and to begin developing a relationship with them. Whereas adolescents often can learn to do this in their counseling groups, most elementary-school children require the counselor's assistance to initiate this process.

Although the same basic principles of group counseling apply to all ages, the counselor must adapt his technique to his clients' social, emotional, and intellectual maturity, their previous experiences in groups, and the development of their communication skills. The writer's counseling experiences with fifth, sixth, seventh, and eighth graders clearly suggests that the techniques used with secondary-school and college students can be used with seventh and eighth graders, but certain adaptations are required for younger children.

The younger the children are, the more structure they require. Preferably this should be done before children are selected for a group. In fact, as he listens to a child trying to convince him that he is ready for group counseling, a counselor can respond to the child who may not understand or accept a therapeutic relationship within a group as follows: "You really have something to talk about, but I wonder if you can sit down and talk about it in a group. If I am going to be able to help you and the others in the group with you, I have to be able to give all my attention to helping you; I can't be scolding you and trying to make you behave. You have to be grown up enough to do that yourself." Some may even be admitted on a trial basis. On the basis of their behavior in one session, the group decides whether these children will be permitted to attend the next.

Facing up to this problem with children enables the counselor to give the children considerable responsibility for helping to develop and to maintain a therapeutic climate in which *he does not* have to enforce limits. An accepting atmosphere is essential, and it cannot be developed in a group in which the counselor enforces limits as teachers and parents do. Even a good explanation of the difference between the relationship with a counselor and the one with parents and teachers is not accepted by children when one or more clients are able to manipulate the counselor into the disciplinary role. When these working relationships are described in terms meaningful to children, even the child who has difficulty accepting limits usually learns to meet the expectations of his counseling group. For him this is an appropriate outcome of counseling, and one that he can learn to apply in his classroom—especially when his teacher learns to reinforce acceptable behaviors instead of attacking inappropriate ones. Moreover, the chances for successful treatment are increased when the counselor takes account of each client's maturity in determining the length of the counseling session, the frequency of the sessions, and the size of the group.

Associated with the need for more structure is the need for more counselor participation. Ohlsen and Gazda found that children are sensitive to others' feelings but cannot detect and respond to significant material as readily as adolescents. However, they do increase their capacity to do this during the treatment period. When, therefore, the counselor fails to help clients learn to be clients and helpers of others, especially during early sessions, children become restless, are easily distracted, and often compete for the counselor's attention.

Children do have some ability to empathize with peers, as Lerner (1937) discovered, and it can be increased during counseling, but they do have greater difficulty than adolescents do in maintaining a sustained interest in others' problems. Ohlsen and Gazda concluded that better results could be achieved with fifth graders in smaller groups (five or six instead of seven or eight) and for shorter counseling sessions (40 to 45 minutes instead of an hour). From even more recent experiences Ohlsen (1968b) concluded that though the length of the period should be adjusted to the maturity of the clients (and this may be lengthened or shortened during treatment), most fourth, fifth, and sixth graders adapt best to a 35-minute counseling period. Primary-school children adjust best to 20- to 25-minute sessions. Two sessions a week are minimum for elementary-school children; three are preferred.

Ginott (1961) reported that the prevailing practice in

clinics is to separate boys and girls for treatment during the latency period. Ohlsen and Gazda found that the girls in their groups were more mature, were more verbal, and tended to threaten boys and to dominate them; hence, it is easier to treat these boys and girls separately. On the other hand, the writer believes that the counseling group may be the best place for boys and girls to learn to express their feelings toward each other and to relate to each other. He sees this as a good example of developmental counseling—helping children learn to cope with problems that most children meet in growing up. When boys and girls are placed in the same group, each learns to understand, to accept, and to relate to the other; this is better than merely accepting the conflict between girls and boys during this period as something normal that must be endured.

Children like to dramatize as well as talk out their problems. Hence, role playing appeals to them. Puppets also may be used effectively in skits that the children develop and act out. Some other play materials that can be used effectively in groups include family dolls, sketching paper, finger paints, and clay. Those who work with older elementary-school children must be wary lest the children consider these materials "kid stuff."

A group of five first and second graders is described here to illustrate how play materials may be used in a group counseling session. Two were having some difficulty with reading problems. All five tended to be shy (in fact, the counselor should have detected this in screening and assigned at least one spontaneous, more self-confident child to the group). Before they entered the counseling room the counselor laid out sheets of brown wrapping paper, finger paints, modeling clay, and various sizes of dolls—some dressed as adults and others as children. Adult "dress-up" clothes also were available for use in role playing. On entering the room each child selected the materials of his choice and sat down to play. Provision was made for the children to sit around a long table in a large office. On this particular day one of the girls and two of the boys decided to play with finger paints. The third boy played with clay and the remaining girl played with dolls.

As the children played, the counselor moved about, responding first to one child, then to another. As he watched a child play, he would try to determine what the child was trying to express and respond to the child in the child's play medium —for example, if the child was playing with finger paints he would respond to him with finger paints. The children also were encouraged to respond to each other, both verbally and with play media. Occasionally one would speak to the entire group—a sort of show-and-tell. When necessary the counselor helped such a client get the attention of the entire group. He also tried to convey to his clients that not everyone was expected to speak to the entire group just because one wanted to do so. For this particular session there was little group discussion. On other occasions most of the counseling session was devoted to discussions and role playing.

The Consulting Relationship

To benefit fully from consultation, the one who seeks it must trust the consultant—must believe that he can talk freely without fear of being criticized or evaluated. For the counselor it is a mutual relationship. He seeks assistance and he gives assistance. He seeks teachers' and parents' assistance in order to better understand his clients and counsel them, as well as to assist the teachers and parents. Wolfe (1966) described the nature of this mutual respect as follows:

> Consultation is concerned with the giving and taking of help in an interpersonal relationship. The outstanding feature of the relationship is its permissiveness. However, regardless of the setting, there are common features of consultation. The consultee is free to seek (or not to seek) the consultant's assistance. After receiving advice or information, the responsibility and decision for using or rejecting such advice remains with the consultee. The consultant has no responsibility for, or authority over, the action of the consultee. Implicit in the relationship, however, is the authority of the consultant's

knowledge, special competence, and professional conscience. Like most human relationships, consultation is a two-way process. Although the balance is usually weighted toward giving by the consultant and receiving by the consultee, both should give and receive. . . . The consultant should serve as a catalyst, stimulator and motivator of ideas. (p. 132)

The mutually sharing nature of the relationship is more relevant for the counselor than for most consultants to teachers. The counselor needs the teacher's assistance in understanding many of his clients. For some teachers the best way to develop this relationship of mutual help is for the counselor to request their assistance in understanding certain clients. However, the counselor must wait until his request for assistance is genuine. He must not use the pretense of needing assistance with a client to seek out a teacher's help, hoping that the teacher in turn will solicit his assistance. Teachers will see through the façade of such manipulation and resent it. On the other hand, a counselor often has good reasons for soliciting a teacher's assistance. Usually, soon after such a genuine request, a teacher identifies someone with whom he needs assistance and initiates a consultation.

The counselor should use his counseling skills to develop a relationship similar, but not identical, to that which he develops with his client. Rather than to help a teacher discuss his personal problems, the counselor tries to help him describe the pupil for whom the teacher seeks assistance, and when more information is needed to decide what additional information should be collected and by whom; to discuss how he feels toward the child; to describe the specific behaviors and attitudes he would like to change; and to plan specific procedures for achieving the desired changes. In other words, when a counselor functions as a consultant to teachers, he often uses behavior-modification techniques [Bandura, Ross, and Ross (1967); and Werry and Wollersheim (1967)]. A counselor also may help a teacher find a referral resource and make the referral.

The same general principles apply to consulting with parents. Many consultations will begin with the counselor seeking parents' assistance. Others will result from the counselor's description of his role to parents on parent nights and at PTA meetings. By encouraging them to ask questions and to explore his various services for them as well as their children, a counselor develops a relationship with parents. These contacts often open lines of communication for individual consultation and for initiating the kinds of groups described in Chapter Ten. Parent discussion groups, parent counseling groups, and teacher seminars also tend to be outgrowths of successful individual consultations.

Teachers' Use of Group Techniques

The effective teacher contributes much to children's normal development. Besides increasing their desire to learn, he can improve their ability to educate themselves. He also can help them understand and accept themselves and what they have a right to expect from themselves; to help them understand, accept, and work with classmates; and to help them discover and develop special interests and aptitudes. With increased use of group guidance techniques he can contribute even more to children's social and emotional development.

Recently Rogge (1965) demonstrated how a counselor can train a teacher to use group methods to motivate learning. The counselor visited a classroom several times and gave the pupils a chance to ask any questions that they wished. Rather than answering their questions he helped them explore where or from whom they could expect to obtain the information they sought. Sometimes several children cooperated in finding the information and reported back to the next discussion session. The counselor's primary purpose was to demonstrate to the teacher how he could use this technique to develop intellectual curiosity. Such discussions can be used for group guidance. They can be used to help children obtain answers to questions that they have wanted to ask, but for which they felt there was no one to whom they could turn for answers.

Since some teachers doubt their ability to field such questions, Rogge recommended that the counselor demonstrate the technique, answer the teacher's questions after the demonstration, and discuss a tape recording of the demonstration. The teacher may also appreciate the counselor's assistance in critiquing a recording of his first group session. When teachers are allowed to suggest other teachers for such critiquing sessions, a counselor can help four or five teachers at once.

Teachers commonly use role playing to help pupils learn to deal with conflict. When, for example, Robert's teacher learned that a bully, Mike, had beaten Robert up on the playground, she used role playing to help Robert learn to cope with Mike. From the description of the event, role-playing the scene several times, and discussing it, all the pupils learned to cope better with bullies. The way in which his classmates rallied behind him also provided support and encouragement to Robert.

Wells (1962) used similar sociodramatic techniques to resolve conflict between pupils, to cope with discipline problems, and to portray occupational roles that were attractive to them. When two boys were sent to her office for fighting, she found that it was much more effective to ask them to show her (to act out without words) what happened than to try to determine who was the culprit so she could punish him. Frequently she asks a pupil to play her role as assistant principal and she then plays one of their roles.

Wells also involves a teacher and his pupils in coping with behavioral problems. In the case of an attention-seeker they decided to look for commendable behavior for which he could be given recogniton. They agreed that he was to be sent to the office every day with at least one piece of commendable written work or a description of some commendable behavior; it really worked.

Rogge's is one example of a group technique a teacher can use to provide children with information about themselves, their environment, and their future opportunities. These aims also can be accomplished by other techniques in informal discussions and small study groups. Perhaps the sociodramatic techniques are even more effective, especially when counselors are available to consult and offer support when teachers first use them.

Summary

Although the elementary-school counselor is concerned about helping all children, he tends to focus on encouraging normal development and on early discovery and treatment of children's problems. He also assists parents and teachers in fulfilling their responsibilities for furthering normal social, emotional, and intellectual development.

When a counselor describes his role for children, they seek his assistance. Frequently, normal children seek his assistance before either parents or teachers recognize that they could profit from a counselor's services.

Children tend to trust the counselor more quickly than do either adolescents or adults, but some counselors have difficulty communicating with children. Though occasionally play materials are needed to communicate with young children, counselors are finding increasingly that children can express their feelings verbally and resolve their problems better than most experts have previously believed. Those who develop effective counseling relationships with children feel comfortable with them; convey genuine respect for them and their ideas; believe in their ability to express themselves verbally; are able to help them express themselves when they have difficulty without feeling condescending toward them; are patient with them; and know how to listen to them.

Best results are obtained from the counseling of children in groups when parents and teachers understand what the counselor is trying to do and are willing to help the counselor achieve his goals by reinforcing the changes he is trying to achieve. The same basic principles apply in counseling clients of all ages, but the counselor must adapt his approaches to his clients' social, emotional, and intellectual development, their previous group experiences, and their communication skills. The text discusses specific adaptations for various age levels.

The consultant relationship is unique. Functioning in this role, a counselor uses his knowledge of human behavior and of counseling techniques to develop a relationship similar to the one that he develops with his clients, but he does not counsel those who seek consultation. When, for example, he consults a teacher, he tries to help the teacher describe the pupil involved; to discuss how he feels toward the child; to determine whether or not he needs more information about the child and, if so, what; to describe the specific behaviors and attitudes he would like to change; and to plan the specific procedures required for achieving the desired changes. A consultant also can help teachers learn to use group techniques in their classrooms.

References

ACES Sub-Committee Report on the Preparation of Elementary School Counselors, mimeographed report, American Personnel and Guidance Association, 1967.

Bandura, A., D. Ross, and S. A. Ross "Vicarious Reinforcement and Imitative Learning," *Journal of Abnormal and Social Psychology*, 1963, 67:601–607.

Dreikurs, R. *Psychology in the Classroom*, New York: Harper & Row, Publishers, 1957.

Ginott, H. G. "Play Group Therapy: A Theoretical Framework," *International Journal of Group Psychotherapy*, 1958, 8:410–418.

Ginott, H. G. *Group Psychotherapy with Children*, New York: McGraw-Hill, Inc., 1961.

Guerney, B. "Filial Therapy: Description and Rationale," *Journal of Consulting Psychology*, 1964, 28:304–310.

Kaczkowski, H. R. "Dimensions of the Counselor's Relationships," Chapter 7 in *Elementary School Guidance in Illinois*, Springfield: Office of State Superintendent of Public Instruction, 1965.

Krumboltz, J. D., and R. E. Hosford "Behavioral Counseling in the Elementary School," *Elementary School Guidance and Counseling*, 1967, 1:27–40.

Lerner, E. "The Problem of Perspective in Moral Reasoning," *Journal of Sociology*, 1937, 43:294–299.

Mayer, G. R. "An Approach for the Elementary School Counselor: Consultant or Counselor?" *The School Counselor*, 1967, 14:210–214.

McCandless, B. R., and R. D. Young "Problems of Childhood and Adolescence," in L. A. Pennington and I. A. Berg (eds.), *An Introduction to Clinical Psychology*, New York: The Ronald Press Company, 1966.

Moustakes, C. E. *Psychotherapy With Children*, New York: Harper & Row, Publishers, 1959.

Ohlsen, M. M. *An Evaluation of a Counselor Program Designed for Prospective Elementary School Counselors Enrolled in 1965-1966 NDEA Institute*, Project #6-8087, U. S. Office of Education, College of Education, University of Illinois, 1967.

Ohlsen, M. M. "Preparation of Elementary School Counselors," *Counselor Education and Supervision*, 1968a, 7:172-178.

Ohlsen, M. M. "Counseling Children in Groups," *The School Counselor*, 1968b, 15:343–349.

Ohlsen, M. M., and G. M. Gazda "Counseling Underachieving Bright Pupils," *Education*, 1965, 86:78–81.

Rogge, W. "Building Professional Behavior," Chapter 11 in *Elementary School Guidance in Illinois*, Springfield: Office of State Superintendent of Public Instruction, 1965.

Sonstegard, M. "Group Counseling Methods with Parents of Elementary School Children as Related to Pupil Growth and Development," Mimeographed report, State College of Iowa, 1961.

Wells, Cecilia, G. "Psychodrama and Creative Counseling in the Elementary School," *Group Psychotherapy*, 1962, 15:244–252.

Werry, J. S., and Janet P. Wollersheim "Behavior Therapy with Children: A Broad Overview," *Journal of American Academy of Child Psychiatry*, 1967, 6:346–370.

Wolfe, H. E. "Consultation: Role, Function, & Process," *Mental Hygiene*, 1966, 50:132–134.

Chapter Twelve

Appraisal of Group Counseling

This chapter discusses some common weaknesses of research designed to appraise outcomes of group counseling and group psychotherapy and suggests some actions to correct these weaknesses. It also reviews the findings of selected studies and discusses their implications for counseling practices.

The research designed to appraise outcomes of individual counseling and psychotherapy (and for that matter all applied psychology) is plagued with the same problems as the research on group counseling and psychotherapy. The practicing counselor (and psychotherapist) tends to prefer helping people on the basis of his own and his colleagues' professional experiences to testing how efficacious his treatment methods are for whom under what circumstances. If, however, he is conscientiously to meet his professional ethical standards, he must ask himself, in selecting each client for each group: Is this a client whom I can help best by this method? During the course of treatment he must continue to ask himself this same question. After treatment has ended, he must ask: Who was helped most by this technique? Who failed to profit from it? Who was hurt by it? What information about these clients might have enabled me to predict who would have been helped or hurt? To what extent did my personal needs and behaviors contribute to or interfere with the clients' growth?

In other words, an investigator must ask more precise questions than "Was group counseling effective?" or "Did group counseling really change clients' attitudes and behaviors?" Instead, an investigator must ask: For whom was this particular group counseling effective, and with what other clients and under what kinds of circumstances? Were some counselors more effective than others? How did the successful counselors differ from the others? What professional preparation and experience are required to provide it? Who profited most from it? Who may be hurt by it? How was readiness for counseling assessed? To what extent were clients committed to change their behavior and to help fellow clients change their behavior? To what extent were they convinced that they could be helped, and that their fellow clients could be helped? To what degree did each participate in defining his treatment goals and accept these goals as reasonable for him? To what extent did the actual treatment focus upon each one's own idiosyncratic goals? To what degree was the counselor able to develop a therapeutic relationship with each client, to help each to relate therapeutically to the others, and to help each accept responsibility for developing and maintaining a therapeutic climate within the group? Were adequate criteria developed to appraise each client's growth in terms of his goals? Were adequate appraisal techniques used to appraise each client's growth in terms of relevant criteria for him? Was the research design adequate to fulfill the researcher's purposes? Did he use appropriate statistical methods?

Obviously it is difficult for researchers to meet all of these conditions in appraising outcomes of group counseling. When one considers the practitioner's commitment to service, the limited time and financial support available to him for research, and the difficulties involved in appraising counseling outcomes, one can readily understand why some practitioners avoid systematic appraisal, and why some who attempt it overlook avoidable errors in their research design. Though no study even approaches perfection, counselors can improve their appraisal of clients' growth, and design much better studies for formal appraisal of group counseling, conducted for specific clients under specified conditions by adequately described treatment methods and counselors. Within its limited space, this chapter merely tries to identify the most serious problems involved and offers some practical suggestions for solving them. Those who want a more thorough review or evaluation of the research will find the following sources helpful: Carkhuff and Berenson (1967), Hoch and Zubin (1964), Rubinstein and Parloff (1959), and Stollack, Guerney, and Rothberg (1966).

Definition of the Problem

Increasingly counselors recognize the need for a much more precise statement of their problem. They are beginning to formulate some carefully stated hypotheses with reference to defined population, specific treatment methods used within a clearly defined setting, and carefully described counselor or counselors. They also must be able to explain why the study is worth doing at this time and within this particular setting. Stating the problem clearly and developing a rationale for it is a slow, painstaking process. Though this clear statement is important for communication to funding agencies and colleagues, it is probably more important to the investigator; it insures that he sees clearly what he expects to do before he begins it.

To give meaning to the statement of the problems, the investigator must spell out his procedures in detail—stating precisely what he expects to do during each stage and defending the procedures selected to fulfill each objective for the study. Pepinsky (1953) outlined the steps in this process as follows:

> 1. . . . a careful definition and delineation of the problem.
> . . . Like other phases of the project, this may have to be

reworked many times before the researcher can be satisfied with it. . . .

2. . . . we should be careful to limit ourselves to the statement of hypotheses that are testable, and to make our
statements so explicit that the research operations follow
directly and unequivocally from them. . . .

3. . . . we ought to set up our design in such a way that it
provides a relatively unambiguous test of our hypothesis.
Here some of us might be old-fashioned: the notion of
systematically controlling independent (predictor) variables to see what effect they have on dependent (criterion)
variables might have strong appeal. . . .

4. . . . we should do a compulsive job of planning our
research: how the data will be collected, how they will be
analyzed, and even how they will be interpreted. Lacking
careful planning, we may be tempted to improvise as we
go along. This can lead us far afield from our original
hypotheses. Pilot studies are strongly recommended.
Finally, we would do well to exercise restraint in discussing our results and in generalizing from them. If
we have decided in advance upon the criteria for accepting
or rejecting the original hypotheses, the obtained results
should be interpreted in the light of that prejudgment.
(p. 293)

Although the definition of criteria and selection of research subjects will be discussed further later in this chapter,
Goldstein's (1959) discussion of laxity with respect to error in
applied psychology relates directly to Pepinsky's suggestions
on design:

. . . applied psychology has developed a tradition of hasty
approximation, and laxity with respect to error. This special
tradition within psychology appeals to many applied sponsors
and often assumes the status of a norm from which departures
can be effected only after painstaking justification. It is routine
for a nonrigorous applied psychologist to ask himself: "How
much sloppiness can I permit and still have something?" Indeed,
this type of question underlies some of the concern over "reliability" of measurement. Passable reliabilities are accepted as
evidence enough that the sloppiness permitted was tolerable.

It must be granted that scientific discoveries can be made, on occasion, in spite of abundant experimental error. It is also true that error is so familiar in all experimental disciplines as to have warranted the development of various formal procedures to treat it analytically. Nonetheless, error must properly be viewed as a matter for discomfort and admitted only when there is no alternative. Psychologists working in the applied tradition repeatedly miss opportunities for progress, because they sample where they might have controlled or accept imperfect connections where avoidable error has prevented them from investigating the possibility of full determinacy (p. 275)

Many of these design problems, and those concerned with analysis of the data, could be avoided by use of competent research consultants during the planning phase of a research project. However, even well-funded agencies rarely have been able to employ uninvolved researchers to evaluate for them the unique features of their services. In order to use the results of research to improve the agencies' services, the staff must help formulate the research problems as well as apply the findings of the research. Goldstein discussed this point as follows:

By the time a man is found to state problems well, he is also one of the few who both care to and know how to solve them. As a matter of fact, problem formulation and solution interact with each other; reformulations are often a main outcome of attempted solutions. It is quite bizarre to seek division of labor between formulators and solvers of problems, especially at this early stage in the development of psychology. (p. 274)

Finally, in defining the problem there is no substitute for a thorough review of the related research literature. Every graduate student should know this, but even many experienced researchers have failed to do it, or they have had the literature reviewed by assistants who focused on results and missed subtle design errors that could have been corrected. A thorough review of the related literature can help the researcher clarify and sharpen the statement of his problem, identify and separate interacting elements, define the treatment process, discover theories to be tested, clarify the hypotheses to be tested, turn up clever methods for improving research design and evaluating change, and identify improved statistical methods for analyzing his data.

Definition of the Treatment Process

Group counseling was defined in Chapter One. The reader will recall that the writer distinguished between group counseling and group psychotherapy, not on the basis of process, but primarily with reference to those selected for treatment. For group counseling the writer selects reasonably healthy clients and expects them to help develop and maintain a therapeutic climate; to talk openly about the problems that bother them; to seek improved ways of behaving; to learn and practice the interpersonal skills required to apply these improved ways of behaving; to develop the will and self-confidence to apply what they have learned; to apply outside their counseling group what they have learned in group counseling; and to help fellow clients discuss their problems and change their behavior. When, therefore, he reviews the research on group counseling, he includes some studies on group psychotherapy that he feels are relevant for group counseling, but he does not include the research on other group techniques such as activity therapy, guidance groups, and T groups. Although these group techniques can be useful, they should not be confused with group counseling.

In order to generalize another's findings to his own situation or to replicate the study, a counselor must know what was done, how it was done, under what circumstances, and something about the person who did it. Unfortunately, researchers often fail to describe these elements. Furthermore, they often use the term group counseling for very different treatments. For example, the titles assigned to the following three studies suggest that they were all concerned with appraisal of group counseling:

1. Teacher-counselors who had very little specialized preparation for counseling gave educational and vocational
   information to students in guidance classes of approximately thirty students each.
2. Well-qualified counselors interpreted tests to students in
   small groups—usually less than ten in each group. The
   counselors also encouraged each group to discuss the
   relevance of the information for vocational planning.
   Nothing in the paper suggested that students were
   encouraged to discuss their feelings concerning what
   they learned about themselves.
3. A well-qualified counselor conducted intensive group
   counseling for one semester within a highly favorable
   setting for carefully selected clients. The treatment process and the size of groups were clearly defined.

Obviously, the treatment processes in these three studies were
not even similar, and those who provided the treatment differed markedly. Certainly no reader could generalize about
group counseling from these very different treatments. If,
however, the relevant elements in the various treatments had
been described adequately, a reader could have used each
investigator's data to judge for himself the relevance of the
treatment method for his staff in his setting. Readers have
the right to expect such from investigators.

The Counselor as a Treatment Variable

Rarely have researchers adequately described the counselors (or psychotherapists) used in their studies. A treatment
can be fairly appraised only when it is provided by competent
counselors, and various treatment methods can be compared
only when the counselors used in the experiment accept each
method's worth and are qualified to use each method. In one
study, for example, well designed in most of its aspects, the
researcher compared the efficacy of the same counselors providing individual and group counseling for a specific type of
client, but failed to describe the competencies of his counselors.

Correspondence with the researcher revealed that all the counselors were beginners who possessed minimal professional preparation. They had a background of formal course work and supervised practicum in individual counseling, but none had had formal course work, supervised practicum, or experience in group counseling. Neither those treated on an individual basis nor those treated in groups improved significantly over the control subjects. Had those treated on an individual basis improved significantly, readers would have assumed that individual treatment was superior for these clients under these circumstances. Obviously, this conclusion would have been unwarranted.

If, therefore, one is to appraise a specific technique, he must describe his counselors' professional preparation, including their didactic instruction, the nature of their supervision in practica and internships, and their posttraining professional experiences. Readers must also know to what degree each counselor was able to establish a therapeutic relationship with each client treated in his group.

Carkhuff and Berenson's (1967) findings stressed the importance of the elements noted above. They noted that treatment can hurt as well as help clients. In order to understand what they discovered about counselors and therapists, one must know how they defined the points on their five-point scale:

1. Describes the severely disturbed client who is essentially immune to constructive human encounter, and the retarding therapist
2. Describes the distressed client who distorts reality but lives in the world of reality, and the moderately retarding therapist
3. Describes the situationally distressed client who functions moderately well, and the minimally facilitative therapist
4. Describes the more potent client who relates effectively—has a positive influence on others—and the therapist who facilitates change in those he tries to help
5. Describes the person who is involved in a lifelong search for self-actualization for others as well as himself

Using this scale, they found that their typical client was slightly lower than 2, with a range between 1 and 3, and that counselors and therapists varied in their facilitating functioning from 1 to 4, with a mean of approximately 2: "The average discrepancy, then, between the counselor and the client would appear to be minimal, with the main difference being the higher levels of functioning to which counselors may range." (p. 52)

> Thus, those facilitators offering the highest levels of facilitative conditions tend to involve the persons to whom they are relating in a process leading to constructive behavior change or gain, both affective and cognitive, or intellective. At the highest levels, these facilitators communicate an accurately empathic understanding of the deeper as well as the superficial feelings of the second person(s); they are freely and deeply themselves in a nonexploitative relationship; they communicate a very deep respect for the second person's worth as a person and his rights as a free individual; and they are helpful in guiding the discussion to personally relevant feelings and experiences in specific and concrete terms. These facilitators, are, ideally, our parents, teachers, or counselors. We say "ideally" because many parents, teachers, and counselors offer very low levels of these conditions; others offer only some of these conditions at relatively high levels and other conditions at relatively low levels. (p. 45)

Carkhuff and Berenson's findings could account for Eysenck's (1952, 1965) and Levitt's (1957) distressing conclusions. These findings should cause counselor educators to ask themselves these questions: What can we do to improve our counselor selection techniques? How can we identify better facilitators of change? What changes must we make in our program to develop and reinforce counselor behaviors and attitudes that facilitate client growth? What can we do to encourage and reinforce continued growth on the job?

First of all, counselor educators (and those who educate therapists) can look at themselves. They can use instruments like those developed by Carkhuff, Berenson, and their associates to assess their impact upon their students. Where they, or their preparation programs, are discovered to be deficient, they can do everything possible to correct the deficiencies. They also can use everything that is known to select the best possible students. Finally, they can appraise the didactic content, students' opportunities to learn from fellow students as well as the staff, students' laboratory experiences with clients, and the quality and nature of supervision provided in practica, internships, and early employment.

Carkhuff and Truax (1965a, 1965b) described and evaluated a promising short-term program for laymen and graduate students. They concluded that within a relatively short training period (approximately 100 hours) both laymen and graduate students can be brought to function at therapeutic levels nearly commensurate with experienced therapists. Nevertheless, the group performed in the following rank order: (1) experienced therapists, (2) graduate students, and (3) lay personnel.

> While a hierarchy of performance was established, the experienced therapist did not effect significantly better process levels than the graduate students on any dimensions, and the latter were not significantly higher than the lay group on any indexes. The only significant difference was found in the comparison of the experienced and the lay groups on the therapist self-congruence dimension.
>
> That the experienced therapists are significantly higher than the lay personnel, as well as relatively higher than the graduate students, on the self-congruence dimension, suggests that with experience the therapists come to be more freely, easily, and deeply themselves in the therapeutic encounter. In this regard, one handicap with which the lay personnel may have been operating is the lack of any real theoretical orientation to indicate to them where they were going in their encounters. The very notion that counseling and therapy may take place devoid of any theoretical knowledge is currently being assessed in a lay group counseling treatment study. While the present program did not emphasize outside readings, the graduate students tended to glean from other sources some direction for themselves and their activities. [Carkhuff and Truax (1965a), pp. 335–336]

In summary, the present research has demonstrated the effec-

tiveness of time-limited lay group counseling, evolving from a
short-term integrated didactic and experiential approach to
training. It is felt that the results indicate great promise for
the possibly critical role which lay personnel might play in
coping with our evergrowing mental health concerns. The
results point to the need for further and continued search and
research into this potentially vast and untapped resource.
[Carkhuff and Truax (1965b), p. 431]

As Chapter One indicated, it is not sufficient to help
beginning counselors merely learn to play the counselor's role.
They must learn to live it, to have the best counselor behaviors
and attitudes reinforced on the job, and to improve their
counseling skills on the job. If any of these are not found in
the work setting, even those who perform adequately when
they complete their professional preparation are not apt to
continue to function effectively on the job.

Goals for Counseling

Failure to define specific goals in *precise measurable or
observable* terms for each client is one of the most serious
weaknesses of the research designed to appraise outcomes of
counseling. Such goals are necessary in order to define the
precise criteria needed to develop and/or to select instruments
and observation methods to appraise changes in clients. From
their efforts to develop educational objectives for the affective
domain of education, Krathwohl, Bloom, and Masia (1964)
argued thus:

. . . We are aware that all too frequently educational objectives
are stated as meaningless platitudes and cliches. Some view
them as an opportunity to use a type of prose found frequently
in the superlatives employed by advertising men and the builders
of political platforms. . . . (p. 6)
We believe that objectives of education might gain meaning
through two rather distinct processes. One process is that of
defining the objective in behavioral terms and then describing

the evidence (i.e. tasks, tests, observations, etc.) which is relevant in judging whether students have or have not "achieved" the objective. This is a type of operational definition which has been an integral part of curriculum and evaluation work for the past three decades. A second process is that of trying to place an objective within a large over-all schema or matrix. It is this second process to which the classifications in the proposed taxonomy were addressed. Here it was hoped that placing the objective within the classification schema would locate it on a continuum and thus serve to indicate what is intended (as well as what was not intended). (p. 4)

School counselors, especially those who work with elementary-school children, can apply Krathwohl, Bloom, and Masia's model. From a review of the theoretical and research literature they can identify the developmental tasks and the broad general principles of mental health into which they can fit specific goals for individuals. In some instances they also will be able to develop scales on which they can portray a child's continuous development. Both the client and his counselor need specific goals in order to appraise its effectiveness during counseling and to determine whether continuing it is worthwhile. More and more counselors are accepting their clients' reasons for seeking counseling, for helping them translate these reasons into specific goals stated in terms of specific behaviors, attitudes, or skills, and for helping them recognize and develop new goals during counseling. When such specific goals are developed cooperatively, clients can assess their own progress, and their counselors have a better chance to develop meaningful criteria to use in appraising changes in their clients. Obviously, this is more difficult *to do* than it is to discuss, but a genuine effort to apply these principles will improve efforts to appraise outcomes of counseling.

Criteria

A review of the research concerned with appraising outcomes of counseling and psychotherapy suggests that some researchers use available instruments, and thus they use as their criteria whatever these instruments measure. Five other obvious weaknesses in choice of criteria were evident: (1) use of global criteria, (2) use for all clients of criteria appropriate for only some clients, (3) use of criteria such that growth for some clients cancelled out growth for others, (4) use of measures for which no evidence of either reliability or validity is presented, and (5) use of measuring devices insensitive to the changes anticipated.

When one reads the literature by practitioners for practitioners, one gets the notion that they know what they are trying to do for their clients. They also seem to be committed to help their clients with the problems with which they sought assistance and to take account of individual differences in appraising clients' growth. In other words, helping clients with their distressing problems must be an essential criterion for appraising growth. Most of them also seem to agree on the general goals for treatment presented in Chapter Two. Hartley and Rosenbaum's (1963) analysis of criteria used by group therapists supports this latter point:

> For the group as a whole, the top three criteria for judging improvements in patients are improved interpersonal functioning in and out of the therapy group; self-acceptance, self-confidence, self-reliance; and flexibility, the ability to cope with and adapt to a variety of experiences. The gap between frequencies with which these criteria are selected in comparison to those that come lower in the order: symptom-reduction, insight and self-awareness, expression of feelings, and working through of transference, is quite marked and may represent a truly significant difference among therapists. (p. 83)

Nevertheless, there is disagreement regarding acceptable criteria for appraising changes in clients. Bergin (1963) concluded that criteria are selected on the basis of subjective value judgments, that disagreements on criteria are traceable to personal values, and that specific criteria are required to correct these deficiencies:

> The present studies are suggestive of how such a state of affairs produces great diversity in indices of psychotherapy's effect. The outcome measures in these reports include self-ideal discrepancy, a TAT index of adjustment, social effectiveness, personal comfort-discomfort, MMPI indices, number of arrests or court appearances, behavior rating scales, and therapists' judgments.
>
> It is no longer original to conclude from such evidence that outcome can mean many things, that different and important outcome criteria tend to be uncorrelated, and that discrepant research results are to be expected under such conditions. All this is well demonstrated and simply punctuates the need for as much specificity with regard to measured consequences as is needed with regard to antecedent conditions of therapeutic promise. . . . (p. 248)

Some failures to detect significant change can be traced to use of vague, general criteria. Usually these investigators have used some type of personality test, an inventory, an anxiety scale, or global clinical judgment. Edwards and Cronbach argued against global criteria as follows:

> Some investigators have tried to keep broad measures and yet stay within conventional statistics by pouring their data into a single overall index of adjustment. This is not recommended, for such an index blurs together the strengths and weaknesses of each method and provides no guide for improvement. Experience in predicting teacher success is a case in point. Hundreds of studies produced negligible correlations or contradictory results so long as a global rating of success was the criterion. As soon as investigators went to more specific criteria which dealt with aspects of the teacher's performance, they began to get appreciable validities, where a mixed criterion lumping intellectual, emotional, and administrative contributions is not predictable. In therapy an overall index is not a good criterion if progress of a patient away from anxiety is concealed by negative scores assigned for an increase in expressed aggression. (p. 56)

The need for using criteria that do not cancel out growth achieved by some clients with changes (and perhaps even appropriate changes) achieved in others is discussed later. Edwards and Cronbach also call for the definition of precise goals for each client and the use of criterion measures by which changes in each of the relevant components can be assessed separately. Cartwright (1957) addressed this problem very convincingly (and perhaps with more enthusiasm than the measuring instruments available today justify) :

> We think that at the present stage of the science of evaluation, it is of major strategic importance to analyze that global dependent variable called personality change into its discriminable, independent components if such exist. And we think they do exist. A good student with no study problems who experiences difficulty in interpersonal relations is not likely to improve his work efficiency very much as a result of counseling. He is very efficient to start with. But he is likely to improve his interpersonal skills, for that is where he needs to change and can change for the better. And if he does come out with greater ease and facility in his relationships, who knows: he might even be less efficient (or less compulsively efficient) in his work. And "successful counseling" for him would likely mean very different changes in his behavior from what it would mean for a student who started with nothing but study problems. (p. 266)

The measurement of change in grades is but one of several cases in which researchers have used a common criterion for all clients when it was appropriate only for some of them. In many instances, such as the one cited by Cartwright, the researchers should have been able to predict direction of movement when they selected subjects for their groups, and if they felt it was necessary to combine their data for these opposite types, they should have used signed numbers to take account of appropriate, but opposite, movement of clients. Obviously, this approach cannot correct for the concealed differences described by Edwards and Cronbach; those call for instruments to evaluate the different components separately.

The behavioral therapists can teach other therapists a lesson on definition of goals for treatment and on the consequent selection of criterion measures. They have not attempted to improve the global adjustment of clients. They have merely focused their attention on one or two precise behaviors, for which they usually have had adequate measuring devices to assess predicted changes.

In reference to the fourth deficiency listed above, adequate validity cannot readily be established for the instruments commonly used to assess changes in clients. This, however, does not excuse disregard for the problem. Forgy and Black (1954) concluded that agreement of experts was sufficient evidence of content validity. Jensen, Coles, and Nestor (1955) also argued for efforts to establish construct validity.

Reliability can be established much more easily, but it often is not done—or at least it is not reported in the literature. Regardless of content validity, the results mean nothing without adequate reliability. Jensen, Coles, and Nestor described four methods for assessing reliability: internal consistency, stability, equivalence, and agreement between two or more raters. With increasing emphasis upon observation of behavior outside the treatment setting by significant others or judges, the latter has taken on increased importance. Though as Jensen, Coles, and Nestor indicated, correlations of ratings for judges may still be better understood, the writer's experience suggests that the percentage of agreement between judges on each decision is a more severe test of reliability.

Paul's (1967) conclusion highlights the need for researchers to attend to this problem: ". . . Subjective reports of change by clients or therapists are notorious for their lack of reliability and validity, and specific problems negate the use of psychological tests." (p. 112)

The fifth weakness listed is use of instruments insensitive to the desired changes requested by clients. Two quite different measurement problems account for this difficulty. In the first case the researcher selects an instrument that was designed for personality assessment of seriously disturbed patients and tries to use it to assess change in reasonably healthy clients. Pretest scores leave so little ceiling for change that the researcher cannot expect to obtain significant change. The other problem resides in the way tests are constructed to achieve stability or status. Bereiter (1962) concluded that present methods of construction tend to produce tests insensitive to the differential changes that educational and guidance services are supposed to produce. Thus, he argues for development of tests that converge on the factor of change rather than the factor of status. Hopefully, this can be done and still produce instruments with acceptable reliability.

Counseling's worth rests on the notion of furthering *individual* development and helping individuals face and learn to deal with painful and distressing problems. Therefore, appraisal must focus upon individual change. Involving clients in defining treatment goals (the basis for defining criteria to appraise change) conveys respect for clients and encourages them to discuss termination when they feel that they should, instead of merely quitting—either because they believe they have obtained the assistance they require or because they do not believe they can be helped. When, for example, George, a very bright tenth grader, asked to join a counseling group to improve his grades and his relationship with his teachers and parents, the counselor helped him determine how he would know when he had achieved these goals. They decided that his 3.4 grade point average could be markedly improved—that perhaps a 4.50 would be a reasonable goal for a six- to nine-month period. They also agreed on some specific behavior changes that he would be expected to make and how reactions to these changes might be reflected by his teachers and parents. (These items were incorporated into a behavior inventory, which was filled out periodically by his parents and teachers as well as himself.) After eight or nine weeks George decided that he should revise his goal to 4.00. Though he urged two other members of his group to continue to work for A's because they required scholarships to attend college, he concluded that for him it was more important to pursue some special reading in physics, and also to develop himself as a person by reading in psychology, literature, and political science, rather than to do the conforming tasks required to earn A's. Whereas his new goal decreased the counselor's chances for obtaining significant improvement on one criterion for his groups, the decision was one that George should be allowed to make. Furthermore, criteria for appraising change for individual clients can take cognizance of such idiosyncratic goals, as will be discussed later.

Appraisal Techniques

Once criteria are defined, the researcher can select from among available techniques or develop new techniques, to appraise changes in his clients. If, instead of using whatever devices are available, he takes the time to define relevant criteria, select or develop appropriate devices, test new devices in carefully designed pilot studies, and administer each only to appropriate clients, he will markedly increase his chances for adequately appraising his treatment methods. Hopefully, he will try to avoid all of the weaknesses described in the previous section of this chapter. He also must ask himself whether the data obtained from each technique will enable him to use the statistical analysis required to test his hypothesis.

Leary's (1957) system for classifying levels of personality lends itself well for classifying the type of measures used in assessing changes in clients. His five levels of personality are determined by the sources of his data. Level I, which he labelled as public communication level, concerns the person's impact on others. Typically important others such as classmates, friends, teachers, siblings, parents, and employers have completed sociometric tests, behavior inventories, Q-sorts, and check lists to describe each subject. Leary's level II is self-description; he called it a conscious description. Such self-reporting devices as autobiographies, check lists, Q-sorts, behavior inventories, and personality questionnaires have been used to obtain each subject's view of himself, of his problems, and of life in general. Level III provides a subject's autistic, projective fantasy, or preconscious views. Leary has usually used TAT and Rorschach to obtain these responses. Inasmuch as even Leary agreed that levels IV (unexpressed unconscious) and V (ego ideal) have limited value at present, they will not be discussed; the techniques commonly used to assess changes in clients can be classified into the other three categories.

Perhaps a brief diversion is justified here. Researchers who are acquainted with the techniques for studying group process and content analysis, and can make a video recording of their treatment sessions, may find that Leary's theory of levels of personality lends itself to the study of several prominent theories of adjustment. For example, it may lend itself to studies of Freud's (1957) explanation of neurosis and psychosis; of Horney's (1945) notion that it is not the conflict itself, but the degree of conflict and the subject's awareness of the conflict that determines his ability to function adequately; and of Sullivan's (1953) view of the ways in which communication, and subsequently adjustment, are influenced by both interpersonal and intrapersonal conflicts.

Level I appraisals are usually labelled external measures of change. When counseling is effective, important others should notice some of the changes in behavior and attitudes. However, Broedel, Ohlsen, Proff, and Southard (1960) found that some important others did not notice readily the changes in underachieving adolescent clients; hence, they urged counselors to help such clients convey their new selves to important others:

> . . . each client must learn to live with his new self, communicate this new self to important others, and teach these important others to understand, to accept, and live with the new self. For example, it is difficult for the average teacher to believe that these hostile and uncooperative students have really changed and for distressed parents to believe that these youngsters are willing to take responsibility for their work, and without nagging. (p. 170)

Even in this study trained observers and important others, especially parents, reported some significant changes in clients' behavior. Very likely better results would have been obtained had the items in the behavior inventory been designed especially for these clients and been limited to behaviors for which changes were predicted.

If the counselor involves important others in defining goals for treatment and enlists their assistance in reinforcing specific changes, he can sensitize them to look for specific changes, but at the risk of obtaining biased reports. Rickard (1965) has tried to reduce biased reporting by the use of trained interviewers, and at the same time has tried to enhance cooperation from important others in defining precise, tailored criteria for each client:

> It seems feasible to select a board of judges, not necessarily psychologists, who might interview important figures in the patient's life, examine case material, and interview the patient more precisely to identify stable, sensitive, relevant behavior to be changed. After psychotherapy or the experimental treatment, the same judges without knowledge of which patients were experimental Ss, would again examine sources of evidence which would bear upon whether the behavior had, in effect, changed. Rickard and Brown (1960) have demonstrated that judges may show a high degree of agreement as to whether or not a specific behavior changes as therapy progresses. An additional function of the judges would be to consider the stability of the behavioral change over time. . . . (p. 65)

Meehl (1959) recommended that the type of data obtained from others described by Rickard be recorded on a standard form for more effective statistical treatment. From his observations it would appear that observers' and interviewers' use of a Q-sort improved reporting. The writer prefers to use a behavior inventory that includes precise descriptions of relevant, specific behaviors and that requires observers to indicate the degree to which each item in the inventory describes each subject (and without knowing which subjects were treated and which were used as controls). Where a criterion involves an event that can be observed and counted, such as the number of times a pupil completes his homework on time, this should be reported as a specific number so that it can be compared with behavior during the baseline period.

From content analysis of interactions an investigator can obtain other clients' reactions to a specific client as well as a client's reactions to himself and others. Raimy's (1948), Seeman's (1949), Sheerer's (1949), Snyder's (1947), and Stock's (1949) early studies were concerned with the affect revealed in discussing the topic "self and others." The same method may be applied to various relevant topics for clients. For example, Wigell and Ohlsen (1962) found that gifted, underachieving adolescents who had difficulty with authority figures began counseling by discussing authority figures with significantly more frequent use of negative affect than either ambivalent or positive affect, and concluded counseling discussing the topic with significantly more frequent use of positive affect. When content analysis of interactions is used, arrangements should be made for clients to meet for one or two sessions during follow-up testing in which they are encouraged to discuss those topics for which they sought counseling. Other questions that may be answered by content analysis of interactions are: Did each client discuss the problems with which he sought assistance? Did he report taking any specific actions to resolve these problems? With what affect were these topics discussed? Did the affect change?

Zax and Klein (1960) described external measures as extremely important, but also noted that their use was beset with a host of measurement problems—for example, the development of criteria broad enough to be meaningful and representative of a wide range of functioning and at the same time circumscribed enough to be measured with reliability.

Shoben (1953) also took note of the difficulty in obtaining these level I types of evaluations, but concluded that they were essential:

> Until the operational criteria used in specific studies are related to the realities of the clients' actual world, their meaningfulness remains moot and controversial. . . . (p. 289)

Thus we are brought full circle to our central point that research in counseling effectiveness must be concerned with the valuations the client makes of his experience of counseling and the valuations placed upon the client before and after his counseling experience by what Sullivan (1947) calls his "significant others." . . . (p. 289)

Investigations of counseling effectiveness will bring proper returns only when they involve considerations of how the client deals with himself and his associates in the world beyond the clinic's doors. . . . (p. 291)

Level II measures involve many of the same problems as level I measures—especially since they may involve the same or similar instruments. When a counselor has established a good relationship with clients or when clients wish to terminate counseling, they may describe themselves in a positively biased manner, and when a good relationship has not been developed they may deny its benefits even when they have been helped. Zax and Klein (1960) analyzed the use of level II measures as follows:

Perhaps the simplest and most direct means of assessing a client's progress in treatment is to ask him to evaluate his own status. Such a phenomenological approach has often been used. Unfortunately, on close analysis, this deceptively simple procedure is seen to be fraught with serious pitfalls. Standards for such assessments will vary both among clients and between client and researcher; clients will vary in the extent to which they can report what they feel; the reports of many clients will be subject to the various unconscious distortions; finally, the client's evaluation of his condition may be affected by conscious or semiconscious motives. In positing the "hello-goodbye" effect, Hathaway (1948) has warned of the subtle social influences which limit the reliability of many of the phenomenological measures which have been made. On entering, the client is under the conventional pressure to justify his appeal for help so that problems are discussed freely. When seeking to terminate, however, he feels an obligation, out of courtesy toward one who attempted to help, to express gratitude and satisfaction. A fundamental weakness of the phenomenological approach would, therefore, seem to reside in the difficulty in obtaining reliable assessments. It seems likely that the content of such assessments depends greatly upon who asks for it and the circumstances under which it was requested. (p. 443)

Much work must be done to establish satisfactory validity and reliability for level III types of measures. Nevertheless, content analysis of clients' responses to picture-story and incomplete-sentence tests appears promising, and can be reliably scored [Broedel, Ohlsen, Proff and Southard (1960)]. Their findings also suggested some support for Leary's idea of classifying picture-story responses as preconscious. They found that their clients exhibited significantly increased acceptance of self on level III (through their identification figures in picture-story responses) before they exhibited increased acceptance of self on level II (self-reports on the behavior inventory).

Subjects, Design, and Statistical Analysis

When a researcher has defined the prescribed treatment for whom, under what conditions, and by whom, he should know how to select his subjects. However, some researchers still cannot answer these questions: What is my population? How may I sample it in order to make the statistical analyses to test my hypothesis? How large a sample will I require to test my hypothesis adequately? What control subjects do I need? What are my obligations to my controls? How can I be certain that they will not obtain some other treatment while they are serving as controls?

If a researcher is going to use a statistical consultant, his assistance should be sought during the planning stage of the research project in order to insure that the data collected lend themselves to the statistical analyses required to test his hypotheses, and that the sample is selected to meet the necessary conditions for use of the chosen statistical analyses.

Though most researchers seem to accept the need for control subjects, they often fail to take the necessary precautions to insure that they serve this function. If researchers have effectively screened candidates for counseling, their control subjects will recognize and desire treatment. Unless something is done to insure assistance from someone later, they will find and obtain treatment while they are supposed to be serving as controls. For this reason the researcher should explain to controls how chance determined which persons were treated first and make specific arrangements to counsel them later (after post-testing). In addition to exhibiting concern for this inconvenience he should provide free counseling for those who serve as controls (or treat them at a reduced rate). Furthermore, researchers should seriously consider budgeting to pay all subjects for pre-, post-, and follow-up testing and for travel expenses to testing centers: it markedly enhances cooperation. This design, which provides for counseling controls, also enables the researcher to enlarge his number of experimental subjects and to use them as their own controls.

Bergin (1963) concluded that one of the reasons why experimental subjects failed to change more than their controls in many experiments was that controls were not true controls; they, too, had obtained treatment, although probably from someone other than professional mental-health workers. In any case, researchers must investigate the daily life experiences of both control and experimental subjects in order to assess the influence of experiences other than counseling on their adjustment.

Frequently researchers' control subjects have differed from their experimental subjects prior to treatment, and their statistical methods for analyzing their data have failed to take account of these original differences. For example, subjects who volunteer for counseling usually differ from those who do not volunteer.

The above studies suggest that voluntary participation in counseling is likely to be associated with grade improvement and that nonvoluntary participation is not likely to be so related. One of the problems is to obtain a control group which volun-

teers for counseling, but does not receive it. The study by
Spielberger (1962) does have this feature and positive results
were obtained [Ewing and Gilbert (1967), p. 236].

Ewing and Gilbert also found that students who cooperated
in their project improved their grades whether they were
counseled or not, but counseled students improved more than
noncounseled students.

The obvious solution is to select a pool of subjects and
use a table of random numbers to divide them into two groups.
Of course, it is always a good idea for the researcher to determine whether or not chance can account for an observed
difference in relevant characteristics between controls and
experimental subjects prior to treatment. This enables him to
decide whether to take account of observed differences by
sampling differently or by statistical controls.

Rarely do researchers describe the population from which
their sample is drawn to an extent that allows meaningful
generalizations about their results. Furthermore, they tend to
use such a small sample that it is difficult to procure the
changes necessary to achieve significance [Cohn (1967) ; Cartwright (1957)].

Paul (1967) presented a strong case for selecting a homogeneous sample to focus upon a *specific change* in behavior of
a specific type of client. This approach enables a researcher to
assess the impact of specific treatment on certain clients and
to compare various treatments for such clients. The writer
accepts the advantages of Paul's model but prefers to give his
research subjects a chance to participate in defining additional
idiosyncratic goals and to help develop criteria that may be
used to assess changes with reference to these goals. If, for
example, a client were a member of a high school group in
which all were concerned about learning to cope with test
anxiety, the researcher would use a common criterion to
appraise changes pertaining to their common goal, but he
would have defined with each client's assistance other specific

goals (such as improved skills in relating to parents and teachers) and specific criteria to assess these changes, too. Prior to treatment a counselor should decide with each client's assistance what would be considered to be significantly changed behavior with reference to each of these idiosyncratic goals. Then he merely compares the number of instances in which experimental subjects achieved these idiosyncratic goals (for example, improved grades from 3.4 to 4.3 or increased reading comprehension by 1.5 years in three months) with the number of instances in which controls achieved theirs during the treatment period to determine whether chance can account for the observed differences. Obviously, there is no way of assessing whether these achievements have equal worth, but this approach does take account of clients' individual needs, recognizes their responsibility for helping to decide what specific behaviors and attitudes are to be changed, involves them in the treatment and appraisal processes, and conveys respect for their judgments.

Finally, could it be that some treatment methods are more effective for some clients than others? Are some methods of treatment more effective for certain types of clients when provided by a certain type of counselor? Edwards and Cronbach (1952) suggested a factorial design to answer the first question. A three-dimensional analysis of variance is a natural for answering the second.

To answer the kinds of questions raised by Bergin (1963) and Cartwright (1957) calls for use of multivariate statistical methods. Because of the numerous process variables that are interacting with outcome variables Cohn and his research team (1967) also recommended the use of multivariate statistical methods. Since they recognized that the use of such methods may discourage counselors and psychotherapists, they pointed out the mutual advantages for counseling psychologists and quantitative psychologists collaborating on research: ". . . Counseling psychologists will probably find it easy to entice quantitative psychologists to collaborate with them on well-planned, extensively supported research programs, as methodologists usually do not have their own substantive problems." (p. 21)

In the final analysis Edwards and Cronbach concluded that those who appraise outcomes of counseling must be the suspicious, tough-minded scientists when they decide what is proven fact, but sensitive enough *not* to discard unproven ideas merely because their experiments were not powerful enough to reveal significant relationships:

> If this tender-minded soul is gullible, believing in what has met no significance test, he will end up with a science stuffed with superstitions. But if he holds these yet-unproven ideas in the air, as notions which may guide him in the next experiment or the treatment of the next patient, he is more likely to be correct than the man who casts the idea from his mind as soon as one experiment fails to provide significant confirmation. (p. 57)

Results

This section cites the conclusions of some reviewers, reviews selected studies in which reasonably healthy clients were counseled in groups, and discusses the implications of research findings for improving counseling practices.

When Eysenck reported in 1952, and reaffirmed in 1965, "that roughly two-thirds of a group of neurotic patients will recover or improve to a marked extent within about two years of the onset of their illness, whether they are treated by means of psychotherapy or not," and concluded that the data failed to prove that psychotherapy facilitates recovery, he shocked the profession. Difficult as it is for some to accept his conclusions, all should note that he also registered concern about the skills possessed by the therapists and called for carefully planned and executed further studies to assess therapists' effectiveness.

Levitt (1957) reached a similar conclusion concerning the effectiveness of psychotherapy for children (preschool to

21 years, with very few patients over 18, and not many over 17 years) :

> It now appears that Eysenck's conclusion concerning the data for adult psychotherapy is applicable to children as well; the results do not support the hypothesis that recovery from neurotic disorder is facilitated by psychotherapy. . . . (p. 193)
>
> The present evaluation of child psychotherapy, like its adult counterpart, fails to support the hypothesis that treatment is effective, but it does not force acceptance of a contrary hypothesis. The distinction is an important one, especially in view of the differences among the concerned studies, and their generally poor calibre of methodology and analysis. Until additional evidence from well-planned investigations becomes available, a cautious, tongue-in-cheek attitude toward child psychotherapy is recommended. (p. 194)

In his reply to Eysenck, Rosenzweig (1954) rephrased the conclusion much as Levitt did: ". . . The only safe deduction on the basis of currently available data is that, in view of the diversity of methods and standards in the field of psychotherapy, broad generalizations as to the effectiveness of treatment are to be avoided." (p. 303) Rosenzweig criticized Eysenck's paper chiefly for his criteria for selecting subjects from the various studies, his failure to describe the treatments used and the varied conditions under which treatment was provided, and the criteria he used to evaluate improvement.

With specific reference to group psychotherapy, Pattison's (1965) recent review is frequently cited in the literature. The seven points in his conclusion were:

> First, evaluation studies of group psychotherapy have lagged behind studies of individual psychotherapy. . . .
>
> Second, studies of therapeutic outcome continue to rely on primary clinical data. . . .
>
> Third, in terms of behavioral criteria, a group psychotherapeutic effect has been demonstrated. However, these were "fairly" sick populations and the effect of other general

therapeutic factors does not appear to have been ruled
out.

Fourth, the usual psychometric tests have proved disap-
pointing. It is found that tests of functions most close to
awareness or actual performance are most applicable.
At best, it is doubtful that such global assessments will
discriminate between general therapeutic change and
any unique therapeutic assets of group psychotherapy.

Fifth, the use of specific construct criteria appears promising. . . .

Sixth, the global problem of assessment needs to be dissected
into variables, such as the type of patient population,
the types of group therapy, the context of therapy, the
effect of time, and the phase effect of group process.

Seventh, a continuum exists in terms of patients, treatment
goals, and treatment techniques, which parallel each
other. Evaluation studies require a consideration of each
of these factors in framing hypotheses. (p. 392–393)

Gundlach (1967) found that most of the research papers
he reviewed on outcomes of group psychotherapy dealt with
treatment of hospitalized schizophrenics. However, best results
were obtained in treating delinquent youth. He identified
research design as a critical problem for research in this area.

Psathas (1967) expressed disappointment with group
therapists' slowness to accept and use social psychologists'
findings. Though other reviews concerned with process studies
are not mentioned here, this one is because many of Psathas'
ideas have relevance for those who wish to investigate the
relationship between process variables and outcome variables:

There is a need for more than the inclusion of control groups
in research; there is a need for a systematic analysis and comparison of a wide range of groups, with special focus on those
concerned with producing behavioral change, so that it may be
learned what processes they have in common and what processes
differ. We should not assume that only therapy groups are
"therapeutic." (p. 228)

What I think is needed in the study of group process is dis-

covery of the rules of the games that people play. The discovery
of these rules will have two effects: one is that we will develop
better methodologies for their discovery, and second is that,
once discovered, teaching these rules to participants in the
games enables them to "see" the game. The latter is important
for producing changes in game behavior, i.e., "therapy." (p. 230)

Chapter Four discussed the significance of clients' understanding *expectations* in order to acquire an adequate basis
for deciding whether to join a group and to accept their full
responsibility for developing a therapeutic climate within their
counseling group. The research on rules of the game suggested
by Psathas should clarify such expectations.

Rogers' (1957) hypothesis concerning the necessary and
sufficient conditions for effective therapy were tested in the
Wisconsin studies. Truax and Carkhuff (1964) reviewed these
findings and reported on the project initiated by Truax on
group psychotherapy in which they evaluated the significance
of the therapist's accurate empathy, unconditional warmth,
genuineness, and intimacy of interpersonal contact. They
also investigated the degree of the patient's intrapersonal
exploration:

> The findings from 30 studies to date are surprisingly uniform:
> each of the therapist "conditions" was significantly related to
> both the amount of patient intrapersonal or self-exploration,
> and most importantly, each of the therapist conditions was
> significantly related to the degree of client improvement as
> measured by a wide variety of standard psychological tests
> including both the Rorschach and the Minnesota Multiphasic
> Personality Inventory, as well as such concrete and objective
> behavioral indices as length of hospital stay.
>
> In comparing patients who received high levels of therapeutic
> conditions with patients who received low levels of therapeutic
> conditions and matched control patients, very disquieting find-
> ings emerged. Patients who received low level conditions
> throughout psychotherapy tended to show clear negative change
> in personality functioning. This latter finding has special signif-
> icance since if comparisons had been made only between the

combined therapy group and the control group, no differences
in outcomes would have appeared. . . .*
One finding of particular significance was that the relationship between therapist conditions and case outcome was the
same for schizophrenics as for counseling cases. . . . (p. 862)

In his review Patterson (1966) deplored the artificial
separation of counseling and psychotherapy. He contended that
one could not differentiate between these processes. As Truax
and Carkhuff noted, findings discovered in one often apply to
the other. Hence, counselors and psychotherapists must know
one another's findings.

Gazda and Larsen's (1968) abstracts included approximately a hundred outcome studies. They found that about half
the studies reported positive change or growth. These changes
included improved grades or academic achievement, acceptance of self, acceptance of others, family and peer relations,
relations with authority figures, school behavior, and school
attendance. They also reported decreased anxiety in meeting
life's challenges. However, they were disappointed with the
number of instances in which positive changes were based on
general description rather than on precise testing or carefully
controlled observations. In other words, they were disappointed with the criteria that investigators used to assess
clients' growth.

Shaw and Wursten (1965) also were disappointed with
the quality of the research, but concluded that some of this
trial and error should be expected when practitioners attempt
to evaluate outcomes for a relatively new treatment. They
summarized their conclusions as follows:

*Readers should take special note of those instances in which chance
can account for changes in means, but not for changes in standard devi-
ations, between pre- and post-testing and/or follow-up testing. The
writer has observed a number of instances in which the evidence suggested that the researchers had failed to notice this condition, the very
one that may support the findings reported above by Truax and
Carkhuff.

Current research leaves essentially unanswered many of the elemental questions related to use of group procedures in schools. In addition, it is difficult to accept at face value the reported outcomes of many studies due to inadequate controls, inadequate statistical procedures, and inadequate outcome criteria. In spite of these shortcomings most studies reported "successful" outcomes. Whether these outcomes are as successful as stated or whether they are the result of inappropriate procedures is impossible to say. The possible screening out of "unsuccessful" group experiments in schools as a result of the unwritten publication policies of some psychological journals can likewise not be ignored as a possible contributing factor to the preponderance of "successful" outcomes reported. (p. 32)

Turning next to a brief review of specific studies, we begin with studies in which children were treated. Until very recently most schools have failed to provide counseling for elementary-school children. Chapter Eleven discussed why this situation must be changed.

Although it involved a very small sample, Davis' (1948) study is reviewed because it was among the early studies with children, and the investigator did use relevant criteria for growth. She counseled nine children in two groups: thirty minutes for each session twice a week for ten weeks. She asked: "Can the degree of social acceptance within a first grade be increased?" Then she used a sociometric test to appraise change in pre-, post-, and follow-up testing. She also used teachers' daily reports and photographed the children periodically during a free-play period. She concluded that she did improve social acceptance for the counseled pupils.

In spite of the brief treatment period and their experimental and control groups, Kranzler, Mayer, Dyer, and Munger (1966) obtained significant results. They provided group counseling twice a week for six weeks for eight fourth graders and group guidance by the teacher for the other group. Those counseled in groups improved, and maintained their improvement in a seven-month follow-up, more than either the control group or those given group guidance.

Ohlsen and Gazda (1965) appraised the impact of group counseling upon bright, underachieving fifth graders. Twenty-two experimental subjects were counseled twice a week for eight weeks. Compared to their controls they failed to exhibit significant change in grades, behavior-inventory scores, perceptions of self, social acceptance, and achievement-test scores, but they did reveal increased congruence between perceptions of self and ideal self, increased acceptance of peers, and marked improvement in psychosomatic illnesses—such as asthma attacks, stomach cramps, and headaches. Selection of clients more highly committed to change attitudes and behaviors would have increased their chances for successful treatment.

Novick (1965) compared the changes achieved by treating both good and poor prospects in individual and group counseling. The children were behavior-problem cases who were treated as outpatients in a community mental-health center. Groups varied from three to five in size. Observers rated each child on nineteen behavioral characteristics (such as bullying, cheating at school) at three different intervals: before therapy, after ten sessions, and after twenty sessions. By the end of ten sessions no significant changes occurred. After twenty sessions significant changes were obtained for some patients. Best prospects (high ego strength) responded to treatment better than poor prospects. Chance could account for any observed differences in scores for those who received individual and group psychotherapy. Generally the various therapists agreed upon their treatment approach as:

> . . . the establishing of a friendly, warm, and emotionally comfortable climate, the maintenance of a reasonably permissive atmosphere with some restrictions, calm acceptance of the young patients and of the nondesirable aspects of their behavior, avoidance of judgmental attitudes, and flexible combination of activity-play and verbal communication. The content of the verbal discussion centered around either specific problems or feelings and attitudes in general which were not necessarily directly related to the problem areas. (p. 369)

Perhaps even better results would have been obtained had the therapists focused on the problems that brought the children to therapy. At least that is what Harth (1966) and Shaftel and Shaftel (1967) tried to do. Harth used role playing to help nine- to eleven-year-old disturbed children change their attitudes toward school and their classroom behavior and to cope with their frustrations at school. Shaftel and Shaftel recommended confronting an entire class with a specific dilemma and using role playing to increase empathy for the primary character and to involve pupils in discovering various solutions to specific problems.

Sonstegard (1961) found that group counseling for fifth-grade underachievers improved reading achievement, classroom behavior, and work habits when parents and teachers also were actively involved in the treatment program.

Winkler, Tiegland, Munger, and Kranzler (1965) identified 121 underachievers in 22 classrooms. These pupils were randomly assigned to five groups: group counseling, individual counseling, remedial reading, Hawthorne effect, and a control group. Those counseled were provided 14 half-hour sessions by six male counselors. It appeared that these were beginning counselors with limited experience counseling children. None of the treatments resulted in significant improvement either in grades or personality-test scores. In many respects this is a very well-designed study. Perhaps it should be replicated with carefully screened clients who really are committed to change their behavior, with experienced elementary-school counselors, and with more precise criteria (in addition to GPA), such as Novick (1965) used.

Chapter Ten made a case for counseling adolescents in groups. During the past decade there has been a marked growth in use of group counseling for treating adolescents. This surge has been supported by an increase in research pertaining to its efficacy for adolescents.

Bates (1968) investigated the effect of time distributions on results obtained. Clients who were treated by two group methods were compared with controls: one met weekly for a class period for thirteen weeks, and one met in continuous session during school hours for two days. The 36 students who were treated by each method were divided into three sub-groups for counseling. Except for responses to the Rotter sentence-completion test, for which their responses improved over those of controls, the marathon groups failed to produce significant changes. For the regular counseling approach positive changes were obtained with reference to attendance, citizenship, vocational choice, acceptance of self, and acceptance of others. Those who were treated by the traditional method maintained their GPA's, while those treated by the marathon methods and the controls deteriorated:

> . . . apparently the accelerated interaction group members were not able to sustain any effect that group counseling process may have had on them, at least when translated into the amount of effort that the teacher saw demonstrated in the classroom. On the other hand, the traditional group members, who were periodically reinforced through weekly interaction, seemed to be able to sustain their efforts to improve behavior to a degree that was obvious to the teacher. (p. 751)

Baymur and Patterson (1960) used underachieving high school students to compare individual and group techniques. They did not obtain significant results from this well-designed study, but, as they said, the limited experience of the counselor with American adolescents could account for their results. Selection of clients with greater commitment to change also could have increased their chances for success.

Benson and Blocher (1967) appraised the effectiveness of developmental group counseling for tenth-grade low-achieving boys. They defined their process as follows:

> Developmental counseling is aimed at helping clients perform more effectively in one or more social roles. It is primarily concerned with helping clients to master developmental tasks and consequently to acquire a more adequate repertoire of coping behaviors. (p. 215)

In spite of the small N (twelve experimental subjects treated in two groups of six), Benson and Blocher's experimental subjects improved their grades, decreased discipline referrals, improved their feelings of adequacy, and persisted in school better than their controls.

Broedel, Ohlsen, Proff, and Southard (1960) provided group counseling (twice a week for eight weeks) for gifted underachieving ninth graders and compared their appraised changes with those of carefully chosen controls. Though their subjects were given the alternative of not participating, these investigators failed to make it the prospective client's responsibility to demonstrate readiness for counseling. Significant positive changes were observed with reference to improved achievement-test scores, acceptance of self and others, and ability to relate to peers, siblings, and parents, but no significant increase was obtained in GPA's. Follow-up data obtained in from fifteen to eighteen months indicated that changes obtained were maintained.

Caplan (1957) compared changes noted in unruly, antisocial, junior high school clients with controls who were matched on the bases of age, sex, intelligence, and school record. His treatment subjects were counseled once a week for fifty minutes for ten weeks. Improved agreement between perception of self and ideal self and improved citizenship were obtained, but not improved GPA. No follow-up was reported to determine whether gains were maintained.

Catron (1966) used a Q-sort to appraise the impact of group counseling with co-counselors upon thirteen groups of high school students. Though the clients' stated purpose was educational-vocational counseling, they were much more interested in discussing (and were permitted to discuss) parent-child relationships, variation in quality of their teachers, peer relationships, and social attitudes. The counselors helped their clients deal with their feelings, especially feelings underlying choice-making and problem-solving. Catron's analysis of his data revealed that perception of self changed significantly for improved adjustment, but no significant changes were noted for perception of either ideal person or ordinary others. He also raised the question whether adolescent girls may be affected differently than boys by group counseling, presenting evidence to support this notion. Few of the studies reviewed meet the previously described standards for research on outcomes as well as this one does.

Clements (1966) evaluated the usefulness of group counseling for preparing college-bound high school seniors for their college environment. He selected randomly 180 students out of a group of 225 from one high school class. These were divided into a treatment group of 60 (six groups of ten each) and two control groups. Group discussions (six sessions while in high school, and additional ones for volunteers as college freshmen), focused on attitudes, fears, and aspirations. Those counseled showed significantly less anxiety concerning self both prior to college entrance and after beginning college.

Gersten (1951) found that juvenile delinquents in the experimental group changed significantly, and in a positive direction, whereas members of the control group did not change with reference to their scores on the Wechsler-Bellevue, Stanford Achievement Tests, and Haggerty-Olsen-Wickman. In general, those who were counseled became less inhibited and evasive, more productive, more responsive to mature promptings from within, and better able to establish wholesome relationships with others.

Gilliland (1968) found that after one year of group counseling Negro students enrolled in a public high school demonstrated significant gains in vocabulary, reading, English usage, occupational aspiration, and vocational maturity. Experimental subjects also moved positively toward self-involvement in the group process. Seven boys were counseled in one group and seven girls in another group. A random sample of Negro boys and girls were used as controls. No attempt was made to equate for age, ability, achievement level, GPA, or school attendance. Two of the investigator's clinical observations are quoted:

> It was found that one of the primary expressed concerns of adolescent Negro males was vocations and vocational planning;

adolescent Negro females verbalized greater concern regarding social adjustment and social acceptance. . . . Group counseling appeared to produce in males a revised conceptual model of the ideal self, prompting them to acquire and use, near the end of the year, such academic skills as listening and studying to the degree that functional classroom success was achieved. The implication for counselors and educators is that such educational endeavors as group activities, counseling, remedial study skills, and vocational information projects may be appropriate for Negro adolescents even though they appeared unwanted at first. (p. 150)

Hansen, Zimpfer, and Easterling (1967) investigated the relevance of relationship conditions to changes in self-concept congruence for secondary school students (50 students from six high schools—each of the six groups being counseled in its own school) :

The results indicate that (a) students' perceptions of the relationships are important to their growth in real-ideal self-concept congruence, (b) if a negative relationship is perceived, students' self-concept congruence will remain the same or decrease, and (c) students expecting a positive relationship make more gains in self-concept congruence than those expecting a negative relationship. (p. 461)

Krumboltz and Thoresen (1964) assessed the effect of both individual and group behavioral counseling on volunteer eleventh graders from six high schools near Stanford University. Two types of treatment were used on both individual and group basis: reinforcement counseling (for information-seeking behavior) and model-reinforcement counseling. They also provided for a special control for the Hawthorne effect. Individual and group counseling were both effective, but males who received model-reinforcement counseling were stimulated more by the group than by the individual setting. Model-reinforcement counseling was generally more effective for males than females. However, the model was a male, hence it may have been easier for the male students to identify with him. This is another unusually well-designed study.

Laxer, Quarter, Isnor, and Kennedy (1967) failed to obtain significant improvement for experimental subjects over controls on any variables when they treated junior high school boys who were behavior problems. Perhaps the treatment period was too brief for clients of this type (40 minutes twice weekly for $7\frac{1}{2}$ weeks) and possibly they were not committed to change their behavior before they began counseling. The writer also has had better results when he combined such youngsters in groups with more conforming clients.

Lodato, Sokoloff, and Schwartz (1964) tried to modify slow learners' attitudes through group counseling. Their subjects varied in age from eight to sixteen: three groups from grades 7 or 8, one from grades 4 or 5, and two groups from grade 3. They only compared pre- and post-test scores for their subjects. On the basis of teachers' ratings they improved pupils' attitudes toward learning and authority figures. They also improved the self concept, school attendance, and teachers' tolerance for students.

McCarthy (1959) divided 24 bright, underachieving ninth-grade boys into four groups (two experimental and two controls) and provided six one-hour treatment sessions in which subjects' attention was focused on disguised case materials based on the boys' own problems. The clients' task was to try to diagnose the reasons for failure and to plan ways of helping these boys. Though they were not told that these were their own problems, they became defensive when their own case materials were discussed, and perhaps insufficient attention was given to helping them discuss these feelings. In any case, significant changes were not obtained. This study reminds the writer of a pilot project in which he provided a seminar for ninth-grade underachievers, who served as tutors for seventh- and eighth-grade children who requested assistance with arithmetic and English. As these underachievers talked about the problems with which they were confronted in helping others, they also often discussed what they could do to improve their own performance. In other words, the seminars became counseling for them. Perhaps both of these approaches should be evaluated by carefully designed research and with more specific behavioral criterion measures.

Mezzano (1967) discovered a statistically significant relationship between investment in group counseling and improvement in GPA. His subjects were low-motivated high school students (18 received individual and group counseling, 18 received group counseling, and 28 served as controls).

Thoresen and Krumbolz (1967) investigated the relationship between counselor reinforcement of certain responses and specific behaviors with volunteers from six high schools near Stanford University. Counselor reinforcement of information-seeking responses was positively associated with information-seeking behavior outside of counseling. Model reinforcement produced significantly more information-seeking behaviors than reinforcement alone did.

Walker (1959) evaluated the effect of group counseling for juvenile delinquents who volunteered for group counseling with their probation officer (three groups of 11 clients each). Though he did not have a control group and did no systematic pre- and post-testing, he concluded that his subjects exhibited marked improvement in relationship to authority figures. They also demonstrated better-than-average probation records.

The final group of studies reviewed here are concerned primarily with evaluation of outcomes of group counseling for college students and adults.

Chestnut (1965) evaluated the effect of structured and unstructured group counseling for gifted college under-achievers. Whereas those assigned to the unstructured group were permitted to discuss whatever originated spontaneously in their group, the counselor for the structured group encouraged clients to discuss, and to develop skills for coping with, the genesis of poor achievement. By the end of treatment only those in the structured group had improved grades significantly more than their controls. At the three-month follow-up their grades were still significantly better than those of the unstructured group.

Dickenson and Truax (1966) assessed the efficacy of

time-limited group counseling for underachieving college freshmen. By comparison with their controls more counseled students tended to earn passing grades and to improve their GPA's. Furthermore, those clients who experienced relatively high levels of therapeutic conditions (accurate empathy, unconditional positive regard, and genuineness) showed the greatest improvement.

Fiedler (1949) provided preventive group psychotherapy for college students faced with comprehensive exams at the University of Chicago. Three of his four groups profited from the treatment, but one client in the fourth group blocked the development of a therapeutic climate, and hence his entire group failed to profit from treatment.

Gazda and Ohlsen (1961) appraised the effects of group counseling on four groups of prospective counselors (34 clients). By comparison with their controls those counseled improved significantly their manifest needs in the predicted direction: increased autonomy and decreased abasement and succorance for all four groups, but other changes for only two groups: increased heterosexuality for two groups and decreased nurturance for two groups. Changes assessed by the picture-story test and the behavior inventory failed to achieve significance for either post-testing or follow-up. When, however, the interviewer (in a fourteen-month follow-up) requested clients to describe specific ways in which they had been helped or hurt, all but two clients were able to describe some specific ways in which they had been helped.

Gilbreath (1967) reported on a study in which he assessed changes in underachieving first- and second-year college males. Two counselors participated in the group counseling projects; each counseled two groups by the high-authority, leader-structured method and two groups by the low-authority, group-structured method. Those counseled by the leader-structured method experienced a higher rate of increase in GPA's and greater ego strength than did either the group-structured clients or the controls. At the three-month follow-up the leader-structured group's rate of increase in GPA's was not significantly greater than that for those counseled by the group-structured method. Furthermore, the investigator concluded that his dependent clients improved GPA's in leader-structured groups but not in group-structured groups. By contrast, his independent clients seemed to improve GPA's more in group-centered groups than in leader-centered groups.

Gorlow, Hoch, and Teleschow (1952) counseled 17 graduate students in three groups twice weekly for from 18 to 20 sessions. After prospective clients volunteered, the counselors used an intake interview to determine whether or not they were deeply concerned about some problems on which they were willing to work. After counseling, all clients perceived themselves and their fellow clients in a more favorable light. The investigators also developed a reliable method for dividing clients into two groups: most profited and least profited. Most-profited clients exhibited a significant decrease in negative behavior and increase in positive behavior, whereas no significant change was noted in the behavior of least-profited clients.

Leib and Snyder (1967) compared the effectiveness of group counseling and of experiences in a lecture discussion course on reading and study skills for underachieving undergraduates. Those treated by both methods improved their GPA's significantly, but chance could account for any observed differences in growth between the treatment methods.

Muro and Ohnmacht (1966) investigated the effects of group counseling on college freshmen enrolled in teacher education. One group was counseled once a week and the other was counseled twice a week. Compared to the controls, neither group improved significantly on acceptance of self, the dogmatism scale, or preference for complexity.

Ofman (1964) tried to appraise the impact of group counseling on college students. Owing to the design of the experiment and the statistical methods used, it is difficult to assess the impact of counseling. The investigator's study should alert future researchers to some of the differences between experimental subjects and those who are selected as controls. He made a good case for a baseline group and for researchers' making a greater effort to control motivational factors. At the beginning of his study there were no significant differences between volunteers in his treatment and control groups, but his subjects in the baseline group earned significantly higher GPA's than the volunteers. By the end of the experiment his treated subjects had improved their grades sufficiently so that there was no longer a significant difference in GPA's between treated and baseline subjects. Furthermore, his treated subjects earned significantly higher GPA's at the end of his experiment than did his control group.

Sheldon and Landsman (1950) found that failing college students who were counseled in groups improved their grades significantly more than their controls who were enrolled in a study-skills course. Furthermore, a one-year follow-up revealed that significantly fewer of the counseled students had dropped out of college than their controls.

Roth, Mauksch, and Peiser (1967) provided group counseling for bright, underachieving undergraduates (52 counseled in groups of from 7 to 12, and 52 controls). Counseling groups met twice a week for approximately one hour. The investigators concluded that these students do poorly in order to avoid risk-taking and to maintain a dependent relationship with their family. Hence, the counselor tried to provide help with both study skills and these dynamics. Those counseled improved their GPA's more than their controls, and the follow-up appraisal revealed that they maintained their gains.

Spielberger, Weitz and Denny (1962) evaluated the effectiveness of group counseling for anxious college freshmen. Volunteers who were provided group counseling showed greater improvement in GPA's than did the controls, who volunteered for group counseling but were not provided it. The investigators also found a significant relationship between the number of sessions clients attended and the improvement in their GPA's (a Pearson r of .63). From their analysis of MMPI scores they concluded that high attenders may be tentatively described as active-repressive, middle attenders as passive-rebellious, and low attenders as passive-withdrawn and ruminative. In their later study Spielberger and Weitz (1964) appear to have added subjects from another group of freshmen and to have made additional analyses of their data. Besides finding additional support for the findings reported above, they found proportionately fewer severe underachievers among the anxious than among the nonanxious underachievers; failure dropout rate for anxious volunteers in 1959 was less than for nonanxious students; and failure dropout rate in 1960 was lower for anxious volunteers and anxious nonvolunteers than for nonanxious students. Their rationale for providing counseling at the very beginning of college for these students is quoted below:

> There is little evidence, however, that personality problems are direct and immediate causes of poor academic performance. It seems more likely that, in response to the pressures of college life, students with personality problems are predisposed to develop maladaptive study habits and attitudes which, in turn, interfere with the learning process and lead to underachievement. For college students identified as having personality problems, preventive measures implemented at the beginning of the freshman year would come at a time when the potential for serious maladaptive behavior is heightened by new environmental stresses. (p. 1)

Teahan (1966) evaluated the effects of group psychotherapy on first-semester college sophomores who were in the top quarter of their high school class, but were not successful as freshmen. Because he believed that certain aspects of their personality interfered with college success, the counselor focused attention on personal and emotional problems. He obtained significant improvement in GPA's. Those whose GPA's improved described their fathers as more dominating and ignoring than those whose grades did not improve. Those who improved most also tended to obtain high Ma scores on MMPI. The higher F scores on MMPI suggest, the investigator concluded, that those most helped were more ready to discuss their personal problems, and their Si scores suggest that they were drawn into the group to satisfy their need for social interaction.

Thelen and Harris (1968) identified and contacted by letter 127 underachievers: 52 did not respond; 38 responded and completed the 16 PF, but were not interested in group psychotherapy; and 37 completed the test and volunteered for group psychotherapy. The latter were divided randomly into treatment subjects and controls—with dropouts these became $C=13$ and $E=19$ (four counseling groups). Those counseled improved their grades. The investigators concluded that those helped had less apprehension about treatment, were more self-accepting, and accepted the notion of obtaining assistance. Those who volunteered for group psychotherapy have the most to gain from it and the most to lose from not obtaining it.

Winborn and Schmidt (1962) investigated the effectiveness of short-term group counseling for bright, underachieving college freshmen. They did not obtain significant improvements on either GPA's or personality measures. However, they only provided six sessions over a two-month period.

For the 38 studies reviewed here the results are summarized briefly in Table I.

Review of Findings for Studies Reviewed

	Children	Adolescents	College students and adults
Significant results	4	10	11
Significant results on some criteria	1	3	2
Nonsignificant results	1	4	2

Summary

Considering his commitment to service, the time required to obtain adequate financial support for research, the difficulties involved in appraising outcomes of counseling, and his own feelings about his research skills, one would not expect the practitioner to do much research.

Even when he does research it is not sufficient for him to ask: "Is group counseling effective?" As a very minimum an investigator must try to assess the effectiveness of a clearly defined treatment provided for a distinctive sample of subjects (and compared to appropriate controls) within a specific setting by a carefully described counselor. A treatment method can be fairly appraised only when it is provided by a competent counselor under reasonably favorable conditions. Moreover, various treatments can be compared only when the counselors used in the experiment are qualified equally well to use each method and accept each method's worth. Unfortunately, many researchers fail to describe both the treatment method and the counselor's competencies to provide it.

The research reviewed in this volume suggests the need for better screening of prospective clients and improved preparation for those who do group counseling. A number of the studies also gave the impression that those who provided the counseling had very limited counseling experience. When, therefore, these inexperienced counselors failed to obtain significant results, the study should be replicated with well-prepared, experienced counselors, and even these experienced counselors should be supervised to insure that they provide the treatment described.

Greater care in the formulation of the questions to be asked or hypotheses to be tested could markedly improve most studies. Such planning, supported by a frank evaluation by an advisory board before the study is begun, improves the design, identifies weaknesses that can be corrected, helps the investigator collect the data he needs to test his hypotheses with the statistical techniques chosen, and helps insure that the investigator and his coworkers understand precisely what they are to do at each step in the experiment. If statistical consultants are to be used effectively, their assistance must be sought before a sample is selected and before the collection of any data.

Subjects must be selected with care—and larger samples are needed. Frequently controls differ from the experimental subjects prior to treatment; hence, statistical procedures selected for analysis of the data must take account of this fact. Investigators also must be alert to insure that controls do not also receive treatment during the experiment. Volunteers seem to profit more from counseling more than do those who are encouraged or coerced to accept counseling. Perhaps even volunteering for counseling is not sufficient. Though no study focused on this specific point, the writer infers from the evidence cited earlier that those who profit most from group counseling are those who are committed to attend every session, to talk openly about their problems, to help others talk about their problems, and to change their behavior.

Failure to define specific goals for each client in precise measurable or observable terms is one of the most serious weaknesses of the research designed to appraise outcomes of counseling. Once such goals are defined, an investigator can define the specific criteria he needs to select and/or develop measuring devices and observation techniques for detecting specific changes in his treatment subjects and their controls. By contrast, investigators are tempted to use as their criteria whatever the available tests measure. Five other weaknesses noted in criterion measures were: (1) vague, global measures, (2) common criteria for all clients when some are appropriate for only part of the clients, (3) failure to use signed numbers when appraising growth for clients who should be expected to make opposite movement, (4) unreliable and/or invalid tests or observation techniques, and (5) insensitive measuring devices. In other words, lack of relevant and adequate measurement techniques handicaps efforts to appraise outcomes of counseling.

Another related weakness of the research is failure to conduct adequate follow-up studies. It is not sufficient to demonstrate that counseling changes behavior. If clients are really helped by group counseling, the new improved behavior must be maintained following treatment.

Finally, the following impressions stood out as the writer tried to pull together his reactions to the research: (1) before prospective clients are asked to decide whether to participate in group counseling, they should understand what will be expected of them in group counseling; (2) within their group they should be expected to help develop a therapeutic climate and to maintain it; and (3) they should be expected to talk openly about their problems, to change their behavior and attitudes, and to help their fellow clients change their behaviors and attitudes—they should be expected to accept responsibility for achieving improved adjustment for themselves and their fellow clients. In other words, clients should be selected with care and be better prepared to meet their responsibilities within their counseling group. Furthermore, better data are needed to determine who are the best prospects for group counseling, with whom and by whom each may best be counseled, and how those who are not ready may be prepared to make the necessary commitments to profit from group counseling.

References

Bates, Marilyn. "A Test of Group Counseling," *Personnel and Guidance Journal*, 1966, 46:749–753.

Baymur, Feriha B., and C. H. Patterson "A Comparison of Three Methods of Assisting High School Students," *Journal of Counseling Psychology*, 1960, 7:83–90.

Benson, R. L., and D. H. Blocher "Evaluation of Developmental Counseling with Groups of Low Achievers in High School Setting," *The School Counselor*, 1967, 14:215–220.

Bereiter, C. "Use of Tests to Measure Change," *Personnel and Guidance Journal*, 1962, 41:6–11.

Bergin, A. E. "The Effects of Psychotherapy: Negative Results Revisted," *Journal of Counseling Psychology*, 1963, 10:244–249.

Broedel, J., M. Ohlsen, F. Proff, and C. Southard "The Effects of Group Counseling on Gifted Underachieving Adolescents," *Journal of Counseling Psychology*, 1960, 7:163–170.

Caplan, S. W. "The Effect of Group Counseling on Junior High School Boys' Concept of Themselves in School," *Journal of Counseling Psychology*, 1957, 4:124–128.

Carkhuff, R. R., and B. G. Berenson *Beyond Counseling and Therapy*, New York: Holt, Rinehart and Winston, Inc., 1967.

Carkhuff, R. R., and C. B. Truax "Training in Counseling and Psychotherapy: An Evaluation of an Intergrated Didactic and Experimental Approach," *Journal of Consulting Psychology*, 1965a, 29: 333–336.

Carkhuff, R. R., and C. B. Truax "Lay Mental Health Counseling: The Effects of Lay Group Counseling," *Journal of Consulting Psychology*, 1965b, 29:426–431.

Cartwright, D. S. "Methodology in Counseling Evaluation," *Journal of Counseling Psychology*, 1957, 4:263–267.

Catron, D. W. "Educational-Vocational Group Counseling: The Effects on Perception of Self and Others," *Journal of Counseling Psychology*, 1966, 13:202–207.

Chestnut, W. J. "The Effects of Structured and Unstructured Group Counseling on Male College Students' Underachievement," *Journal of Counseling Psychology*, 1965, 24:388–394.

Clements, B. E. "Transitional Adolescents, Anxiety and Group Counseling," *Personnel and Guidance Journal*, 1966, 45:67–71.

Cohn, B. *Guidelines for Future Research on Group Counseling in the Public School Setting*, Washington, D.C.: American Personnel and Guidance Association, 1967.

Davis, Ruth G. "Group Therapy and Social Acceptance in First Grade," *Elementary School Journal*, 1948, 49:219–223.

Dickenson, W. A., and C. B. Truax "Group Counseling with College Underachievers," *Personnel and Guidance Journal*, 1966, 45:243–247.

Edwards, A. L., and L. J. Cronbach "Experimental Design for Research in Psychotherapy," *Journal of Clinical Psychology*, 1952, 8:51–59.

Ewing, T. N., and W. M. Gilbert "Controlled Study of the Effects of Counseling on the Scholastic Achievements of Students of Superior Ability," *Journal of Counseling Psychology*, 1967, 14:235–239.

Eysenck, H. J. "The Effects of Psychotherapy: An Evaluation," *Journal of Consulting Psychology*, 1952, 16:319–324.

Eysenck, H. J. "The Effects of Psychotherapy," *International Journal of Psychiatry*, 1965, 1:99–144.

Fiedler, F. E. "An Experimental Approach to Preventative Psychotherapy," *Journal of Social and Abnormal Psychology*, 1949, 44: 386–393.

Forgy, E. W., and J. D. Black "A Follow-up after Three Years of Clients Counseled by Two Methods," *Journal of Counseling Psychology*, 1954, 1:1–8.

Freud, S. *Collected Papers*, vol. 2, London: Hogarth Press, Ltd., 1957.

Gazda, G. M., and Mary J. Larsen "A Comprehensive Appraisal of Group and Multiple Counseling," *Journal of Research and Development in Education*, 1968, 1:57–132.

Gazda, G. M., and M. M. Ohlsen "The Effects of Short-Term Group Counseling on Prospective Counselors," *Personnel and Guidance Journal*, 1961, 39:634–638.

Gersten, C. "An Experimental Evaluation of Group Therapy with Juvenile Delinquents," *International Journal of Group Psychotherapy*, 1951, 1:311–318.

Gilbreath, S. H. "Group Counseling, Dependence, and College Male Achievement," *Journal of Counseling Psychology*, 1967a, 14:449–453.

Gilbreath, S. H. "Group Counseling with Male Underachieving Volunteers," *Personnel and Guidance Journal*, 1967b, 45:469–476.

Gilliland, B. E. "Small Group Counseling with Negro Adolescents in a Public High School," *Journal of Counseling Psychology*, 1968, 15: 147–152.

Goldstein, M. "Some Characteristics of Research in Applied Settings," *American Psychologist*, 1959, 14:272–278.

Gorlow, L., E. Hoch, and E. Teleschow *The Nature of Non-directive Group Psychotherapy*, New York: Bureau of Publications, Teachers College, Columbia University, 1952.

Gundlach, G. H. "Overview Studies in Group Psychotherapy," *International Journal of Group Psychotherapy*, 1967, 17:196–210.

Hansen, J. C., D. G. Zimpfer, and R. E. Easterling "A Study of the Relationships in Multiple Counseling," *Journal of Educational Research*, 1967, 60:461–462.

Harth, R. "Changing Attitudes Toward School, Classroom Behavior, and Reaction to Frustration of Emotionally Disturbed Children through Role Playing," *Exceptional Child*, 1966, 33:119–120.

Hartley, E., and M. Rosenbaum "Criteria Used by Group Psychotherapists for Judging Improvement in Patients," *International Journal of Group Psychotherapy*, 1963, 13:80–83.

Hathaway, S. R. "Some Considerations Relative to Nondirective Psychotherapy as Counseling," *Journal of Clinical Psychology*, 1948, 4: 226–231.

Hoch, P. H., and J. Zubin (eds.) *The Evaluation of Psychiatric Treatment*, New York: Grune & Stratton, Inc., 1964.

Horney, Karen *Our Inner Conflicts*, New York: W. W. Norton & Company, Inc., 1945.

Jensen, B. T., G. Coles, and Beatrice Nestor "The Criterion Problem in Guidance Research," *Journal of Counseling Psychology*, 1955, 2:58–61.

Kranzler, G. D., G. R. Mayer, C. O. Dyer, and P. F. Munger "Counseling with Elementary School Children: An Experimental Study," *Personnel and Guidance Journal*, 1966, 44:944–949.

Krathwohl, D. R., B. S. Bloom, and B. B. Masia *Taxonomy of Educational Objectives:* The Classification of Educational Goals, Handbook II, Cognitive Domain, New York: David McKay Company, Inc., 1964.

Krumboltz, J. D., and C. E. Thoresen "The Effect of Behavioral Counseling in Group and Individual Settings on Information-Seeking Behavior," *Journal of Counseling Psychology*, 1964, 11:324–333.

Laxer, R. M., J. J. Quarter, Catherine Isnor, and D. R. Kennedy "Counseling Small Groups of Behavior-Problem Students in Junior High Schools," *Journal of Counseling Psychology*, 1967, 14:454–457.

Leary, T. *Interpersonal Diagnosis of Personality*, New York: The Ronald Press Company, 1957.

Leib, J. W., and W. W. Snyder "Effects of Group Counseling on Underachievement and Self-Actualization," *Journal of Counseling Psychology*, 1967, 14:282–285.

Levitt, E. E. "The Results of Psychotherapy with Children: An Evaluation," *Journal of Consulting Psychology*, 1957, 21:189–196.

Lodato, F. J., M. A. Sokoloff, and L. J. Schwartz "Group Counseling as a Method of Modifying Attitudes in Slow Learners," *School Counselor*, 1964, 12:27–29.

McCarthy, Sister Mary V. *The Effectiveness of a Modified Counseling Procedure in Promoting Learning among Bright Underachieving Adolescents*, Research Project #SAE-6401, Washington, D.C.: Department of Health, Education, and Welfare, 1959.

Meehl, P. E. "Some Ruminations on the Validation of Clinical Procedures," *Canadian Journal of Psychology*, 1959, 13:102–128.

Mezzano, J. A. "A Consideration for Group Counselors: Degree of Investment," *School Counselor*, 1967, 14:167–169.

Muro, J. J., and F. W. Ohnmacht "Effects of Group Counseling on Dimensions of Self-Acceptance, Dogmatism, and Preference for Complexity with Teacher-Education Students," *Journal of Student Personnel Association for Teacher Education*, 1966, 5:25–30.

Novick, J. I. "Comparison of Short-Term Group and Individual Psychotherapy in Effecting Changes in Nondesirable Behavior Children," *International Journal of Group Psychotherapy*, 1965, 15:366–373.

Ofman, W. "Evaluation of a Group Counseling Procedure," *Journal of Counseling Psychology*, 1964, 11:152–159.

Ohlsen, M. M., and G. M. Gazda "Counseling Underachieving Bright Pupils," *Education*, 1965, 86:78–81.

Patterson, C. H. "Counseling," *Annual Review of Psychology*, 1966, 17:79–110.

Pattison, E. M. "Evaluation Studies of Group Psychotherapy," *International Journal of Group Psychotherapy*, 1965, 15:382–393.

Paul, G. L. "Strategy of Outcome Research in Psychotherapy," *Journal of Consulting Psychology*, 1967, 31:109–118.

Pepinsky, H. B. "Some Proposals for Research," *Personnel and Guidance Journal*, 1953, 31:291–294.

Psathas, G. "Overview of Process Studies in Group Psychotherapy," *International Journal of Group Psychotherapy*, 1967, 17:225–235.

Raimy, V. C. "Self-Reference in Counseling Interviews," *Journal of Consulting Psychology*, 1948, 12:153–163.

Rickard, H. C. "Tailored Criteria of Change in Psychotherapy," *Journal of General Psychology*, 1965, 72:63–68.

Rickard, H. C., and E. C. Brown "Evaluation of a Psychotherapy Case in Terms of Change in a Relevant Behavior," *Journal of Clinical Psychology*, 1960, 16:93.

Rogers, C. R. "The Necessary and Sufficient Conditions of Personality Change," *Journal of Consulting Psychology*, 1957, 21:95–103.

Rosenzweig, S. "A Transvaluation of Psychotherapy: A Reply to Hans Eysenck," *Journal of Abnormal and Social Psychology*, 1954, 49: 298–304.

Roth, R. M., H. O. Mauksch, and K. Peiser "The Non-Achievement Syndrome, Group Therapy, and Achievement Change," *Personnel and Guidance Journal*, 1967, 46:393–398.

Rubinstein, E. A., and M. B. Parloff (eds.) *Research in Psychotherapy*, vol. I, Washington, D. C.: American Psychological Association, 1959.

Seeman, J. J. "The Process of Non-Directive Therapy," *Journal of Consulting Psychology*, 1949, 13:157–168.

Shaftel, Fannie R., with the assistance of G. Shaftel *Role Playing for School Values:* Decision Making in Social Studies, Englewood Cliffs, N. J.: Prentice-Hall, Inc., 1967.

Shaw, M. C., and Rosemary Wursten "Research Procedures on Group Procedures in Schools: A Review of the Literature," *Personnel and Guidance Journal*, 1965, 44:27–34.

Sheerer, Elizabeth T. "An Analysis of the Relationship Between Acceptance of and Respect for Self and Acceptance of and Respect for Others in Ten Counseling Cases," *Journal of Consulting Psychology*, 1949, 13:169–175.

Sheldon, W. D., and T. Landsman "Investigation of Nondirective Group Therapy with Students in Academic Difficulty," *Journal of Consulting Psychology*, 1950, 14:210–215.

Shoben, E. J. "Some Problems in Establishing Criteria of Effectiveness," *Personnel and Guidance Journal*, 1953, 31:287–290.

Snyder, W. U. "A Comparison of One Unsuccessful and Four Successful

Nondirectively Counseled Cases," *Journal of Consulting Psychology*, 1947, 11:38–42.

Sonstegard, M. "Group Counseling Methods with Parents of Elementary School Children as Related to Pupil Growth and Development," mimeographed report, State College of Iowa, 1961.

Spielberger, C. O., H. Weitz, and J. P. Denny "Group Counseling and Academic Performance of Anxious College Freshmen," *Journal of Counseling Psychology*, 1962, 9:195–204.

Spielberger, C. O., and H. Weitz *Improving the Academic Performance of Anxious College Freshmen*, Psychological Monograph #590, Washington, D.C.: American Psychological Association, 1964.

Stock, Dorothy "An investigation into the Interrelations between the Self-Concept and Feelings Directed Toward Other Persons and Groups," *Journal of Consulting Psychology*, 1949, 13:176–180.

Stollack, G. E., B. G. Guerney, and M. Rothberg *Psychotherapy Research:* Selected Readings, Skokie, Ill.: Rand McNally & Company, 1966.

Sullivan, H. S. *Conceptions in Modern Psychiatry*, Washington, D.C.: William Allen White Psychiatric Foundation, 1947.

Sullivan, H. S. *The Interpersonal Theory of Psychiatry*, New York: W. W. Norton & Company, Inc., 1953.

Teahan, J. E. "Effect of Group Psychotherapy on Academic Low Achievers," *International Journal of Group Psychotherapy*, 1966, 16:78–85.

Thelen, M. H., and C. S. Harris "Personality of College Underachievers Who Improve with Group Psychotherapy," *Personnel and Guidance Journal*, 1968, 46:561–566.

Thoreson, C. E., and J. D. Krumboltz "Relationship of Counselor Reinforcement of Selected Responses to External Behavior," *Journal of Counseling Psychology*, 1967, 14:140–144.

Truax, C. B., and R. R. Carkhuff "The Old and New: Theory and Research in Counseling and Psychotherapy," *Personnel and Guidance Journal*, 1964, 42:860–866.

Walker, G. J. "Group Counseling in Juvenile Probation," *Federal Probation*, 1959, 23:31–38.

Wigell, W. W., and M. M. Ohlsen "To What Extent Is Affect a Function of Topic and Referent in Group Counseling?" *American Journal of Orthopsychiatry*, 1962, 32:728–735.

Winborn, B., and L. G. Schmidt "Effectiveness of Short-Term Group Counseling upon the Academic Achievement of Potentially Superior but Underachieving Freshmen," *Journal of Educational Research*, 1962, 55:169–173.

Winkler, R. C., J. J. Teigland, P. F. Munger, and G. D. Kranzler "The Effects of Selected Counseling and Remedial Techniques on Under-

achieving Elementary School Children," *Journal of Counseling Psychology*, 1965, 12:384–387.
Zax, M., and A. Klein "Measurement of Personality and Behavior Changes Following Psychotherapy," *Psychological Bulletin*, 1960, 57:435–448.

Author Index

Caplan, S. W., 275, 288
Carkhuff, R. R., 2, 12, 16, 27, 242,
    247, 248, 249, 250, 269, 270, 288,
    292
Caron, P., 64, 75
Cartwright, D. P., 39, 47, 49, 52, 74,
    78, 84, 86, 87, 88, 94, 95, 97
Cartwright, D. S., 254, 264, 265, 288
Catron, D. W., 275, 288
Chenault, Joann, 21, 27
Chestnut, W. J., 279, 288
Clark, D. H., 5, 30, 173, 192
Clements, B. E., 276, 288
Cohen, Mabel B., 143, 148
Cohn, B., 264, 288
Coles, G., 255, 289
Corman, B. R., 194, 221
Cornish, Mary J., 21, 27
Corsini, R., 41, 47, 218, 222
Cronbach, L. J., 253, 254, 265, 266,
    288

Damrin, Dora E., 22, 27
Daniels, M., 108, 109, 114
Davis, Ruth G., 271, 288
Deabler, M. L., 152, 159, 162
Demos, G. D., 13, 14, 27
Dennis, C., 15, 28
Denny, J. P., 102, 106, 282, 292
Dickenson, W. A., 259, 288
Dickerman, W., 59, 62, 76
Dilley, J. S., 15, 27
Dinkmeyer, D., 198, 222
Dittes, J., 86, 97
Dole, A. A., 15, 27
Donaghty, R. T., 14, 30
Dowse, Eunice, 13, 29
Drabkova, H., 151, 153, 162
Dreikurs, R., 33, 47, 53, 74, 89, 97,
    198, 215, 218, 222, 238
Dunbar, F., 194, 222
Durkin, Helen E., 4, 27, 133, 148,
    184, 191
Dyer, C. O., 271, 290

Easterling, R. E., 277, 289
Edwards, A. L., 253, 254, 265, 266,
    288
English, Ava C., 130, 131, 148
English, H. B., 130, 131, 148
Ewing, T. N., 101, 105, 114, 264, 288
Eysenck, J. J., 248, 266, 267, 288

Fenichel, O., 184, 191
Festinger, L., 86, 87, 97
Fiedler, F. E., 10, 27, 54, 55, 74, 105,
    114, 280, 288
Foley, W. J., 13, 15, 27
Fonte, N., 154, 162
Forgy, E. W., 255, 288
Frank, J. D., 4, 27, 33, 47, 62, 75,
    78, 83, 89, 90, 97, 98, 106, 115,
    124, 129, 165, 190, 192
Frank, L. K., 194, 222
Frank, M. H., 194, 222
Freedman, M. B., 109, 114, 120, 123,
    129, 133, 148
Freeman, V. J., 217, 222
French, J. P. R., 84, 97, 151, 162
Freud, S., 10, 129, 165, 191, 258,
    289
Fried, Edrita, 137, 148
Fritz, M. F., 195, 223
Fullmer, D. W., 218, 222

Gadpaille, W. J., 204, 222
Garrison, K. C., 195, 222
Gazda, G. M., 108, 229, 231, 232,
    239, 270, 272, 280, 289, 290
Gersten, C., 276, 289
Gesell, A., 194, 222
Gibb, J., 7, 27, 49, 53, 74
Gilbert, W. M., 101, 105, 114, 264,
    288
Gilbreath, S. H., 280, 289
Gilliland, B. E., 276, 289
Ginott, H. G., 107, 114, 215, 222,
    226, 231, 232, 238
Glasser, W., 33, 41, 47, 84, 97
Glatzer, Henriette T., 130, 137, 148,
    184, 186, 191

Subject Index